Robert Moffat

The Standard Alphabet

Robert Moffat

The Standard Alphabet

ISBN/EAN: 9783744750417

Printed in Europe, USA, Canada, Australia, Japan

Cover: Foto ©Andreas Hilbeck / pixelio.de

More available books at **www.hansebooks.com**

THE
"STANDARD-ALPHABET"
PROBLEM:

OR THE PRELIMINARY SUBJECT OF A

GENERAL PHONIC SYSTEM,

CONSIDERED ON THE

BASIS OF SOME IMPORTANT FACTS IN THE SECHWANA LANGUAGE OF SOUTH AFRICA,
AND IN REFERENCE TO THE VIEWS OF PROFESSORS LEPSIUS,
MAX MÜLLER, AND OTHERS.

A CONTRIBUTION TO PHONETIC PHILOLOGY,

BY

ROBERT MOFFAT, Jun.,

SURVEYOR,

Fellow of the Royal Geographical Society.

"The loss of the living traditional pronunciation implies a loss of much more than what we generally call pronunciation."—*Bunsen.*

" But the linguistic scholar will prefer to follow the written system fixed by literature, and to neglect the varying deviations and shades of modern pronunciation."—*Lepsius.*

Publishers.

LONDON ....TRÜBNER & Co., PATERNOSTER ROW.
SOUTH AFRICA. { J. C. JUTA, CAPE TOWN.
{ J. O. BROWNE, NATAL.

1864.

Unavoidable delays, contingent on the work being edited in a foreign land, have delayed its publication. The concluding sheets have been revised by the Rev. J. FRÉDOUX, of Motito, S.A.

THE PRINTER.

October, 1864.

GEORGE UNWIN, GRESHAM STEAM PRESS, BUCKLERSBURY, LONDON.

TO HIS EXCELLENCY

SIR GEORGE GREY, K.C.B.,

A SCHOLAR IN AFRICAN PHILOLOGY, AND AT THE SAME TIME ITS
DISTINGUISHED PROMOTER,

THIS HUMBLE ATTEMPT TO ARRIVE AT SOME OF THE FUNDAMENTAL
PRINCIPLES OF HUMAN SPEECH,
UPON THE BASIS OF A NEW ORDER OF FACTS,
THE RESULT OF PERSONAL RESEARCHES INTO THE LANGUAGE OF A REMOTE
PORTION OF THOSE INDIGENOUS SOUTH AFRICAN TRIBES WHICH
HAVE LATELY BENEFITED BY HIS EXCELLENCY'S RULE,

IS (BY PERMISSION)

MOST RESPECTFULLY DEDICATED, BY HIS OBLIGED SERVANT,

THE AUTHOR.

CONTENTS.

CHAPTER IV.

CHAPTER V.

[*No MSS. have been found for this.*]

INTRODUCTORY REMARKS.

It is in the nature of man and his prerogative to generalize, however limited the range of his observation; and in proportion as this is extended, is he enabled the more or less confidently to demonstrate the truth of his knowledge, or the degree of credibility of what he anticipates. Therefore, I presume that fresh statements, whether of facts or inferences, will be welcome from any individual in a new field of research, however obscure or diffident he may be; especially in this golden age of inductive science, when particulars, and instances, and data, in every department, are being scrambled after by all classes of students.

I have been prompted by such considerations as the above to publish, for the information of others devoted to the study of language, the results of my observations during a few years of assiduous research in an elementary branch of the subject. This I had long selected for my own amusement and instruction in leisure moments of a professional vocation; and having recently been engaged in an active trading life on a wide frontier, among native tribes, the destruction of whose language is as inevitable as their speedy social dissolution, I have enjoyed unusual facilities for the prosecution of my object.

While the quotations, which confront each other on the title-page of this treatise, present in a concise form the opinions of two of the first continental scholars on the same subject, they will also serve to convey an idea of the nature of the task I have now undertaken. Where such absolute difference of opinion exists between men possessing stores of learning, there must rather be a deviation in the researches of either of them, than a deficiency in his materials. The one, in a special case, proposes to explain an ancient rock-engraven literature by means of an investigation into the actual relations of the material elements of human speech, as "transcribed * * * from the lips" of those "among whom it has been traditionally preserved;" * the other attempts to establish an "absolute rule" of phonetics on the historical relations of those elements, as represented to the eye by letters in various existing literatures. I need not proceed to argue the question as to which is suggesting the proper path of research for the collection of data, in order to arrive at the laws of "a natural science," as that of phonetic philology undoubtedly is ; and whether the rudiments of this science are to be conveyed to the mind by the artificial means of letters to the eye, or rather the more legitimate one of sounds to the ear.

Dr. Lepsius, by means of an immense command of ancient and modern graphical materials, of both dead and living languages, and taking the Indian grammarians as a guide, has arrived at the construction of a "*universal linguistic alphabet;*" but truly elaborate as it is, and however convenient it may be for students whose attention is confined to the historical forms of the Indo-European tongues, there is decidedly something of an artificial nature about it, which must necessarily be discordant with the views of others who, in confining their investigations to the "living traditional pronunciation" of primitive tribes like those of South Africa, are led to arrive at conclusions of a more demonstrative character. The quotation to which his name is attached sufficiently explains the basis of his system, and the difficulty of his labours.

---

* Dr. Lepsius's researches (1835) into the relation between the Egyptian and Coptic, after all, I believe, only extended to the comparison of literatures—viz., the hieroglyphics and the liturgy.

The following treatise is the result of a mode of research suggested by the pointed remark of the late Baron de Bunsen, contained in the other quotation. It is a survey of the elements of articulation as they occur in the crude and simple speech of a barbarous people, and the principles which enter into their various mutations and combinations; which, in an order analogous to that usually pursued in all natural science, must precede a consideration of the more complicated or syntactical stages of the material forms of human language. It maintains at the outset, that "we can understand the historical forms of speech only by watching and comprehending the process of utterance as it goes on even now in the individual speaker;* but rather by observing the effects of the process on the ear, and in the various permutations of the elements of articulation, than the cause in the physiology of the voice which pre-supposes the anatomy of the organs. It, in fact, claims for the humble *Sechwana* language, spoken by numerous degraded tribes on the south-eastern borders of the South African desert (or Khalagare wilderness),—and why not for other unwritten tongues?—that perfection of phonic purity which Professor Max Müller concedes only to the *Vaidik Sanskrit*, whose historical orthography is more than two thousand years old; and for the very same reasons, viz., that it (can be) "studied by means of oral tradition only, and . . . . in the absence of a written alphabet, the most minute differences of pronunciation (have) to be watched by the ear," and "it (has) suffered less from the influence of phonetic corruption than any tongue from which *we* can derive our observations."† While it does not deny that the phonic forms of the ancient vernacular Sanskrit *were* perfect, whatever corruptions may since have crept into their phonetic representations, it holds that those of the Sechwana, and some other barbaric dialects, *are*

---

* The *Saturday Review*, June 29, 1861, p. 673.
† *Proposals for a Missionary Alphabet,* &c., by Max Müller, M.A., p xxii.

perfect, and still accessible to the inductive philologer, but at an immeasurably further advanced stage of inductive science. It therefore deals only with natural facts, discovered *in situ* by personal observation.

As thus treated, the subject may be found to have some new phases when viewed by men of learning, for whose consideration I would with becoming reserve and humility submit my views. It is just possible that a few of the facts, and such conclusions as have been arrived at, or to which they may come, may account for various phenomena in the accidence of those written tongues, in which the development of the *essential form* has greatly modified the *accidental* structure. Though I have availed myself of the common prerogative of generalizing, and even speculating to the utmost of my ability, and presume to state such a possibility, I have given every particular that has fallen under my notice, to enable the reader to arrive at his own conclusions, by the aid of such accessory knowledge as he doubtless possesses beyond me.

In craving the candid attention of the reader, and lest the title of this treatise should lead him to expect more than it contains, I would beforehand state—

a. That the object of the work is not to prescribe a new system, but rather to contribute to the construction of one,* or to illustrate the science of universal phonics by the collection and arrangement of instances from the phonology of the Sechwana language of South Africa. It is an attempt to treat inductively on a subject, which, by being usually based on the physiology of the human voice, has hitherto only been examined deductively; nevertheless, reserving to myself the privilege of employing the

---

* On reference to the tables of consonants in Chapters IV. and V., the letters in *bold type* will show the reader the extent to which the classification is based on data furnished by the language; those in *italics*, the mode in which I have attempted to complete it by a train of speculation suggested by them.

latter speculative mode of analysis, besides so much of classification as the extent of my train of facts will have admitted.
Without - venturing to assert that, by a consideration of the
elements of articulation of any one spoken language, a correct
system of phonics may be framed applicable to all, it will satisfy
me to intimate that at least an imperfect, and not-incorrect or fragmentary, system may thus be framed; and that the consideration
of other languages, containing additional elements, would, by in-
creasing the number of instances, contribute to a more copious
induction. I have, therefore, proceeded upon the principle that
it is absolutely necessary, for the purposes of this elementary
branch of the science, to arrive at fixed results in one pure and
living dialect, before advancing to a comparative view of different
tongues. This will, I trust, obviate, in my case, a common
objection urged against writers whose observations are confined
to a single language.

_b._ However I may feel the want of some fixed mode of re-
gistering my researches, as a saving of both time and labour, a
graphic scheme is entirely secondary to my immediate object.
Anything of the kind, even though it may emanate from a
master-mind in philology, must be regarded as immature, till
suggested by a phonic system resulting from an inductive survey,
similar to, but of a far more comprehensive nature than, that I have
attempted. It is in vain to expect it so long as men seek to arrive
at the nature of vowels and consonants exclusively, either by
experiments on the action of the vocal organs, or by artificial
contrivances to imitate them, or by the comparison of existing
historical _alphabets_.

To the self-experimenting phono-physiologist in the one case,
the facetious advice of Professor De Morgan to the metaphysical student is particularly applicable, viz.: —" I would not
dissuade a student from * * * inquiry ; on the contrary, I would
rather endeavour to promote the desire of entering upon such

subjects : but I would warn him, when he tries to look down his own throat with a candle in his hand, to take care that he does not set his head on fire."*   In the second case, it happens that though the ingenious contrivers of speaking machines "have succeeded in imitating a great part of the sounds used in speech," they confess that "every simple and independent sound and consonant requires a special apparatus ;" they must, consequently, admit that the production of the unique combination and operation of the different apparatus would be a task about as hopeless as that of any optician who would attempt to devise a means of imitating the peculiar structural arrangement of the eye, whereby the automatic alteration in the curvature of the crystalline lens adjusts it to different ranges of vision ; in fact, that what the telescope with its sliding focal adjustments (spite of its comparative perfection) is to the wonderful structure of the visual organ, so are "reed tubes" and "vibrating tongues" to the complicated organism required in the perfect enunciation and articulation of the most simple elements of voice.   In the third case, it may be urged that the fact of the English, or any other historical *alphabet,* only indicating a limited number of elements, does not necessarily imply that the language does not contain several additional elements, though these may be represented by irregular combinations of letters.   In the transliteration of such, "where," to use the words of Professor Müller, "for reasons best known to the archæologist, one sign may represent different sounds, and one sound be expressed by different signs, new and entirely distinct questions are involved, and capable of solution by archæological and philological research alone."†   Hitherto the advocate of historical orthography has as little to show as either the physiological observer or the artificial experimenter, in any attempt to establish a natural classification of the elements of speech.   The one mode of research has only

---

* " Formal Logic," p. 27, Note.   † " *Proposals,*" &c., p. 20.

shed a few rays of light on the other, and phonology, instead of being already " reduced to its last analyses," as a learned American writer remarks, is, in his own words, as echoed from Sir Robert Taylor's Institution, Oxford, verily and without equivocation, "*exactly the same* that Sanskrit grammarians more than two thousand years ago defined its elements to be in their own primeval tongue ;"* but not what it may be, if the modern philologer will base his inferences on facts of a proper description.†

In corroboration, it may be alleged that the whole system of phonetic philology, as at present based on ancient and existing alphabets, and physiological classifications, is but a labyrinth of graphic schemes. To the various powers given to the Roman letters in different European alphabets, and various letters representing the same power, there may be added—(1) both letters and sounds introduced by travellers and navigators of different nations, in lists of words collected irregularly and carelessly from uncivilized tribes; (2) the more complete alphabets of

---

* *Bibliotheca Sacra*, Oct., 1859, p. 673. (See also *Proposals*, &c., by Max Müller, p. 22.)

† The following, from the pen of no less distinguished a philologer than the late Rev. Richard Garnett, of the British Museum, and which has occurred to me since the above quotation was written, approaches more to the sober and truthful :—

" It is presumed that enough has been advanced to show that the scale of permutations in the Indo-European languages, as laid down by Grimm and Pott, will admit of being considerably extended beyond the limits which they have assigned; and that it is very unsafe to fix upon Sanscrit, or any other known language, as a model to which all others are to be referred. It is believed that there are numerous phenomena in language of which neither Sanscrit, Greek, Teutonic, nor all in conjunction, can furnish a satisfactory solution ; and that the real original articulations of speech have in many cases yet to be ascertained. This can only be attempted by a copious induction of all known varieties of cognate forms, and all that we can rationally expect to achieve is an imperfect approximation to the truth."—*Philological Essays*, p. 254.

missionaries and priests labouring under the same disadvantages of a diversity of plan; (3) the host of cumbrous alphabets of Oriental languages, dead and living; and (4) the numerous "transliterated" forms of these alphabets introduced by Oriental scholars of different schools, each according to a "method of notation peculiar to himself," not to mention the orthoëpical schemes of many authors; so that it may truly be said, the operations of the linguist are trammelled by his own materials.* This complexity of his phonetic materials has been especially increased since the efforts of Sir William Jones, in 1788, and of Count Volney, in 1795. Missionaries labouring among conterminous tribes have often made attempts to arrive at uniformity, and philologers have as frequently seen the absolute necessity of a universal alphabet for the analytical purposes of their science; but the general public, with Isaac Pitman before them, are too prone to suspect every innovation as only a preliminary to the practical "abrogation" of the ancient forms of literature. Therefore, such characters as I have made use of, or even any suggestions on modes of writing the elements of articulation, must be regarded as arbitrary, though, as much as possible, in keeping with the Roman graphic system; at all events, most of my remarks upon them are confined to the foot-notes. It will, nevertheless, be seen that, by working on a new basis, I have attempted to provoke a little discussion on a subject which every student of unwritten tongues must be most anxious to see satisfactorily settled ; in order that the constant trouble of making myriads of alterations may be dispensed with in the collection or publication of orthographical data.

c. Much less do I presume to enter into the controversy on the subject of "Romanizing" existing ancient and cumbrous

---

* The numerous comparative tables, occurring in this work, of letters intended by different authors to represent the same series of sounds, will alone show the confusion of alphabetic systems.

alphabets, in which some of the first Oriental scholars have been engaged.* Independently of all the arguments which it is possible to allege for or against such an innovation on Oriental graphic systems, it must be confessed that it would amply repay the labour of any man with the necessary ability, and possessed with the " phonetic crotchet," as it has been called, to reduce the " *twenty* different vernacular tongues" of India, having now "*fifteen* various alphabets," to the same phonetic system, based upon identical phonic principles, without consulting one volume of philosophy, poetry, or theology.   He would verily be examining them *in situ*, and classifying them by a most rigid analytic formula ; while, by giving his attention to *Pali*, *Sanscrit*, and *Arabic*, he would have to resort to the "*books*" of the Buddist, the Hindu, and the Mussulman—which ancient literary repositories, in point of value, bear the same relation to the living dialects, that a few drawings of fossils in a museum would have to originals still imbedded in the rock.   It cannot, then, be denied that a body of men, by a division of labour, and acting upon preconcerted views of a phonetic system, would arrive at still more comprehensive results, which no existing literatures could ever afford.   In the same manner as the learned Bunsen showed that a knowledge of the traditional Koptic, gathered from the priests, would be necessary to enable the Egyptologer to decipher the illegible groups of hieroglyphics, so it would be easy to prove that a still surviving colloquial dialect would shed light on the most ancient sacred literature ; for " all sacred language is   *   *   * essentially, nothing but an earlier stage of the popular dialect,

---

* *For:* Sir William Jones, Volney, Gilchrist, Monier Williams, Sir C. Trevelyan, H. T. Prinsep, Dr. Yates, Dr. Duff, Dr. Caldwell, Max Müller, Lepsius, the " Times," and others.
Against: J. Prinsep, J. Tytler, Dr. Jarrett, H. H. Wilson, Mohl, and others —See *Evangelical Christendom*, May, 1860, p. 237.

preserved by means of the sacred books,"* only in an imperfect and fragmentary, however correct, form.

d. Nor do I attempt to expatiate on the necessity of introducing a uniform phonetic system for the practical purposes of the missionary. If we are to credit the opinions of many writers of the present day, as to the qualifications of a missionary—for example, in India—then he requires the preparation of a *savan.* He has not only to master the root language of the people among whom he is labouring, but also that from which its theology has

---

* "Egypt's Place in Universal History."—*Bunsen*, Vol. I., p. 258.

Indeed, if we would wish to form an idea of the objective value of a sacred literature, in a philological point of view, and compared with the traditional language of the people among whom a new religion has been introduced, we have only to examine any elaborate modern translations of the Bible into unwritten tongues, such as the Sechwana, for instance, which will bear comparison with many. The missionary acknowledges that, in order to maintain the tenor of Scripture, he is compelled in a measure to mar the colloquial idiom in a few cases; *ex gr.*, to indulge in circumlocution, where a curt phrase would convey the identical meaning more elegantly. It cannot be otherwise, as, in the colloquial idiom, there is so involved a reference to the instinctive customs, habits, and modes of thought of the barbarian, that it would often be inappropriate, and in many cases unnecessary, to introduce it; for, excepting the book of Job, with its host of allusions to the scenes of the outer world, the subject of all sacred books is generally too confined to allow of the introduction of more than a *fourth* part of the spoken words in a comprehensive language.

Bearing this in mind, and the fact that a sacred literature is a *new subject* in the language of an ancient or barbarous people, it is not surprising that we hear of slurs cast by scholars in India on *missionary vernacular*, and in this country on *school Kaffir*. In South Africa, I have heard an intelligent missionary, after one year's application to the " book," or otherwise "sacred," Sechwana, convey the simple truths of Scripture to the natives in the most intelligible strain, because, during the acquisition of the language, his phraseology has been confined, almost exclusively, to that *new subject ;* while, again, I have heard some, comparatively uneducated, of a few years' standing, so attached to this *book*—or *sacred*—idiom, without at the same time making themselves daily more acquainted with the common idiom for colloquial purposes, that their garrulous repetition of it *on all subjects* was absolutely disgusting. It is sometimes as well that a translator is as much at home in the one as in the other.

been derived, and, of course, their respective *alphabets*. Of the six systems of Indian philosophy, the Nyâya, with its excess of logic; the Sânkhya, with its excess of metaphysics; and the Mîmânsâ, with its excess of theology,* all claim his versatile attention.† To accomplish his object, he must study those tongues thoroughly, for a smattering is often no better than, absolute ignorance. But, in order to understand the true end of his exertions, it is as well to compare his calling and sphere with those of the philologer.

The vocation of a missionary, who provides an unwritten language with an alphabet, or finds one imperfectly prepared, is entirely independent and peculiar; his aim is the communication of Divine truth to the instinctive ignorance of heathens; to substitute—for the vague impressions which exist on their minds of impersonal " rude powers," or subtle deities, the revealed fact of a personal God, or supreme moral Governor—for a superstitious adherence to any human method of expiation, a living faith in His incarnation and redemptive act—for a servile willingness to appease aught that will quiet conscience, the spirit of penitence and reformation—for the fear of death, the hope of future existence. Whatever the medium, he seeks to address man, " be it an A'rya or a Sudra." His teachings have to be conducted, not so much by an " argumentative exposition " of his doctrines, and an " elaborate confutation " of those of his opponents, as " in the form of a *testimony* * * with respect to the mode of exhibiting it, though not in the spirit of the teacher * * *dogmatic.*"‡ He has to declare " intrinsic

---

* " Indian Logic," by Max Müller. Appended to " Laws of Thought, by W. Thomson, D.D.," p. 363.

† " Moreover, as is well known, the peculiar philosophical notions of the learned Hindus must be understood by those who would effectively evangelise that race."—*Evangelical Christendom*, May, 1860, p. 244. See Ibid., Oct., 1860, p. 524.

‡ Works of Rev. Robt. Hall, by Olinthus Gregory, LL.D., &c., Vol. I., p. 302.

primordial truths," without the aid of a "syllogism, or quotation"* of human wisdom, and by the mere external means of a new vernacular. Therefore, in many cases he considers it immaterial to him what orthography he may use,† as his practical operations differ from those of the philologer, of whose science he *applies* such a knowledge as he happens to have acquired to suit his own peculiar plans. Moreover, as to his sphere of duty, what is true of human nature in South Africa, where the most rigid statist would be compelled to admit it, will be true of man in all lands—viz., that it is only amongst poor, or isolated, or dismembered communities, that the missionary has been most successful. One would think, therefore, that—as he has more immediately to explode popular notions, and not systems of philosophy ; to dispel the superstitious polytheism of the "unthinking multitude," rather than the atheism and pantheism of philosophic sects : in fact, to deal with the vulgar rather than with the learned—he would endeavour to command a knowledge of the popular dialect, independently of existing ancient vernacular literatures, in which "the spelling of words is no longer phonetic but traditional." Indeed, if the fact admitted by the "*Friend of India*," and cited by Sir C. E. Trevelyan,‡ may be regarded as an approximate estimate of the proportion of the educated classes to the ignorant masses in India—viz., "that only *one* million out of the *thirty* millions of Bengal can read" their indigenous literature, the missionary can have no doubt as to which ought to engage his attention, and the mode of writing speech most likely to facilitate his labours. The amount

---

* Vinet.

† "But as it is so immaterial how the language is written, and the only essential point being that the Word of God may be taught in it, I entirely waive the question as to the mode of writing, &c."—*Rev. H. C. Knudsen, R.M.S., in Corres. S. A. A. B. Society,* p. 5.

‡ Papers originally published at Calcutta in 1834 & 1836, on the application of the Roman Letters to the Language of Asia. London, Longman, 1854.

of success which has attended the labours of missionaries in South Africa during the last half century, in the introduction of a native literature, is only a proof that as much could be accomplished among the illiterate of every nation by any who would choose the same course; for it must be patent to all, that what is communicable to the vulgar must be intelligible to the learned.

The aim of the philologer is far otherwise. While, on the one hand, he has solved some most interesting ethnologic problems, such as the identification of the radical language of the " rude Kelt" of the corners of Britain, with that of the " effeminate Bengáli" of the Indian promontory; and, more recently, the stock of the Hottentot of the Southern extremity of Africa, with that of the ancient Egyptian of the extreme North — and discerns in the future still greater triumphs; on the other hand, he feels assured that if " *truth* consists in the conformity of the names by which the representations of the mind are expressed to the representations themselves," and if " language is the only external condition on which philosophy is dependent,"* he has the whole range of mental science at his feet. To effect these objects, the analysis of language, phonetic as well as grammatic, is his great power; the former, by the comparison of the *material* forms of human thought, as are to be found in the various sets of combinations of the elements of articulation, and in the collocations of words, which distinguish different tongues; the latter, by an inquiry into the *essential* form, or the law of the process, by which the varieties of names and syntactical constructions in different languages are but different expressions for similar cognitions in all.† His sphere of re-

---

* Sir William Hamilton's Lectures, Vol. I., p. 382.

† This will perhaps be the fittest place for me to append, in explanation of my meaning here, the following remarks, which I have extracted (slightly modified) from a letter addressed in February, 1857, to a distinguished individual greatly interested in the study of aboriginal tongues :—

search alone is analogous to that of the missionary's duty. As with the missionary, the more unsophisticated and humble the people, the more successful he is likely to be; so with the philologer, the more simple and primitive the language in which he works, the more correct are his conclusions likely to be in all cases; for in it the various forms and combinations of either sound or meaning* are more easily discernible, and resolvable

---

"It has often appeared to me that many of the so much misunderstood elementary principles of universal grammar, which are the subject of great diversity of opinion among scientific men in Europe, may be explained and proved, and in some instances discovered, by a clear investigation of such hitherto unwritten tongues, when carefully reduced to writing; e.g.,

'Mr. Horne Tooke's idea of prepositions and conjunctions is, that they do not form distinct classes of words, but are merely abbreviations of nouns and verbs."—*Encyc. Brit.*, Vol. X., p. 673.

Page 657.—"It has been proved, by such evidence as leaves no room for doubt, that *if*, though called a conjunction, is in fact a verb in the imperative mood, of the same import with *give*, so that we may substitute the one for the other without in the smallest degree altering the sense."

The identical word holds good in the Sechwana, in the sentence *ha ki bobola nka shwa* (If I sicken, I may die); **ha**, the equivalent of our conjunction *if*, is nothing else than the verb **ha** (*give*), which is in a measure obsolete in the language, and is usually employed in asking a gift, or at meals, as *mo ha* (help, or give him), **naea** being the more common word on other occasions.

AGAIN—"*From* (the preposition) merely means *beginning*, and nothing else." . . . . . "As *from* always denotes *beginning*, so *to* and *till* always denote *the end*. There is, however, this difference between them, that *to* denotes the end of any thing; *till*, only the end of time."—*Ibid.*, p. 681.

Now, in the Sechwana sentence, *ki le ka ea* **go cwa** (or *go simolola ka*) *Kuruman* **go ea** *Khatwe*, the words *go cwa* and *go ea*, which are nothing else than prepositions in their primitive forms, respectively mean *to come out* (or to *begin with*), and to *go to*. *Go tsamaea* (to be in *the act of going*), which is used for till or until, implies *time*. These are coincidences showing that, however the accidental forms of language may vary, the essential form or meaning is the same.

* In illustration I add the following from my note-book, with an example from the primitive dialect of the *Sechwana* :—

Nothing is more common in writings on mental science than a reference to the connexion between thought and language; but this seldom exceeds 'half belief and feeble assertion.' The remark of Professor de Morgan,

into their elements. I have somewhere met with the remark, that "the concerns of barbarians, unconnected and remote from all contact with literature and civilization, and destitute of all

"I doubt whether we could have made thought itself the subject of thought without language," (Formal Logic, p. 34) is, however, more bold and suggestive ; and he surely speaks here of language in its essential form. But though we are told by another able author that logic is a science of "the structural laws according to which man thinks," and by the above profound logician that "logical truth depends upon the *structure of the sentence*," I doubt whether either of them would concede that logic "can but result as a generalization * * * from an inductive survey" of the science of universal grammar, *i.e.*, language in its essential form. To any inclined to this opinion, as well as to those who maintain that language "is not essential to thought," and go so far as to say "it must not be supposed that an examination of the rules of language would answer every purpose of a logical system," the undermentioned facts cannot be devoid of interest. For it is to be expected that parties holding such opposite views must be at variance as to whether or not the modality of a judgment belongs to the copula—in other words, whether "logic can take cognizance of the probability of any given matter ;" that is, more plainly speaking, to say, whether the expressions *will be* and *may be*, and their negatives, are not also *simple* forms of the copula as much as *is* or *is not*.

The *Sechwana* auxiliary verb, deprived of a host of accessory particles, may be simply classified under *two tenses* and *three moods* (proper).

Moods.	Tenses.	
	Past.	Present.
1. INDICATIVE.	*ki le ka tsamaea.*	*ki ea tsamaea.*
	I did go (= I went.)	I am going.
2. P	*ki le ki tla tsamaea.*	*ki tla tsamaea.*
	I (did) shall go.	I shall go.
3. POTENTIAL.	*ki le ki ka tsamaea.*	*ñka tsamaea.*
	I (did) may go.	I may go.

It is evident, from the above, that there is no such thing as a "*future tense*;" but rather, besides what are popularly called the *indicative* and *potential moods*, another *mood*, of which this "*future tense*" has all along been the erroneous representative, and which might, for common grammatical purposes, be called the *conjectural mood*. There is very little doubt, in my own mind, that these *three moods* express "modality," or degrees of knowledge, *at times past and present*, viz., certainty, probability, and possibility ; but, as my attention is for the present confined to phonology, I cannot here enter more fully into the subject. The fact will also, no doubt, be

historical records, will scarcely be thought to require any great portion of attention from a philosophical inquirer." True—judging from the fate of such nations and tribes as have in many countries been discovered by the traveller and navigator, and which have dwindled before the approach of the colonist, very much in the same manner as the herds of elephants, ostriches, and antelopes, before the repeated sallies of relentless hunters—such a remark carries with it a phase of plausibility; but it is a false conclusion, based upon the assumption that, inasmuch as a barbarian is a degraded being, everything pertaining to him must be correspondingly liable to depreciation. Civilization has advanced to such a consummation, through all its stages of improvement, from writing and printing, to the electric, and more recently the printing telegraph, that distance and time alike have become annihilated in human intercourse, and enlightened man has forgotten his ancient position, wherein, without the means of constructing the symbols of his thoughts, he spoke in native fluency and simplicity the language he now transmits, in all its complexity, with the speed of lightning, across continents and seas. Each science and art, in the historical order of its occurrence to the human mind, and its application to the supply of human necessities, has developed and modified, and in fact, destroyed the original language to such an extent—and his facilities of intercommunion have increased so amazingly by means of the various modes of expressing thought—that he is apt to magnify the nature of the idiom he speaks, forgetting that it

---

interesting to those writers who have lately been speculating on the nature of the auxiliary verbs *shall* and *will*, as they occur in English. "Whether Aristotle's rudiments of logic have not antecedent rudiments—which time may yet bring to light—is a somewhat unsettled problem in speculation."—(See *Ferrier's* "*Institutes of Metaphysic,*" p. 14.) Where, but in the principles of universal grammar, are such rudiments to be found? and whether more likely in the primitive dialect of the barbarian, or the complex idioms of the civilized?

is only the measure of its power that has been enhanced by the means of its communication ; that its development and complexity are the result of the development of mind, and the accession of new kinds of knowledge ; that, whether man avail himself of electricity or printing, or his organs of speech, he cannot surpass the rapidity of his thoughts, and in this respect the degraded Bushman can vie with the philosopher. When, therefore, we are told that Horne Tooke conceived an "original thought" regarding the significance of the particles in his native tongue, and, though "ignorant of the characters even of the Anglo-Saxon and Gothic languages," acquired their crude and barbarous forms, "to ascertain whether he had made a discovery," and this most successfully; and again, that Jacob Grimm was indebted for his "law" to his researches into the ancient forms of the German language, it seems surprising that students in philology have not, ere this, inferred from such facts the probability that, in the simplicity of the barbarous and unwritten tongues of newly discovered regions, are to be found most of the data necessary for the solution of some of the difficult problems in their science.* It seems not unreasonable for us to expect that, just as men are indebted for the greater part of what they know of metaphysical

* I am enabled to fortify these remarks by the following quotations from able authorities :—" The language of tribes who roam wild in a condition of savage life, is necessarily simple and primitive. So long as they continue separate and distinct from a civilized race, it is marked by the genuine impress of nature ; but as soon as they mix with nations more refined than themselves, in proportion as they gain morally or mentally by the inter-course, it is observable that, in the same degree, the parent language becomes vitiated or changed. Modifications and inflexions, unsanctioned additions, tralatitions, and neologisms, like parasitical plants adhering to an ancient and venerable stock, are then first observed disfiguring the natural root; and, as the genius of modern literature has become disdainful of indigenous compounds, a kind of hybridous vocabulary takes the place of the old tongue."—*Edinburgh Review*, April, 1844, p. 455.

" It is in the ruder languages that the important phenomena of development and growth—the laws of language—are best studied."—*R. G. L.*, *Encyc. Britann.*, *8th Ed.*, Vol. XIII. p. 195.

science to so much of what the ancients knew as was preserved in the monasteries of the middle ages, so they will have to look to the perspicuous structure of these primitive languages, which have hitherto remained concealed in the dark recesses and shades of history, for any principles elucidative of the laws of speech and thought.

But the condition of barbarous man is ephemeral! Guided by the knowledge of the past, we can only rest our hopes or fears of him on sheer probabilities. That his normal constitution will be annulled, and his social system dismembered, and that this will result in his gradually disappearing from the dismal scenes of his degradation, the whole tenor of modern history only convinces us. This ephemeral nature renders him the more interesting to both the missionary and the philologer. The former redoubles his efforts in scattering the seeds of knowledge, and raising the bright cloud in the path of the benighted to futurity; the latter, in grasping at each new appearance of truth, is rendered impatient by the conviction that "every day destroys a fact, a relation, or an inference." It is not to be wondered, then, that the missionary occasionally anticipates the duties of the philologer, and that the philologer sometimes borrows his materials from the missionary. It appears impossible that all that would be "acceptable to the scholar" in a uniform system of notation could be "convenient to" the evangelist; for the one requires a perfect and elaborate system of phonetic symbols as a means of etymological analysis, the other "a commoner alphabet, more suited to a work-day age" of missions; nevertheless, if the two can accommodate their plans to each other, it is to be expected that mutual facilitation must result.

In conclusion, it cannot be denied the subject which I have chosen is an unusually dry one, inasmuch as it is an attempt to arrive at the laws of a process which the great Macaulay would have said " is not likely to be better performed merely

because men know how they perform it ;" and cannot, therefor e
be expected to command the attention of more than a few of the
most zealous students of phonetic science, much less of those
who are indifferent to the gratification of " finding out laws
from facts, causes from effects, necessary truth from fleeting
occurrences of the day." At the same time, it must be admitted
that a writer on such a subject could never hope to realise anything remunerative, beyond the gratification of having embodied
opinions, based on his own researches, and of anticipating discussion in imparting them to others. But if even the materials
contributed are turned to account, without regard to my own
opinions, I shall consider myself fully compensated for my labours.

Throughout the work, which will be issued in three separate
parts, it will be my endeavour to trace the facts and phenomena
of the language to first principles. In the following pages on
the *Consonants*, I have worked upon a few materials which have
been known to missionaries for the last forty years—viz., the
permutations of *Initials ;* especially as they have occurred to my
own observation during the last four years. I have dealt only
with simple consonants and their mutual combinations, as well
as other elements affecting them. It may be thought that, in
confining my generalization of particulars to *initial* consonants,
I have made an arbitrary selection, and avoided any reference
to numerous permutations which are perceptible in the
comparison of different tribal idioms of the Sechwana—such, for
instance, as may be seen on a considerable scale in the comparison
of the " three members of the Bantu family of languages," which
Dr. Bleek considers " can be brought under certain laws,
similar, to some extent, to those detected by Jacob Grimm, as
affecting the relations between the different Teutonic tongues,
and other members of the Indo-European family of languages,
I have only to allege, in defence, that in the one class of instances
which I have chosen for analysis, the changes are constant, and

limited to cognate pairs of consonants—no one initial element being changeable to a third ;* whereas, this cannot be said of the other class alluded to by Dr. Bleek. It must not be supposed that, while thoroughly analysing the constant examples, I am neglecting the dialectical variations, to a proper discrimination of which, however, a far more critical knowledge of the South African languages than has hitherto been published for sacred purposes is absolutely requisite.

I should have preferred to treat of the *Vowels* first, but have found it necessary to reserve the consideration of them for the Second Part. This portion of the work will be based entirely on a series of new facts, the fruits of my own researches into the phonology of the language, on the subject of a peculiar order of mutation existing among the vowels. The Third Part will be confined to " sounds" formed by the combinations of simple or compound consonants, with simple or compound vowels, and which answer to the " Palatals" of some writers, the " Unstable combinations" of Dr. Latham, and the " Specific Modifications" of Professor Max Müller. My peculiarly unsettled circumstances will render the issue of these remaining parts rather uncertain.

As it is the first public essay of one who, during the last twelve years, has seen little of current literature, and still less of society, and the greater part of it has been penned in the native village or at the wild encampment, it will be needless for him to attempt to disarm the censures of critics, by defending himself on the score of style. Having, amidst the harassing vicissitudes of Colonial border-life, long neglected the art of composition, his work might doubtless have been rendered " more readable" had the phraseology been corrected throughout by some literary friend ; but it has not been his lot to find convenient access to any one.

---

* Except in one instance of *h* to *k*, for which I have attempted to account.

After a practical knowledge of this language during the few years of childhood, an alternating use of the low Dutch *patois* and English in the Cape Colony during youth, followed by an education in England, and subsequently by a return to a rude life among South African Boers, and more recently intimate intercourse with the same tribes among whom I was born, it cannot be said that any of these tongues is properly vernacular to me; or that I am open to charges of either national prejudice or organical habit, which would be unfavourable to a proper comprehension and discrimination of new elements. At all events, the desultory nature of my experience will help to explain and palliate any want of literary ability in the execution of a laborious task. The work having been printed in England, during my residence about 600 miles within the South African coast, some allowance will no doubt be made for any lapses and mistakes which I should otherwise have been enabled to rectify.

It was not till the *Second* and *Third* Chapters were in the press that I succeeded in procuring a copy of "The English Language," by Dr. Latham, nor till the first proof of the *Third* had been returned, and the *Fourth* was in the press, that I met with the "Missionary Alphabet" of Professor Max Müller, and the works of Professor Monier Williams, the Rev. Richard Garnett, and Dr. J. Müller, together with an exposition of "Grimm's Law," in the 8th Edition of the "Encyclopædia Britannica." I was, nevertheless, enabled, in correcting the later proofs, to avail myself of any notes or quotations from these works, by interpolations, wherever they appeared to place my own views in relief.

In reperusing it, I have reason to regret that a controversial tenor is perceptible throughout; but it is difficult to see how this can be avoided in a work containing innovations on prevailing notions. However I may have presumed to differ from Dr. Lepsius, I need only say, that its publication was suggested by his able and interesting pamphlet, without the thorough perusal of which I could not have placed the results of my researches in the form in which they now appear.

R. M., Jun.

Natal, South Africa,
January 28th, 1862.

These pages must be offered to the public in an unfinished state. The lamented author did not live to complete what was to him a labour of love. He died in his 36th year, at Mangeeri, near Kuruman, South Africa, after only a few days of acute suffering. In him the aborigines of interior Southern Africa, whose language was his favourite study, have lost a disinterested and enlightened friend.

The attempt is now made, in accordance with the desire of his widow, to present in as complete a form as possible the result of his investigations. As far as the 64th page, the proof-sheets had been fully revised and corrected by himself. Beyond this, it has been deemed best that nothing should be added, but the typographical corrections absolutely required.

Those who may read this attempt to contribute something to the general store of philological facts and inductions, will pass lightly over such imperfections as must necessarily be found under the circumstances.

J. S. M.

D'Urban, Natal,
1st December, 1862.

CHAPTER I.

PRINCIPLES OF CONSONANTAL CLASSIFICATIONS.

§ I. OF CLASSIFICATIONS AT PRESENT IN USE.

IT is not my purpose to discuss at any length the propriety of the distinction usually made between vowels and consonants, as it would suffice for me to assume that they are distinct, in accordance with the opinions of the majority of writers on the subject. The following remarks, in a quotation from an antiquated work, will perhaps be sufficiently distinctive to prepare the reader for the sequel :—

" WHAT thefe Vocal Organs precifely are, is not in all refpects agreed by Philofophers and Anatomifts. Be this as it will, it is certain that the *mere primary and fimple Voice is completely formed, before ever it reach the Mouth,* and can therefore (as well as Breathing) find a Paffage through the Nofe, when the Mouth is fo far ftopt, as to prevent the leaft utterance.

" Now *pure* and *fimple* VOICE, being thus produced, is (as before was obferved) *tranfmitted to the Mouth.* HERE, then, by means of certain *different* Organs, which do not change its primary qualities, but only fuperadd others, it receives *the Form or Character* of ARTICULATION. For ARTICULATION is in fact nothing elfe, than *that Form or Character, acquired to fimple Voice, by means of the Mouth and its feveral Organs, the Teeth, the Tongue, the Lips, &c.* The Voice is not by Articulation made more grave or acute, more loud or foft (which are its *primary* Qualities), but it acquires to thefe Characters certain others *additional,* which are perfectly adapted *to exift along with them.*

" THE *fimpleft* of thefe new Characters are thofe acquired through the *mere Openings of the Mouth,* as thefe Openings differ in giving the Voice a Paffage. It is the Variety of Configurations in thefe Openings only, which gives birth and origin to the feveral VOWELS ; and hence it is they derive their Name, by being thus *eminently Vocal,* and *eafy to be founded of themfelves alone.*

" THERE are *other articulate Forms,* which the Mouth makes, not by mere Openings, but by *different Contacts of its different parts* ; fuch for inftance, as it makes by the Junction of the two Lips, of the Tongue with the Teeth, of the Tongue with the Palate, and the like.

B

"Now as all thefe feveral Contacts, unlefs fome Opening of the Mouth either immediately precede, or immediately follow, would rather occafion Silence than to produce a Voice, hence it is, that with some fuch Opening, either previous or fubfequent, they are always connected. Hence alfo it is, that the *Articulations fo produced* are called CONSONANTS, becaufe they found not of themfelves, and from their own powers, but *at all times in company with fome auxiliary Vowel.*

"THERE are other fubordinate Diftinctions of thefe primary Articulations.

* * * * * *

"IT is enough to obferve, that they are all denoted by the common Name of ELEMENT, inafmuch as every Articulation is from them derived, and into them refolved."—*Hermes, by Iames Harris, Efq.*, p. 318. (1771.)

The above *general* description of the fundamental distinction between the two main classes of the Elements of Articulation, though written nearly a century ago, and founded upon the opinion of one of the ancients,* is perhaps as clear as, if not clearer than, anything I have met with.

According to it, the VOWELS are pure *sounds*, the variations in which are caused by different configurations of the aperture of the mouth; and the CONSONANTS are elements resulting from interruptions of the breath by the *contact of different organs;* and though the vowels can be pronounced without them, they cannot be completely uttered without accompanying vowels. It is, therefore, incorrect to speak of consonants as sounds, inasmuch as they require the apposition of these to render them audible. In speaking of them I therefore retain their common name, or otherwise call them " *explodents*,"† but only in reference to the necessary separation of the organs after contact in every case; and in the same sense may be understood the word " sound " when it occurs applicably to consonants in all my quotations, without distorting the meaning of their authors.

True, some consonants have been called semi-vowels,

---

* Ammonius.

† In this restricted sense I place the word in inverted commas throughout the analyses. The word *dividur*, used synonymously by Dr. Lepsius, would have done just as well, but occurred to me too late.

liquids, &c., because though such are formed by a contact, and are therefore "*explodent*," there is only a partial interruption of the breath, part of which escapes, giving to the otherwise *mute* element a *liquid* or *continuous* nature. There is, however, so much uncertainty attached to the subject of these peculiar consonants, and the most able writers differ so in classifying them, that it is not well to anticipate a proper analysis by any conjectures; and I prefer to base my conclusions respecting them upon a thorough generalization of facts which will come under consideration in the order of this Essay.

Though M. Majendie writes,* "Grammarians distinguish letters into Vowels and Consonants, but this distinction cannot suit physiologists," his division of the elements of sound into "those which are truly modifications of the voice, and those which (as he thinks) may be formed independently of the voice," does not differ materially from that of Harris. Nor does the system of Girard and Beauzée,† who "confine the term '*articulation*' to the Consonants, and designate the Vowels by that of '*sons*,' (sounds)," differ in anything but *terminology* from the distinction made above. For the Vowels, the term *Sonants*, in contradistinction from *Consonants*, would be as suitable as any, were it not also applicable to certain elements which may, perhaps, be proved to be *vocalized* Consonants. More satisfactory terms than those employed by Harris, and still in common use, could scarcely be found.

Among the ancient grammarians, as well as some moderns who have taken it upon them to interpret Grecian and Roman authors, the consonants appear to have been classified upon one or two principles, which have since been introduced into other highly developed living languages, and remained long in vogue among the learned. For a suitable example, it is only necessary

---

* El. Sum. Physiol., vol. i., p. 154. Cited by Sir J. Stoddart.
† Gram. Gén., vol. i., p. 5. Cited by Stoddart.

to refer to a grammar of the Greek. Its *fourteen* consonants were arranged according to *three* organs—*e.g.,*

	Mutes.			Semivowels.
	Tenues.	Mediæ.	Aspiratæ.	Liquids.
Labials.........	p	b	ph	m
Linguals	t	d	th*	n l r s
Palatals	k	g	kh	

Of these consonants, *nine* (viz., those of each organ) were found capable of another ternary arrangement, according to their properties or gradations of breathing, into *tenues, mediæ,* and *aspiratæ;* and a certain relation was thus established as existing among them. These were all denominated *mutes,* in contradistinction from the *vowels.*

Again, " the ancients found, in the humming and hissing of the letters *l, m, n, r, s,*" which did not fall under this second ternary arrangement, " a transition to the vowels, and therefore called them *semi-vowels;* and the first four were named *liquids,* on account of their mobility, and easily combining with other letters."† The sibilant *s* appears not to have admitted of any specific description.

This classification still obtains among some men of learning, who maintain the distinction between " *tenues (p, k, t)*—*i.e.,* slender, weak consonants; *mediæ (b, g, d,)* or consonants requiring a medial quantity of air for their articulation; and *aspiratæ (ph, kh, th,)* or strong consonants."‡ The partiality of many to it has of course been strengthened by their attachment to the classic tongues, as well as by long prescription. Among

---

* The nature of the articulation of the ancient letter θ, has not yet been satisfactorily decided; it may have been either *t*, combined with the *spiritus asper*, or equivalent to *th*, in the English *thin*. I have preferred to assume the former, in accordance with the opinion of Dr. Lepsius.—*See* " *Standard Alphabet,*" p. 37, note 2.

† Buttmann's " *Larger Greek Grammar,*" p. 11.

‡ " Egypt's Place in Universal History."—*Bunsen,* p. 278.

many modern systems which have sought to supplant it, that which retains the same division of the organs, but divides the gradations of breathing into *explosive* and *continuous*, is beginning to obtain among some eminent linguists, and probably owes its introduction to a certain peculiar law of correlation existing between several consonants; but it is difficult to say whether the discovery of this law is to be traced to any deductions from the physiology of the human voice, or to the frequent interchange and approximation of those consonants, which must have been apparent to any observer.

At all events, I must for the present content myself by placing before the reader such explanations of it as have been given by writers upon a physiological basis.

"All the oral consonantal sounds, except *l* and *r*," says **Sir John Stoddart,** " are produced in *pairs*, each pair having the same position of the organs, but with a certain difference of effect. . . . . The difference of effect in each pair is produced in the same manner throughout the whole."— *Glossology*, p. 127.

This principle is elsewhere explained by **Volney,** thus :—" Each contact (or near approximation) of two organs forms two consonants, which differ only by the degree of intensity of that contact, and which, under the names of strong and weak (or the like), are absolutely of the same family."— *Alfab. Europ.*, p. 71, *cited by Stoddart.*

Again, **Dr. Richardson,** in assuring his readers that **Horne Tooke** was guided by some general views of the " interchange of letters," writes as follows :—

" The perpetual change of *t* into *d* is familiar to all, and there is an organical cause for these and other changes—of B into P ; V into F ; G into K ; Z into S ; J into SH ; and the Anglo-Saxon Ð, that is, TH, as pronounced in *that*, into their θ, that is, TH, as pronounced in *thing*. The first of each pair (including D into T) differs from its partner by no variation whatever of articulation, but simply by a certain unnoticed and almost imperceptible motion or compression of or near the larynx, which causes what Wilkins calls some kind of murmur."—*The Study of Language ; an Exposition of the Diversions of Purley*, p. 31. He then describes how Horne Tooke, by illustrating " the whole series of these organic changes,"—viz.,

Of   *v*   *b*   G   *d*   Ð   J   Z   ZZ

Into *f*   *p*   C   *t*   θ   *sh*   *s*   *ss*

in two parallel (but not very elegant) lines, as they would be repeated by an Englishman and Welshman respectively, shows that a Welshman, by

" failing in the compression," changes seven of the English consonants;
" to which compression," he adds, " we owe seven additional letters."—
Ibid. p. 32.*

Having never seen an exposition of "Grimm's Law,"† of which Dr.
Richardson seems to think the above " general remarks" of Horne Tooke
" evidently lay the foundation," I am, of course, unable to judge of the light
which it may have shed on this subject.

This correspondency, or correlation‡ of certain consonants, has
given rise to a variety of terms, which differ according to the
views which the writers seemed to entertain of its nature.   The
following are a few which I have encountered :—

Sharp	flat	{ *Latham.*§ *Sir J. Herschel.*
Hard	soft	} *Lepsius, and others.*
Fortis	lenis	
Breathing	vocal	*Walker.*
Whispered	spoken ...	*Pitman.*
Firm and dry	soft	} *Volney.*§
Strong	weak	
Voiceless	voice	{ *Article, " Stammer," Penny Cyclopædia.*
Hard	weak	*Adelung.*§
Atonic	subtonic ...	*Rush.*§
Mute	semi-mute.	*Bishop.*§
Surd	sonant ...	*Sanscrit Grammarians.*§

* The fact of such crude remarks on this important subject making their
appearance in an able work, so recently as 1854, leads to the suspicion that
the laws of phonics must still be based on imperfect conjecture.

† A writer in an able Review thus speaks of " Grimm's Law:"—
" It consists in a permutation, or, if you will, a play of letters, whereby
almost any word may be made germain to any other. . . . . Not,
however, that the said law, with its machinery of ' nine equations,' is
without a real foundation in the history of language. We only mean that
it is exaggerated, and exactly in the manner of all hypothesis, all analysis,
by being run out into a vicious circle."—*North British Review, Feb.,* 1859.

‡ This is called, by Sir John Herschel, " a constant relationship or
parallelism to each other."—*Richardson's Dictionary,* 8vo., p. 19.

§ These are cited by Stoddart.

The two series of consonants, which are generally supposed to have this correlation, may thus be represented in parallel lines :—

k	p	t		th (thin)	s	sh	ch (-kh)	f	ch (-tsh)
g	b	d		th (this)	z	zh	gh	v	j

By means of a vertical line, I have separated from the rest the first three pairs, each answering to the *tenues* and *mediæ* of the ancient *mutes*, to which the *fortes* and *lenes explodents* of the modern system are identical. Among the remaining instances we find, *of the ancient alphabet*—1, the consonant *s* and its correlative *z*, which latter was considered to be a double consonant ; 2, the *hard* guttural aspirate *ch* (-*kh*). A corresponding *soft* form, *gh* (pronounced like *ch* in *loch* by a Scotchman, or in *buch* by a German), of this aspirate, and *four* other pairs, were thus left to be included in the second division of a more comprehensive classification. This appears to have been suggested—as I have before hinted, and as may be gathered from the tenor of the preceding remarks—by the above explained principle of binary quantities.

I leave the intelligent reader to compare with the above two parallel series of interchanges, obvious to the most superficial observer, the following tableau of the " Simple Consonants in the European Alphabets ;"* and have no doubt he will concur as to the probability of this classification being based as much on a vulgar view of the correspondency of sounds, as on any deduc-

---

* The same, on the graphic system of Dr. Lepsius :—

	Explosivæ or dividuæ.			Fricativæ or continuæ.			Ancipites.	
	fortis.	lenis.	nasalis.	fortis.	lenis.	semivoc.		
Gutturales......	k	g	ṅ	x́(χ) h	x́(γ)	y	r	
Dentales	t	d	n	{ š { s (θ́ (θ)	ž z θ́ (δ)		r	l
Labiales	p	b	m	f	v	w		

—*Standard Alphabet*, p 38

tions of the phono-physiologist—with the exception of, perhaps, the two gutturals above noticed.

	Explosivæ or dividuæ			*Fricativæ or continuæ.*			*Ancipites.*
	fort.	lenis.	nasal.	fortis.	lenis.	semivoc.	
Gutturales ...	k	Ger. *g*	Ger. *ng*	Ger. *ch* h	Danish *g*	Ger. *j*	gutt. *r*
Dentales	t	d	n	Fr. *ch* Sharp *s* En. *th* (-in)	Fr. *j* Fr. *z* En. *th* (-ine)		*r l*
Labiales ...	p	b	m	f	Fr. *v*	Eng. *w*	

Under the *explosivæ*, the only element not in the ancient phonetic tableau is *ng* ;* thus completing the set of nasals *m* and *n*, which were semi-vowels of the old arrangement. The remainder of these—viz , *r* and *l*, are excluded, as they anciently were; and left doubtful as to whether they belong to the *first* or *second* division. The letter *s*, formerly considered peculiar, and more recently called by a distinguished authority† " the last vowel and the first consonant," but to this day still rather inexplicable, sits the basis (phonically) of a formidable array of sibilants. The elements *w* and *y*, sometimes called consonants, at other times vowels, are introduced as *fricative* or *continuous* consonants, guttural and labial respectively.‡

Again, the unfortunate aspirates, which, Volney would say, require efforts of the lungs compatible with the vehement passions and strong desires of the savage or rustic, are excluded from this general tableau ; and only preserved from nonentity by the fact that they occur in such highly important languages as the *Sanscrit, Bengáli*, and *Chinese*, &c., in the phonetic tables of which Dr. Lepsius has inserted them. One of these, before

---

* Its omission was a mere oversight, as it occurred in the living pronunciation in the first syllable of such words as ἄγ-κος, ἔγ-χος.

† Sir John Herschel, in Richardson's Dictionary, 8vo., p. xix. This quotation does not occur in the synoptical table of sounds, in a later volume of " Essays, &c.," by Sir John Herschel.

‡ These, of course, occurred in the ancient living-pronunciation, in the diphthongs υι and ια of such words as νεκυι-α and θῡ-ιας, though not in the phonetic tableau of the grammarian.

referred to—viz., a soft form of *ch* (-*kh*), viz., *gh*, the most common instance of a rough guttural in the European alphabet, has by some mode of analysis been divided into two forms of a gentler and a harsher degree, and, under the letters χ and γ, marshalled in common with the sibilants, under the head of *fricativæ*, as if because swallowed up by the majority, or "democratic test of number" in which the latter exceed them! Nevertheless, we find *h*, the letter equivalent to the *spiritus asper*, huddled up between them, as if tacitly to imply that they are aspirates. If we seek an explanation of this apparent anomaly, we find the latest writer on this system saying—

"The essential distinction of the three fricative formations, *s̄*, *s*, and θ, together with the corresponding soft sounds *z̄*, *z* and θ', from the guttural . . . χ . . . consists in the friction of the breath being formed and heard at the *teeth*."—*Standard Alphabet*, p. 45.

But, to add to the confusion of nomenclature, at p. 33 of the same work, *h*, which I have described as being huddled up between the two gutturals in the above general tableau, is called a " fricative basis."

The principle of this classification is thus explained by Dr. Lepsius, its recent and most able expounder, before referred to. After disposing of the subject of the common and generally admitted organic divisions, he adds—

"There is another essential difference in the pronunciation, in as far as either the mouth at the above-mentioned places* is completely closed and re-opened, or the passage of the breath is only narrowed, without its stream being entirely interrupted by closing the organs. The consonants formed by the first process we call *explosive* or *divisible* (*dividuæ*), because the moment of contact divides the sound into two parts; the others *fricative*, from their sound being-determined by friction, or *continuous* (*continuæ*), because this friction is not interrupted by any closing of the organs."— *Standard Alphabet*, p. 30.

Before placing before the reader some of the elements of another classification founded on incontrovertible natural facts, it

---

* "In the throat, at the teeth, or with the lips."—*Ibid*.

may perhaps not be regarded as presumptuous if I endeavour
to show, on physiological grounds, where the system just described is probably at fault.

As the consonants *k, t, p*, and *g, d, b*, respectively, *fortes* and
lenes of the *division* of *explodents*, differ in no respect except
terminology from the *tenues* and *mediæ* of the more ancient
arrangement of *mutes*, I shall make no reference to them; for
whether viewed in the above binary order, or the ternary one,
according to the organs, they are, *so far as they go*, intact
and indisputable. I have mainly to do with the group of " pairs ;"
which, while they bear an organical relation to the three series
above, are all supposed to differ from them in the gradations of
breathing, and have been denominated *continuæ* or *fricativæ*.

NOTE.—As the gutturals which are included in these terms have only
apparently a different phonical basis from the rest, and it is chiefly in relation
to them that the terms *fricative* and *aspirate* have been confounded, they
will require another line of argument; I, therefore, reserve a further consideration of them for the section on *gutturals* in the following chapter.

By the former term is meant the *non-interruption of a sound ;*
by the latter, that *the sound is determined by friction*. From the
fact of both terms serving to describe the same instances, it is
evident that *partial interruption of the breath* is implied in all.
More definiteness ought to be expected in the treatment of
philological subjects; and, till we succeed in arriving at that, we
may as usual grope in the mazes of sophistication, and be tan-
talized by a play of words. One would think that, of all the
natural sciences, none ought to demand more accuracy in its
rudimental nomenclature than that of language, whether phonetic
or grammatic.

The word *continuæ* includes several elements not classed under
it by those who make use of the term. " Vowels," which I have
assumed to be entirely distinct in their nature from consonants,
" are," in the strictest sense of the word, " continued sounds, produced when the passage of the air through the fauces is unin-

terrupted, the fauces being only *more or less narrowed.*"* Not
only the four " pairs" of sibilants—i.e., *s, z; th*(-in), *th*(is); *sh,
zh;* and *f, v;* the principal examples classed under this term
(in the letters *s, z; θ, δ; š, ž; f, v*)—but also *l* and *r,* which
have been placed under the head of *ancipites,* because they
appear to betray a little of the nature of explodents—and even
the nasals *m, n,* and *ñ* (-ng)—in certain modified forms can all
be proved to be continuous consonants. There can be little
doubt that it is the *" indistinct vowel"* element (whether by the
term be understood action of breath alone or voice), easily assumed
by them all which renders them so, and has led to their being
frequently called *semi-vowels;* at all events, it is very probable
that it is nothing else than their peculiar nature in this respect
which renders them *liquid* with all other consonants.

The term *fricativæ* conveys the idea of the breath being partially confined, as well as, that it may be almost wholly interrupted; but, like the above, it includes elements not admitted by
those who apply it exclusively to some consonants. "Each vowel
requires a different elevation of the tongue, or contraction of
the lips,"† by which different degrees of frication, however apparently imperceptible, are produced. And it follows that all the
above consonants, which easily assume the *"indistinct vowel"*
element, must, where so modified, also be fricatives; with (but
only apparently) the sole exception of the nasals, in the enunciation of which the breath is withheld, and there is no faucal
passage to cause a frication.

The two terms are thus strictly compatible in respect to the
instances I have shown can be included under them both. The
nasals are apparently the only exceptions, being continuous and
fricative in their modified forms, but not faucally.

---

* Encyc. Britann., 7th Ed., article *Physiology,* p. 683. The italics are
my own.
† *Ibid.*

I shall now endeavour to illustrate this position by confronting the two following quotations, which will show where contradiction and confusion exist in the application of these terms. Dr. Lepsius, treating of the "indistinct vowel-sound" attached to some consonants, writes as follows:—

" This vowel is inherent in all **soft*** *fricative* consonants, as well as in the first part of the *nasal explosive* sounds. . . . . It assumes the strongest resonance, as may be easily explained on physiological grounds, in combination with *r* and *l*, which, as is well known, appear in Sanscrit as *r* and *l*, with all the qualities of the other vowels."—*Standard Alphabet*, p. 27.

Again, as follows:—

" It is a decided mistake to reckon *m* and *n* among the *consonantes continuæ*; for in *m* and *n* it is only the **vowel element*** inherent in the first half, which may be continued at pleasure, whilst in all the continuous consonants it is the consonantal element (the **friction***) which must be continued, as in *f, v, s, z*."—*Standard Alphabet*, p. 30, note.

In what precedes, I have implied that the *vowel-element* and some amount of *friction* are inseparable in all articulations partaking of the former, inasmuch as the breath is the medium of the voice. The learned Professor seems to have forgotten, (1) that the consonants *v* and *z* in the latter paragraph were some of the *soft* fricatives of his classification, alluded to in the former as partaking of the "indistinct vowel sound;" (2) that it is as much the "indistinct vowel" element in *v*, and *z*, which is continued, as in any forms of *m* and *n*; (3) a fact amounting to a postulate in the science of phonics, that the consonantal element does not consist in the *friction* but in the *contact*, whether partial or complete, of two organs. In short, the important principle appears to have been lost of, that if we are to regard the *teeth* and the *palate* as organs indispensable to the action of the *lips* or the *tongue*, in forming articulations by interrupting the emission of the breath by their *contact*, it follows the elements produced by them are also " *explodent*," because the moment of contact (of the tongue with either of them, or the lips with one of them)

---

* The bold letters are substituted by me, as italics already occur.

divides the sound into two parts : that they differ from the other
mutes or " explodents," in that the contact is partial, thus causing
a gentle *frication* between them, and prolonged if necessary,
whether in the form of breath or voice, therefore *continuous;*
but these are not reasons sufficient to warrant their exclusion
from the division of " explodents." Dr. Richardson, treating
of the consonants *b, p, f, v ; c (k), g (γ), d, t; l, m, n, r, x; s, z;*
very concisely says—

"Each and every of them requires, however, for its complete utterance,
a breathing (precedent), a closure or collision of some of the organs of
speech, and an apertion or separation of them, with a breathing (subsequent)."—*Richardson's Dictionary,* 8vo., p. xiv.

Moreover, granting, what is implied in the preceding quotation, that " the complete consonant is best perceived when
placed between two vowels,"* and that " the full pronunciation
of an explosive letter requires the closing and opening of
the organ,"† which are both very plain statements on the
part of those who sanction this classification, and tantamount
to saying that the formative process of all consonants is the same,
it follows that those which easily assume the " vowel-element "
are also " explodents ;" this accessory " element " having its
origin in the pliability and mobility of the tongue—an organ
indispensable even in the formation of the pure vowels.

The above train of reasoning suggests that there is something
very unsatisfactory in this classification of elements ; and, consequently, that any graphic system founded upon it must
also be liable to objection. In referring to the two terms
continuous and *fricative,* I have endeavoured to show, (1) that
they include a large number of instances (vowels) having no
essential or generic resemblance to those within the scope of
induction (consonants); (2) that though consonants may possess
a secondary attribute (semivocal), this ought not to exclude
them from classification under a more general attribute (" explo-

---

* Standard Alphabet, p. 30, note.   † Ibid.

dent"), definitive of the nature of the generalizations arrived at by a survey of all the points in which they differ from or resemble each other.

In conclusion, granting, what is generally admitted, that both the vowels and the pure "explodent" consonants ($k, t, p; g, d, b,$) may be aspirated, it follows that the other "explodent" consonants, which easily assume the "vowel-element," may also be aspirated—*i.e.*, those usually called *fricativæ* or *continuæ*.

I thus show that the aspirate "explodents" include some fricatives, the rest of which, therefore, fall under the simple "explodents." A very important question then arises, as to whether the correspondency existing between *s* and *z*, *th*(in) and *th*(is), *sh* and *zh*, and *f* and *v*, (s, z; θ, δ; $\check{s}, \bar{z}$; and $f, v,$ of Lepsius,) is analogous to that between the mute explodents *k* and *g*, *t* and *d*, *p* and *b*. If I have succeeded in raising a doubt in the mind of the reader, I only leave him in a prepared state for the impartial consideration of a few simple facts, the analysis of which, in the following chapter, will perhaps result in a synthetic view of a far more satisfactory nature.

§ II. General Principles of a Classification suggested by the Mutation of Consonants in the Sechwana* Language.

" The transformation of sounds," says Dr. Bleek, " is the main

---

* There has been a good deal of speculation at work on the origin of the name of the people speaking this interesting language. The common opinion among Missionaries is, that the name is derived from *tshudna* (be like each other). Another holds that it is derived from *tshudna*, " a little white, or inclining to white, light coloured—*i.e.*, not black (probably in opposition to the more dark-coloured tribes of the north), a diminutive form, from *tshuéu*, white."—*Sir G. Grey's Library, S. A. Lang.*, p. 184. Mr. Fredoux, of the Paris Missionary Society, writes:—"For our part, we are inclined to give it another origin. In the idiom of the people of whom we are speaking, we find the word *Mochuana* (plural, Bachuana) employed as a kind of diminutive of *Monchu*, black, and signifying blackish, or inclining

characteristic of the Setshuâna,"* and it is probable that in no other existing language is this principle carried to such an extent. It appears surprising that, though so long before the public, it should not have suggested to the attention of philologers the probable existence of some fundamental phonical laws.

This peculiar commutation† of consonants occurs chiefly in certain instances—viz., the formation of verbal nouns, e.g., seeing, &c., and those cases in which the verb is immediately preceded by the " object.-particles" self and me, as in the following examples:—

	Verb.	Verbal Noun.	Verb, with the 1=self.	"Object-particles," m, n, nt=me.	Mutation.
1.	Bòna	Pònòt	Ipòna	Mpòna	b to p
2.	Cola§	Colò	Icola	Ncola	c immutable§
3.	Ndaea	Ntèò			d to t
4.	Gorisa	Khorishò	Ikhorisa	Ñkhorisa	g—kh
5.	Heta	Phetò	Ipheta	Mpheta	h—ph
6.	Kana	Kauò	Ikana	Ñkana	k immutable
7.	Khatla	Khatlò	Ikhatla	Ñkhatla	kh „

to black."—*Bulletin de la Société de Géographie, de Paris,* 4ᵉ Série, t. xiv., p. 371.

The probability is, that Mr. F. has hit upon the correct derivation, upon the following grounds. A black cow is called *chwana*, from *nchu*, black; in the same manner as a red or black cow, with white back, is called *khwana*, from *nkhwè*. Any little black thing would be called *nchunyana;* a little black person, *monchunyana;* but the word being also used as a diminutive of *colour*, a person with a dark brown complexion is invariably called *mochwana.* Had the name been derived from *ohwéu*, or *shweu*, white, it would have become *bashòwána*, in the same manner as *ohòwána*, a white cow, from *chwéu;* or *hòchwána*, a grey cow, from *kwebu*, grey, in which examples *we* becomes *ò*. (In the above examples, *tsh* and *ch* are homophones.)

* Sir G. Grey's Library, S. A. L., p. 116.
† The language also contains other instances of interchanging consonants which may appear to be irregular forms, but allow of classification under euphonical or dialectical laws affecting the relations between the different languages of the Bántu family. These will be noticed in the sequel.
‡ Used by the Missionaries as equivalent to *ng*.
§ The diacritical mark attached to *o* as *ò*, will in every instance, for the purposes of this work, indicate that vowel in the Italian *però*, or the English *a* in *all*.
§ C of the Missionaries=*tsh*, or *ch* in *Charles*.

	Verb.	Verbal Noun.	Verb, with the i=self.	"Object-particles," m, n, ṅ=me.	Mutation.
8.	Loma	Tomò	Itoma	Ntoma	l to t
9.	Metsa	Mecò	Imetsa	Mmetsa	m immutable
10.	Nama	Numò	Inama	Nnama	n ,,
11.	Ṅapa	Ṅapò	Iṅapa	Ṅṅapa	ṅ ,,
12.	**Pitla**	**Pitlō**	**Ipitla**	**Mpitla**	p ,,
13.	Phala	Phalò	Iphala	Mphala	ph ,,
14.	Risa	Tishò	Itisa	Ntisa	r to t
15.	Rata	Thatò	Ithata	Nthata	r to th
16.	Sila	Tsilò	Itsila	Ntsila	s to ts
17.	Shòka	Còkò	Icòka	Ncòka	sh to c
18.	**Tena**	**Tenō**	**Itena**	**Ntena**	t immutable
19.	Thiba	Thibò	Ithiba	Nthiba	th ,,
20.	Tlotla	Tlotlò	Itlotla	Ntlotla	tl ,,
21.	Tlhaba	Tlhabò	Itlhaba	Ntlhaba	tlh ,,
22.	Tsenya	Tsenyò	Itsenya	Ntsenya	ts ,,
23.	Ila	Kilò	Ikila	Ṅkila	— to k

The above are all the consonants found in the phonetic systems of the Missionaries of different Societies. Additions could be made; but I prefer to reserve such for the analysis in the sequel, as they are based on my own researches.

In the above list of *twenty-three* initials, *ten* are mutable, and *thirteen* immutable. If there are excluded from it, for the present, those words with the nasal initials *m, n, ṅ*, and those with compound letters, all of which are in italics, it will be observed that the remaining instances* may be classified upon a few apparent principles:—

1. That the immutable elements *t* and *p* are those which have generally been denominated *fortes*, and the mutable elements *b* and *d, lenes*; and that the language so far confirms the fact of the existence of each in binary quantities, to which I have before alluded. The reverse mutation in the above examples, from *fortis* to *lenis*, never takes place. This holds good in all the remaining instances; therefore the presumption upon which I start, in proceeding to the analysis, is that the commutable consonants are respectively *fortes* and *lenes* in all these other cases not commonly admitted.

---

* All these are indicated in bold type.

2. It may be distinctly observed that some are *aspirate*, and the rest *simple* " explodents ;" that the aspirates have binary quantities corresponding with those of the simple " explodents," and that instances of " fricativæ or continuæ" fall under both divisions. This decides my presumptive arrangement into *simple* and *aspirate* " explodents," instead of into *explosivæ* and *continuæ*. It must be evident that we have thus suggested to us the practicability of arriving at some of the fundamental laws of a general phonic system, without having recourse exclusively to either the physiology of the human voice, or to any " written system fixed by literature," however elaborate and ancient.

The whole of these elements, though gathered from one barbarous language by strict attention to the " living traditional pronunciation," will be found in the following analysis to admit of a simple classification, corroborating partially, but in a striking manner, the views now obtaining, and in other respects entirely upsetting them. In the Sechwana language we have two series of consonants, both possessing binary quantities,* each of which is only in certain circumstances changeable to the other; but the reverse mutation never takes place. Such normal facts are of great importance, and where constancy is thus attributed to their laws, these are rendered the more worthy of being regarded as a basis upon which to plant further investigations.

---

* The reader, if dissatisfied with the above term, is at liberty to substitute the word *values*, or *characters*, or *natures*, provided the same be used throughout.

CHAPTER II.

ANALYSIS OF SECHWANA CONSONANTS.

In accordance with the views stated in the preceding chapter, I have, in the following table, removed from the "European Consonantal System" of Dr. Lepsius, the consonants to which I, for the present, take exception, as not all belonging to the set corresponding with the *Simple "Explodents;"* but have included the few under the head of *Ancipites*.

TABLE OF COINCIDENT CONSONANTS.

	1st Division. fortis.	1st Division. lenis.	2nd Division. fortis.	2nd Division. lenis.	Nasals.	Ancipites.
I. *Gutturals* .	k	— ·	—	g(-gh)	ñ(-ng)	r
II. *Linguals*...	t	d			n	{ r l
III. *Labials* ...	p	b			m	

Thus are presented the points of coincidence between a phonic system based upon the physiology of the human voice, and another arrived at by induction from particulars in the languag of a barbarous people, "in a manner wholly concerning the ear." It is now my purpose to explain and develope this natural system, by treating of each horizontal (or organic) series separately, filling it up according to the principles assumed, and thus completing the vertical sets.

NOTE.—By doing so, I am apparently admitting a division according to the organs; but my use of it is arbitrary, in order to make myself better understood, by adhering as much as possible to the prevailing nomenclature where no dispute exists. So far as regards the classification of the elements of articulation, the views started in this treatise are discordant with those generally h ld, principally upon the subject of the vertical divisions into *simple*—and *aspirate*—" *explodents*." instead of into *explodents* and *fricatives*; and the distinction of each of these into binary quantities, *fortis* and *lenis*, in certain instances not usually admitted. On this account, I speak of 1st and 2nd divisions at the commencement of the section in each series, to avoid confusion in the above terms. At the close of each section, I give the series as developed according to the Sechwana, in the most simple characters that can be suggested.

§ I. The Guttural Series.

1st *Division*.		2nd *Division*.		*Nasals*.
fortis.	lenis.	fortis.	lenis.	
k	—	—	g(-gh)	n (-ng)

The above Sechwana consonants, so far, happen to coincide, as I have said, with the organic order generally admitted.

Under the *First Division* of the Guttural Series, it will be seen that the only exception is *g*, which is usually considered the *lenis* form of *k*, and improperly called in English " hard g." This consonant does not exist in Sechwana, which thus affords another instance of a language possessing an element of articulation in one quantity, without its correlative form.

Note.—But an apparent anomaly presents itself at the outset, in the case of Sechwana verbs with vowel initials, *e.g.*: The verb *ila* (hate), in the noun expressing the action, becomes *kilo;* and with the object-particles, *ikila, ṅkila.* This does not, however, contradict the principle which I wish to maintain regarding the fixed correlation of the instances in every pair; for the above is merely an example of the substitution of a positive consonant where none exists. It is, perhaps, " a mere contrivance for euphony's sake;" something like that in Greek, in the case of the particle οὐ (*not, no,*) which takes final κ before vowels, as in the example οὐκ ἔνεστιν.[*] A reason why *k* is naturally preferred to either *t* or *p* in such a case, may perhaps be alleged, upon a physiological basis, that in the articulation of it the mouth is in a position best suited for the pronunciation of a vowel.

In Sechwana, all verbs with initial k, as kana (*fix together*), retain this consonant in the initial of the noun expressing the action kanŏ, and in the verb itself with the object-particles prefixed—

---
[*] Buttmann.

ikana, ñkana. It thus remains immutable, and its quantity is, therefore, upon the principle I have shown to exist in the phonic system of the language—*fortis*. It is probable that had the Sechwana contained the *simple* "*explodent*," *g* (*lenis*), as an initial, this would, in the inflection, have become *k*. Though I have not the opportunity of thus testing, by this language, the correlation which is universally admitted to exist between *k* and *g*, a collateral, and perhaps sufficiently satisfactory confirmation of it may be found in the two aspirate forms *kh* and *g* (-*gh*) corresponding with them in the series, so far as regards quantity, and which I shall presently notice.—(*Vide* Section ii., Ch. iv.)

Like the rest of consonants, in the confusion of so many orthographic schemes, the instances in this pair, *k* and *g*, have been separately the subject of " nice distinctions," especially among authors reasoning upon a physiological basis, *e.g.* :—

NOTE.—"**Adelung** declares that the German *k* has a double sound;" that in *kaum* (scarcely), and *sack* (a bag), it is different from *k* in *klein* (little), and *haken* (a hook) ; " and on the letter *g* he makes somewhat similar observations."—*Glossology : Sir J. Stoddart, p.* 132. Again, **Mr. Bell** observes " that in *k*, before the close lingual vowel *ee*, the tongue strikes the palate much further forward than before *ah* or *aw*, and that the same will apply to *g*."—*Ibid.*

I shall not presume to question the utility of such phonical divarications, believing that consonants, as well as vowels, are apparently modified, but only slightly influenced, according to their different combinations, their position in the collocation of syllables,* and the capacity of the voice : that is, either the *fortis* or *lenis* form of any consonant may be enunciated with different degrees of distinctness,† but its quantity, relatively to that of the other instance of the pair, remains constant. The importance of adhering to this principle, in order to arrive at a classification

---

* Or, more correctly: their position with respect to the syllabic accent.

† Or, in the words of Sir J. Stoddart :—" It is not to be understood that either the one or the other articulation in each pair does not admit of nice shades and discriminatory touches as it were, perceptible to some ears, and not to others."—*Glossology,* p. 132.

of the normal elements of articulation, and so as to account for the nature of all variable instances, cannot be estimated. To the philologer, the desideratum of the day is a phonic standard, with which to compare undefined sounds; a phonetic formula, or analytic means of explaining apparent exceptions, and bringing them within a synthetic view, as a further means of evolving the principles of the science of etymology.

Under the *Second Division* of the GUTTURAL SERIES, the Sechwana presents probably the normal instances of what are generally considered the most questionable elements in universal phonics ; that is, upon which the opinions of linguists have been most divided.

The data are as follows : —

1. All verbs with initial g* (-gh), as gata *(tread)*, commute this consonant into kh (or aspirate k) in the inflected noun expressing the action, khatò ; also in the verbs with the object-particles—ikhata, ñkhata.

2. Again: All verbs with initial kh,† as khwetsa *(drive)*, retain this consonant in the inflected forms — khweco, ikhwetsa, ñkhwetsa.

In the former instance, the articulation of g *(-gh)* is changed to kh ; in the latter, kh remains immutable. Both instances are constant—*i.e.*, without exceptions; therefore g is a *lenis* form, and kh the *fortis* of the same pair, and consequently they are both aspirates corresponding to the simple " explodents " *k* and *g.* Such laconic inferences may lay me open to a charge of presumption ; but in the sequel I shall have recourse to collateral evidence, and the testimony of able authorities.

---

* Called by Dr. Bleek " a soft kind of guttural . . . . denoted by *g*, as in Dutch."—*Sir G. Grey's Library, South African Languages, p.* 113.

It is the *g* in Dutch *dag=ch* in German *buch.*

† This digraph=*kh* in *milk-house*, with *mil* elided, the accent on *khouse*, and the *h* distinctly enunciated.

*Confusion in Nomenclature and Orthography, in the usual
Classification of the* Guttural *Consonants.**

[Sir John Stoddart, in speaking of a pair of gutturals,
very correctly says—" They are evidently susceptible of modification by slight differences in the position or action of the
organs."† I have already had occasion to refer to them; and
shall do so again in the details of this section, in order to show
that the circumstance of their partaking of the nature of fricatives
as well as aspirates has hitherto led to a classification which, however elaborate, is unsatisfactory to some like myself engaged in
local researches into a language till recently *unwritten,* and to
this day without a proper grammar or vocabulary.

Indeed, it may truly be said of all the gutturals, but especially
of their aspirate forms, that they are of a nature to deceive the
ear more than any other simple consonants, especially on account
of the difficulty of distinguishing them accurately from purely
" palatal "‡ utterances, or other sounds resulting from a combination
of these with gutturals.§

NOTE (*a*).—In German, **Adelung** distinguishes the articulation *ch* into

---

* The reader is at liberty to pass on to page 40, in order to follow the
analysis; or to read this parenthetical section separately, as from its nature
it is treated in a desultory manner.

† Glossology, p. 130.

‡ Whenever this word *palatal* occurs within inverted commas, it is intended to represent a more general term (to which I shall have recourse in
the sequel, Part III.), of which the above word includes only one of the
special meanings.

§ Gutturals are by some writers also called *palatals*, perhaps from this
very circumstance; and by others are made to include *h*, or the *spiritus
asper.*

two degrees, a stronger and a weaker; and **Müllёr** reckous. the three
following modifications of the same :—

1. In *lieblich, selig*, &c.
2. In *tag, suchen*, and,
3. As uttered by the Swiss, Tyrolese, and Dutch.

NOTE (*b*).—**Volney** has two pairs of sounds approximating to those under
consideration—viz., (1), his twelfth class, distinguished by the French term
grasseyement (thickening of utterance), which has also a strong and a weak
pronunciation :—

The stronger (grasseyement dur),—which he compares to the 19th Arabic
letter "غ," and is " common among the Parisians and Provençals, and pre‐
dominates among the Berbers."—*Glossology, Sir John Stoddart*, p. 130.
This is the letter, the power of which **Dr. Lepsius** considers equivalent
to the modern Greek γ.—*Standard Alph ibet*, p. 48.

The weaker (grasseyement doux),—in this "the position of the organs is
very similar to that which produces the vowel *i*."—*Glossology, Sir John
Stoddart*, p. 130. **Dr. Lepsius** appears again to consider the sound
meant here as equivalent to "the modern Greek γ."—*Standard Alphabet*,
p. 13, note 3.

" A transition often takes place from the one to the other of these articu‐
lations, in like manner as we find the Hellenic γέλαν . . . become in
Romaic *yelan*."

(2) His thirteenth class, containing—*The stronger*, as in *buch ; the
weaker*, as in *Metternich.—Glossology, Sir J. Stoddart*, p. 130. Otherwise
expressed by **Dr. Lepsius** thus:—" The German *ch* in *ich*, he (**Volney**)
places as a *soft* sound by the hard sound in *buch.*"—*Stand. Alph.*, p. 13, note 3.

NOTE (*c*) —**Dr. Lepsius** (at page 43, "Standard Alphabet"), in describing
the difference between guttural *k* and a palatal *k'*, adds:—" In most lan‐
guages *k* and *g* before the vowels *e, i, ę, u,*[*] approach the palatal pro‐
nunciation, whilst before *a, o, u,* they remain more guttural, owing to the
formation of these vowels. In the Sanscrit, the guttural and palatal pro‐
nunciation were distinguished before *all* vowels."

Again : (p. 48.) We find the same two sounds alluded to by **Volney**
(13th class) thus classified :—

" χ g. *Buch, ach ;* pol. *chata.*

χ' Sansc. श [†] Ger. *ich, recht.*"

The former as a guttural, the latter as a palatal-guttural, if the diacritical
mark has any value.

Again : (Note 1, p. 43.) The Germans " pronounce, for instance, the *ch*
in all diminutives, even after *a, o,* and *u*, not guttural as in *Aachen, rauchen*,

---

* Of his graphic system.

† This Sanscrit (?) and German sound is again called a *palatal sibilant.—
Stand. Alph.*, p. 42, note 1.

kuchen, but palatal, as in *Mamachen, Frauchen, Uhuchen*, from *Mama, Frau, Uhu.* The guttural *ch* is pronounced after all vowels in the most southern parts of Germany."

The indistinctness of the above remarks arises from this learned philologer not being sufficiently specific in describing what he means by the "palatal pronunciation," or an "approach to the palatal pronunciation." It may mean either, that of the "pure and simple palatal" *y* and its aspirate form *ẏ*, or that of *k* or *g*, "easily assuming a shade of *y*."* If the former, it must fall without the guttural series; if the latter, it becomes a palatal-guttural.† But if the pointed letter *k'* is intended for the sound of *ch* in *choice*, as Dr. Lepsius seems to intimate (p. 41), it is then quite as likely to indicate the "palatal" form of some other compound consonant. It is first necessary to arrive at the nature of elementary sounds, in order to comprehend the manner in which they are transformed or modified by usage.

The matter is rendered still more indistinct by the following (Note 1, p. 37) :—"The modern Greek γ passes at least before *e, ι, υ*, into the corresponding fricative sound." See above example of γέλαν. The terms palatal and fricative, intended by the learned writer to differ in meaning, are thus confounded in reference to the gutturals. The writer elsewhere speaks of a "palatal sibilant," and it is easy to comprehend the nature of a palatal-lingual ; but when (p. 43) he speaks of cases in which "the friction connected with the palatals" is "so inherent, that in the organic structure of the language it may be considered as still forming a *simple sound*,"‡ it is difficult to conceive of what is meant. I think much confusion would be avoided by a distinction being first made between simple or compound consonants, and the modifications in either by the superaddition of the pure "palatals"—a plan I intend to pursue by the assistance of the Sechwana. In the sequel I shall attempt to prove that an element of articulation, exactly equivalent to *ch* in the German *ich* (above alluded to by all these distinguished authors), and which exists in Sechwana, is simply the pure "palatal" *y*, with the *spiritus asper*. A careful perusal of the above quotations and remarks will no doubt suggest the probability that the other few sounds referred to are either different gradations of the soft consonant *ch* in *lachen*, or in some instances combinations of the pure "palatals" with them.

Dr. Lepsius, in his elaborate work, under the series of gut-

---

* Or, as Dr. Bleek more happily expresses it, "*being influenced by a superadded* ẙ."

† *Vide* "Standard Alphabet," p. 44, in which both are confounded in "the series of pure palatal sounds," which cannot surely include compounds of simple consonants with pure palatals. See Part III. of this work.

‡ The italics are my own.

turals, gives, besides his *explodents,* two distinct sets of pairs,
which he denominates *fricatives* and *aspirates ;** but between
these divisions I must confess myself utterly at a loss to comprehend the difference in reference to the *gutturals.* I have, in
the preceding chapter, stated wherein it appears the classification
which he sanctions is at fault. It becomes me to bear out the
truth of my remarks on the details of each organic (or horizontal)
series. As this learned philologer has given a synoptical and
comparative view of the phonetic systems of several languages,
as reduced to his own graphic system, and also as represented
by the authors from whom he gathered his particulars, I cannot
do better than subjoin a compendious abstract of the *gutturals*
under those heads of *fricative* and *aspirate,* in order to enable
the reader to follow my inferences.

AFRICAN LANGUAGES.

	Fricative.		Aspirate.	
	fortis.	lenis.	fortis.	lenis.
1. Hottentot:				
Wuras	kh	ch		
Knudsen		c		
Wallmann		ch		
2. Káfir:				
Appleyard	r	r		
3. Zulu:				
Grout	r, r̕	r		
4. Tšuána :				
Appleyard	kh	g		
5. Kúa:				
Prof. W. Peters	h	—		
6. Swáhili:				
Krapf	c̣	h		
7. Hereró:				
C. Hugo Hahn	h	—		
8. Mpongwe:				
Am. Board on the Gabun.	—	—		

* The latter, it must be remembered, are not included in his " general
tableau," but only in phonetic tables of the few languages in which they
are supposed to occur.

| | Fricative. | | Aspirate. | |
	fortis.	lenis.	fortis.	lenis.
9. Fernando Po :				
John Clarke	h	—		
10. Yóruba :				
S. Crowther	h	—		
11. Ot'i :				
H. N. Riis	h	—		
12. Susu :				
I. W. G., Am. Board	kh			
13. Máude :				
Macbrair	h	—		
14. Vei :				
S. W. Koelle	h	r		
15. Olof :				
Roger	kh hr	h		
16. Hóusa :				
Schön	h	y		
17. Kánuri :				
S. W. Koelle	h	—		
18. Nubisch :				
Lepsius	h	—		
19. Koṅgára :				
Lepsius	(h)			
20. Galla :				
Ch. Tutschek	—	—		
21. Hieroglyphic :				
Lepsius	χ	—		
22. Koptic :				
Lepsius	χ	—	k'	
23. Beǵa :				
Lepsius	—	-		
24. Abyssinian, Gęẹẹz				
Ludolph	h	-	—	k'
25. Abyssinian, Ambāra :				
Isenberg	h	ch	—	k'

NOTE.—By the above list it appears that of **twenty-five** African languages, nine are represented as having both quantities of fricatives, i.e., *fortis* and *lenis;* thirteen contain fricatives of only one quantity, and the remaining three, neither fricatives nor aspirates; but, among the whole number, only three are said to contain *aspirates,* viz., the two Abyssinian dialects, and the Koptic.

From the above, a rather sweeping inference may be drawn,

viz., that about seven-eighths of the African dialects have no aspirated gutturals.

Fortunately for my purpose, the list contains, at the outset, *three* or *four* South African languages, with the *nature* of which I happen to be more or less acquainted—viz., the Hottentot or Namân, the Kafir and Zulu, and the Sechwana; the phonic system of the latter being the subject of my particular attention, I have made it the basis of these investigations. To test the propriety of the distinction between the terms *fricative* and *aspirate* in the case of the gutturals, as well as to show the confusion arising from a mere comparison of *alphabets,* I shall consider each of these languages in succession.

(*a*) SECHWANA.

The pair of consonants in this language, which I have already indicated by the letters *kh* and *g* (in use among the missionaries), and proved, upon a certain principle, to be aspirate-" explodent" gutturals, are indicated in the list by the same letters,* but without a knowledge of their nature, both pláced under the head of fricatives by Dr. Lepsius, and, moreover, represented by the ancient Greek letters χ and γ, in his corresponding graphic system. To say that the consonant thus intended to be indicated by the Greek χ, and called a fricative, is anything but a slight modification by a gentler aspiration—that is, differing only in an insignifioant degree, if at all, from *lenis* aspirate *g* (*-gh*)—is, I think, carrying the habit of phonical " hair-splitting" to an excess. The appropriateness of the letter χ, in any new graphic system, would consist in its being introduced to indicate an element of articulation which bears the closest approximation, if not absolute identity, to that which it anciently indicated. In lexicons, χ is represented as having been " a strong guttural aspirate." Its former identity to *k aspirate*

---

* Mr. Appleyard. the authority cited, probably procured his information on the subject at second-hand, from Mr. Archbell.

seems to be generally admitted;* at all events, I may avail myself of an independent proof of this (especially as it will serve to illustrate the Sechwana), in the fact that the same Greek particle *ού*, previously noticed as taking final *κ* before initial vowels, took *χ* before the same vowels with the *spiritus asper*, e.g., *ούχ ύπεστιν*, which could not of course mean the doubling of an aspirate, but the coalescence of final *κ* with the *spiritus asper* of the following vowel. This is more distinctly shown in the case of *δέκα*, combined with *ήμέρα*, forming *δεχήμερος*. Whereas, *χ* is intended by Dr. Lepsius to indicate a *continuous* consonant— viz., *ch* in the German *lachen*, differing only in degree, if at all, from that I am about to notice (*g, -gh*).

This reference to the orthography of a dead language enables me to explain exactly the nature of the consonant in Sechwana, which I, for the present, call an *aspirate " explodent."* In this language it is at times gently enunciated; at others, forcibly; but the fact of an aspiration accompanying the simple " explodent" *k*, is unmistakeable.

The other consonant *g (-gh)*, which the genius of the Sechwana proves to be a corresponding *lenis* form of the *fortis kh*, and therefore also an aspirate, is more difficult of illustration. An evidently very close approximation to it is that intended to be indicated in Dr. Lepsius's system by the above letter *χ* , and classed as a *fortis* fricative. That the Greek letter *γ*, adopted by him, anciently indicated the same lenis consonant as that now under consideration, is not at all borne out by Greek lexicographers. In fact, the supposed identity of *γ*, in the traditional Greek pronunciation, with the Arabic *غ*, satisfies me that it would only be applicable to a *vocalised* form of the German *ch* in the above example, or to the Cape-Dutch *g†* in *dagen* (days).

---

* See " *Standard Alphabet,*" note 2, p. 37.

† An articulation approximating to what is improperly called the " guttural *r*," but only more gentle.

It must now be evident to the reader that the two letters χ and χ' (γ), which the able linguist has adopted to represent the elements *ch* in Germ. *lachen*, and the Arabic ﻊ respectively, are by him erroneously applied in the Sechwana to other two elements, which, in his graphic system, ought to be written $\dot{k}$ (or *kh*), and χ, respectively; so that only one of the two is correctly regarded as an equivalent, but merely misplaced as to quantity—viz., the latter.

These two consonants in the Sechwana are thus described by Dr. Livingstone, in his " Analysis of the Language of the Bechuanas," (Section 1.)

" *kh* is the *k* strongly aspirated, as in *khakala* (far) ; *g* guttural as *ch*, in *loch* (Scottice), *dag* (Dutch)."

At the end of the section, he calls *kh, ph,* &c., " aspirated explosive sounds," which agrees with the nomenclature I have preferred for explanatory purposes, and, indeed, with the definition of Dr. Lepsius.*

Whereas, Dr. Lepsius's guttural letters χ and χ' (γ) are well illustrated in the Cape-Dutch examples *dag'*, *dag²en*, in which g^1 and g^2 are to each other as *s* to *z*, and as *th* (in *thin*) to *th* (in *thine*).

(*b*) HOTTENTOT (OR NAMĀN).

In this language there are two consonants thus indicated by

Mr. Appleyard, *or rather* Wuras	kh	ch
Mr. Knudsen†	c	
Mr. Wahlmann	ch	

---

* " *Aspirates* are those *explosive* sounds which are pronounced with a simple but audible breath."--*Standard Alphabet*, p. 49. The word *forcible* in place of " *audible*" would convey a more correct definition. The word " *explosive*" omitted, or the words *elements of articulation* substituted for " *explosive sounds*," would include the **vowels.**

† By reference to the " *Correspondence of the S. A. A. Bible Society*," p. 6, containing a letter from Mr. Knudsen, this missionary, in speaking of an orthography, writes thus: " It would also be better to use for *ch* the Dutch *g*, or something else, and for *kh* another single letter." So that it would appear he admits two forms of this consonant. As to Mr. Wahlmann, I believe his observations were based on data furnished by Mr. Knudsen.

These are also both placed under the head of *fricatives* by Dr.
Lepsius in the above list, and thus regarded by him as identical
to *kh* and *g* of the Sechwana. From my own personal observations, in frequent intercourse with both Koranas and Namaqua
Hottentots, as well as the Bechwana, I am able confidently to
confirm the fact that this language has two aspirated gutturals
exactly equivalent to those just described under the Sechwana.
These, Mr. Wuras's* digraphs are, no doubt, intended to indicate ;
but I prefer to add the authority of an individual who, by reasno
of intercourse with natives during his youth, is perhaps not sur-
passed by any other missionary in a knowledge of the Namân
language, whether practical or critical—viz., the Rev. H. Tindall,
of the Wesleyan Society. Mr. Tindall, in describing the two
gutturals of this language, which he indicates by *kh* and *gh*, says :—

" *Gh* is a soft guttural, as in the Dutch word *gaan.*
" *Kh* represents a much deeper and harsher guttural than *gh*. We have
no corresponding sound, either in English or Dutch, by which to illustrate
its power.
" These two letters are simple sounds, though represented by compound
consonants. In spelling they are pronounced at a single articulation,
without separating the combined characters ; thus *ghun* is spelt *gh-u-n*, and
not *g-h-u-n*. *Khap* is spelt *kh-a-p*, not *k-h-a-p*."†

The error of the Professor, detected in his Sechwana examples,
is here repeated in the application of his graphic system to the
Namân gutturals ; and not only are the terms to which I have
alluded confounded, but also the consonants misrepresented.
These two gutturals are identical in the two languages ; but in
both it is only the *lenis* form that coincides with one of Dr.
Lepsius's consonants, viz., his *fortis* χ.

---

* See *Sir George Grey's Library, South African Languages*, p. 19, note,
for some additional information by Mr. Wuras himself, in a letter to Sir
G. Grey.
† "Grammar, &c." See also *Correspondence of S. A. A. B. Society*, p. 8, for
further remarks by Mr. Tindall on these consonants.

(*c*) Kafir and Zulu.

In these dialects, two guttural consonants are arbitrarily represented in the graphic systems of the missionaries, by

Mr. Appleyard*...	*r*	*r* (Kafir)
Mr. L. Grout† ...	*r* or *ṙ*	*r* (Zulu)

These are also denominated *fricatives* in the above list, and are thus regarded by Dr. Lepsius as identical to the Sechwana *kh* and *g*, and the Namân *kh* and *ch*, in his arrangement. I now proceed to add the testimony of a third very able authority, the Rev. J. L. Döhne, in his elaborate and valuable dictionary, published two years later than the "Standard Alphabet," as to their nature:—

"The two gutturals are both harsher than the gutturals in any European tongue. The one, called the softer, is exactly like to the compound sound of the Dutch *gr* in *groot, groet*; Zulu-Kafir *rola, rauka*, &c."

"The other is a hard, ringing, harsh sound, which it is very difficult to describe, and still more so to utter, but by no means impossible for a foreigner to pronounce. It is made by contracting the aperture of the throat, and expelling, as it were, the breath forcibly, so as to produce a harsh rustling of the epiglottis."‡

(1) From this it would appear that the former, which is described as a *lenis*, answers exactly to the Dutch *g*, with a superadded *r*, and therefore to the Sechwana *g*, similarly compounded. But, according to the testimony, not only of all missionaries, but also of Mr. Charles Brownlee, a high authority in the Kafir, "no such sound (as *r*) exists in the language;"§ therefore it would

---

* See Mr. Appleyard's later remarks, p. 107, *Correspondence S. A. A. B. Society*, suggesting *k* and *g*, with *points over them*, to represent them.

† Now indicated in the graphic system of the "Zulu Grammar and Dictionary Commission," as follows:—

The softer, by *h barred*.
The harder, by *k barred*.

See p. 83, *Correspondence S. A. A. B. Society*.

‡ See "*Zulu-Kafir Dictionary*," Letter R (1), p. 306. Also Letter G, p. 90, under which are some remarks on another soft guttural, apparently rather difficult to describe, but referred to in the sequel.

§ *Correspondence S. A. A. B. Society*, p. 78.

perhaps be nearer the mark to liken it to a rough form of the Dutch
or Sechwana *g*, (Germ. *ch* gutt.)   Mr. Grout, in his *Grammar* of
the Zulu, published since Mr. Dohne's work, describes it thus :—

A soft guttural sound, somewhat broader than the German *ch*, in "*macht ;*"
and corresponding more to the guttural sound of . . . *g* in the Dutch
words, " *God*," "*goed*;" thus "χ*ola*," "χ*a* χ*a*'," p. 16.—(*In this Grammar*
he has *adopted Lepsius's orthography*.)

I have since had an excellent opportunity of testing several
Zulu consonants by my own ears, and have ascertained this
element (χ of Lepsius, *r* of the missionaries) in the Zulu to be
strictly identical to the Sechwana (*lenis*) *g* of the missionaries.
I subsequently met with the abridged Zulu Grammar of the
Bishop of Natal, who thus alludes to the same consonant :—

" The . . . letter *r* is taken to represent the guttural which sounds
like the strong German *ch*, as heard in *auch, noch*."—(P. 2.)

So that there can be little doubt as to the strict equivalence of
this Zulu consonant to the Sechwana *g*, and the Namân *gh ;* but,
as in those instances, Dr. Lepsius, by making it his "*lenis*" of *ch*
in *lachen*, has erroneously supposed it to be another example of
the vocalised form, or the Arabic element غ.   Mr. Grout, again,
by making *it* the *lenis* of the two (meaning it to be the equivalent to *ch* in *lachen*), has evidently not apprehended the nature
of the element intended by Dr. Lepsius to be the " *lenis*."   Such
is, consequently, the present confusion in Zulu phonography.

(2) In the pronunciation of the other instance of the pair, the
breath is said by Mr. Döhne to be " forcibly" expelled, and
would thus appear to answer to a harsher form of the Sechwana
and Namân *kh ;* for, even among the Bechwana, both *kh* (*k*') and
g are at times very coarsely enunciated by natives possessing
stentorian voices ; just as we fancy the German guttural *ch* to be
pronounced more forcibly in the Scotch *loch*, or the Dutch *dag*,
though the same in quantity with them.   However, the following is Mr. Grout's own description of the same element, which
he now indicates by χ':—

D

"The letter χ' represents a peculiar, hard, rough guttural sound, which seems to be made by contracting the throat, and giving the breath a forcible expulsion, at the same time modifying the sound with a tremulous motion of the epiglottis, as in *ukuχ'eza, ukuχ'eba, umχ'ezo*."—P. 16, *Zulu Grammar*.

On my own examination of a native I was disposed to think that this element χ' (or *r*) was not, as supposed by Dr. Lepsius, equivalent to the Sechwana and Hottentot *kh* (*k*'), but simply the former (*lenis* of Grout, Germ. *ch*, Sech. *g*), *accompanied by a decided lateral click*, and that it was actually neither of the two guttural elements of Dr. Lepsius, but a double consonant.

As in the preceding instance, I was gratified to observe that my view of this articulation was in a measure corroborated by Bishop Colenso's description of it.

"There is another sound occurring in a few Zulu words, which may be pronounced either as a guttural from the bottom of the throat, or as a click in a peculiar way. But the sound must be heard in order to be imitated. We shall denote it by *x*; and the student may get a native to sound it for him."—*First Steps in Zulu Kafir*, p. 2.

My own description differs from this only in being more definitive. It is decidedly not a simple consonant, and Dr. Lepsius has erred in classifying it as the equivalent of both the Sechwana or Namân *kh* (*k*'), and the German *ch*, under the delusion that the two latter digraphs indicated identical elements. Mr. Grout, again, with the "living traditional pronunciation" of the Zulu at his ear, has evidently never taken the trouble to ascertain the real nature of both elements *intended to be* indicated by Dr. Lepsius's letters χ and χ', the former of which he has in fact reversed as to quantity, and applied that with a diacritical mark to a compound though cognate consonant.

I do not know whether the *vocalised* form of *ch* in *lachen* (that is, the *lenis*-fricative-guttural χ' of Lepsius, Arabic غ), which he has confounded with the Sechwana *g*, is to be found in Zulu; but have ascertained beyond a doubt that this language nevertheless contains the Sechwana or Namân *kh* (*k*'), which he has confounded with his χ, and I have endeavoured to prove is properly the fortis form of this *ch* (gutt.) At page 16 of his Grammar, Mr. Grout says :—" There is also a sound intermediate between that of *g* and *k*." On trying, by my own ear, so accustomed to Sechwana aspirates, the two examples he refers to—viz., *uku ganda* or *kanda*, and *utukela* or *utugela*, I distinctly perceived that the former was pronounced *uku khanda*, and the latter *utukhèla*,* with *k·* in both.

I am afraid I have brought my reader into a phonetic labyrinth, and would rather it had fallen to the lot of some other writer to make an exposure of any imperfections in the graphic systems of men labouring to arrive at uniformity; but conceive it to be

---

* Lest, in the above statements, I should lay myself open to a charge of obsequiousness and party-spirit, I append the following facts :—In the course of a short visit to Natal (August, 1861), I took the opportunity of riding out about twenty miles or more from Durban, to the mission station of the Rev. Mr. Rood (who was at the time absent). My object was to become satisfied, before committing myself to print, of the true nature of the two gutturals *r·* and *r* of the American missionaries, or *χ* and *χ'* of Lepsius. As Mr. Grout's Grammar had just been published, I carefully went through his letters of the alphabet with an intelligent native ; especially as I had my doubts of the correctness of his descriptions of the Zulu elements ; for I had on one occasion observed the written words *isipingo* and *tina* distinctly pronounced by some gossiping natives *isip'ingo* and *'tina*. The result of my observations respecting the *two* gutturals is stated above. As also shown above, I found that Mr. Grout's " sound intermediate between *k* and *g*" was *kh* (*k·*). In addition to these facts, I observed (2) that his " sound intermediate between the genuine *p* and *b*" was *ph* (*p·*), *e.g.*, his word *popoza* was what I should write in Sechwana *phò-phoza* (*p·op'oza*) ; (3) that *tina* was really pronounced *thina* (*t'ina*), and *utixo* really *uthixo* (*u·tixo*) ; in fact, that not only the simple mutes *k*, *t*, and *p*, existed in the language, but also their unmistakeable aspirate forms, *the equivalents of those in the Sechwana*—viz., *k·*, *t·*, *p·*. I not only stated these facts to my relative, Mr. Laurence Platt, my companion on the jaunt, but the morning after to Dr. Mann, the able superintendent of education, while riding a short distance with him from the Isipingo, in the direction of Durban. A day or two subsequently, I received a kind letter from Bishop Colenso, (in reply to an application for his Dictionary,) enclosing also a copy of his " *First Steps in Zulu-Kafir*," which I had never previously seen. This, in addition to other corroborative quotations, of which I have already made use (at p. 2), contained the following paragraph :—

" There is a slight aspiration heard in very many words (as in Hebrew) after either of the letters *b*, *g*, *d*, *k*, *p*, *t*. This will account for some roots, which in the dictionaries appear identical, having a difference of meaning, which a native would distinguish by his enunciation, though it will require a fine ear to detect it.

Ex. *kona*, it ; but *kona* (pronounced *khona*), these.
kwako, its ; but *kwako* (pronounced *kwakho*), thine."

D 2

my duty to divest this important subject of a confusion worse confounded by an obsequious attachment, on the part of those who have the living speech within hearing, to "written systems fixed by literature," and the authority of great names. I do not, however, flatter myself that any will wade through all my remarks, but shall attempt to give as synoptical a view of the subject as possible, employing the letters of Dr. Lepsius's system, and in brackets those of the missionaries, &c. :—

		fortis.	lenis.	
1. ....:......	....	χ	χ' (γ)	of **Lepsius.**
	fortis.	lenis.		
2.	kͨ (kh)	χ (g)	....	of the Sechwana.
3.	kͨ (kh)	χ gh)	....	of the Namân.
	compound.		lenis.	
4. { ...... χ' (rͨ)	....	χ (r)	....	of **Mr. Grout.** ⎫ In the
....	kͨ(kh)	Observed by **Bishop Colenso,**		⎬ Zulu.
		and more recently by myself.		⎭

The instances which I have observed for myself are quite as strong as the *aspirated* mutes in the Sechwana, though I have no doubt slighter aspirations would be found to occur in unaccented syllables. I am not sufficiently acquainted with the Zulu to be able to give an opinion as to whether the *lenes* mutes g, d, b, occur, but I need not say I was most agreeably surprised to find my views respecting the *fortes* corroborated by the authority of an able scholar.

This will perhaps be the fittest place for me to express an opinion which I have long entertained. It is much to be regretted that, in the compilation of his elaborate and interesting Dictionary, the Rev. Mr. Döhne has not, by means of diacritical marks, or other expedients, shown, in the case of every word in which they occur, the variations of the following letters: e, g, m, o, r (gutt.), hl, &c., &c., to each of which he attributes two or more powers. The importance of such distinctive marks in the search after *roots* cannot be estimated; and is moreover enforced by a reference to precedents, in which phonetic distinctions in such a language as the Arabic are shown to clear up apparent difficulties in several cases of the Hebrew having one word with entirely different meanings. Unless Zulu scholars look to their *phonography*, the cognate Sechwana will doubtless, ere long, have the advantage, like the Arabic; simply because of greater attention having been paid to phonetic distinctions.

All the confusion consists in the instances of the 2nd, 3rd, and 4th pairs being reckoned by Dr. **Lepsius** the equivalents of those of the 1st pair respectively, and in kͨ having entirely escaped the notice of the American missionaries; whereas, the vertical columns show the real *phonical* equivalents.

There can now be very little doubt as to the strict equivalence in quantity of certain pairs of rough guttural consonants in the three species of languages I have just examined. I have shown those in the Sechwana to be combinations of the *simple* "*explodent*" gutturals *k* and *g* (*gh*) with the *spiritus asper;* personal intercourse with the natives, and the authority of Mr. Tindall, enable me to identify with them the two harsh gutturals of the Namàn language; and the descriptions of able linguists among the missionaries, added to my own observation, lead me to conclude that the " Kafir species" also contains them both.* Therefore I have considered myself justified in concluding that they are, *in every case,* formed by a combination of the *spiritus asper* with the simple "explodents" *k* and (a form of) *g.* But in no case are they the exact equivalents in quantity of the pair under which Dr. Lepsius has classified them in his tables, except that his *fortis* form χ answers to their *lenes* forms, though differently indicated—(*g, gh,* or *r.*) It will no doubt have been observed that all the authors quoted speak of the softer form of the two, *i.e., g* (-*gh*) being simply a guttural, or a soft guttural; the proof of its being a *lenis* form of the aspirated guttural, *kh,* and therefore *also an aspirate,* is alleged by me solely on the principle existing in the Sechwana phonic system, and which I hope to maintain throughout this treatise. .

As to the remaining African languages in the list, I must of course plead absolute ignorance, in the absence of the living pronunciation, which would enable one to compare for himself; but, so far as regards the absence of authentic facts, my disadvantages are surely not greater than were those of Dr. Lepsius, when compelled to base his conclusions on second-hand data, contributed, of necessity, by different and various authors, at several intervals, and of course without a preconcerted plan.

* Since the above was in type, I have met with Dr. Van der Kemp's list of Kaffir gutturals—viz., " G, g, (like ye Dutch *g* in *groot*); Q, q, (like ye English *g* in *great*); X, χ, (like ye English *ch* in *chlorosis,* being ye same as the Greek χ) ; and K, k."—*Sir G. Grey's Library, S. A. Lang.,* p. 47.

If out of his list of these languages I have shown him to have fallen into egregious errors in regard to the four first, there is surely some probability that his remaining examples, based on the researches of others, will also be erroneous. However, having endeavoured to prove that these two consonants, distinguished by him as *fricatives* in **twenty-five** African languages, are *aspirates* in about **one-sixth** of the number, I am left to surmise that they are so in all or most of the remaining instances, and that the difference between the two terms is, in the case of the *gutturals*, merely imaginary.

I have thought proper to subjoin also a compendious abstract, similar to that preceding, of the gutturals in the Asiatic languages, as arranged, by the same learned author, under the two heads of *fricative* and *aspirate*, in order to place the matter in another light.

ASIATIC LANGUAGES.

	Fricative.		Aspirate.	
	fortis.	lenis.	fortis.	lenis.
1. Hebrew :				
Without points	ח			
With points	חֿ	ג		
2. Arabic :				
Ancient Literature	ح	غ		
Smith and Robinson ⎫	*kh*	*gh*		
Act. pronunciation ⎭				
8. Persian :				
Mirza M. Ibrahim	*ḵ*	*ġ*		
4 Sanscrit :				
Oriental Literature			ख	घ
Bopp, 1833			*k*	*g̣*
H. H. Wilson			*kh*	*gh*
5. Bengáli :				
G. C. Haughton			*kh*	*gh*
6. Zend :				
Oriental Literature	ڬ	٢		
Burnouf	*kh*	*gk*		
Bopp, 1833	*c*	*gh*		
Brockhaus	*kh*	*gh*		
7. Armenian :				
Ancient Pronunciation	խ	ղ		
Actual Pronunciation ⎫	*ch*	*ġ*	*k'*	
Petermann ⎭				
8. Georgian : '				
Rosen	*ch*	*gh*	*k'*	

	Fricative.		Aspirate.	
	fortis.	lenis.	fortis.	lenis.
9. Albanian :				
J. G. v. Hahn	χ	γ		
10. Hindustáni :				
W. Yates	kh	gh		
Gilchrist	kh	gh		
H. H. Wilson	kh	gh		
11. Malayau :				
J. Crawfurd	x	g		
12. Javanese :				
J. Crawfurd.................				
13. Turkish :				
A. Jaubert	kh	gh		
14. Mongolian :				
J. J. Schmidt	ch	gh		
15. Chinese :				
Rev. J. Gough ....}	χ	—	kʾ	
Rev. T. McClatchie ......}				
Stephen Endlicher	ᴄ	—	kʽ	

NOTE.—Of **fifteen** Asiatic languages, one is represented as containing neither fricative nor aspirate gutturals; eleven as having *fricatives* of both quantities, *i.e.*, *lenis and fortis;* one as having a fricative of one quantity. Again, two are represented as having *aspirated* gutturals of both quantities; three, aspirates of one quantity. The inference from this is, that **two-thirds** of the Asiatic languages have no guttural aspirates.

Counting single instances, the proportion of *aspirates* to "*fricatives*" is as seven to twenty-three in the fifteen Asiatic languages. In the twenty-five African languages they are as three to thirty-one. The inference must then be, that more than **four-fifths** of the rough guttural consonants in all these languages are fricatives, and less than **one-fifth** aspirates! I admit the possibility, but not the probability of its truth.

It must strike any one at all given to generalising, that, with the exception of the Armenian, Georgian, Chinese, the two Abyssinian dialects, and the Koptic, which are represented as having one guttural aspirate each, besides the one or two fricatives, those languages which are stated as having *fricatives,* have no *aspirates,* and *vice versâ;* an inference which has all the appearance of being based upon a spurious arrangement of instances. It appears the more evident, from these comparative lists taken together, that confusion exists in the use of the terms fricative and aspirate, in regard to the *gutturals*. It may be gathered from what preceded them, that the terms fricative and palatal are also at times used synonymously when applied to that series. For my own part, I should feel myself lost in a maze of conflicting terms of *fricatives, aspirates, and palatals*, were it not for the light which appears to me to be thrown upon the subject by the simple and primitive nature of the phonic system suggested by the Sechwana.]

Under the *Nasals* in the guttural series, the Sechwana has the same element as we find indicated by *ng* in English in the word *sing*, and in German in the word *enge*. It is indicated in the literature of the missionaries by *ñ*. It may be said to occur more frequently than any other consonant in this language.

The whole series of simple gutturals, according to the arrangement suggested by the Sechwana, will now be as follows:—

	Simple "Explodents."		Aspirate "Explodents."		
	fortis.	lenis.	fortis.	lenis.	
Gutturals	k	*g*	k‘	‘g*	ñ (-ng)

§ II. The Lingual Series.

1st Division.		2nd Division.			
fortis.	lenis.	fortis.	lenis.	Nasals.	Ancipites.
t	*d*			*n*	*r* *l*
					r

To the extent above represented, the Sechwana gives the same linguals, but, as will be seen, contains the elements of a more consistent and satisfactory series. These consonants have been variously classified. *T* and *d* have as frequently been called

---

* It may be observed I have called this consonant *a* lenis form of *k‘*. In order not to confound it with the *mute* lenis form *g̊*, and till enabled in the sequel to explain its real nature, I shall indicate it by '*g̊*.—(Sechwana *g*; German *ch*, gutt.)

dentals as linguals. In the words of Sir John Stoddart, " the sound expressed by *t* throughout Europe is unvaried, and the same may be said of that expressed by *d.*" *L* and *r* have usually been called linguals; though they are included in the " Standard Alphabet" under the series of dentals.

The following quotations, from the same distinguished author, will show that there are few consonantal elements so little understood as the linguals *r* and *l* :—

" All the oral consonantal sounds, except *l* and *r*, are produced in pairs, each pair having the same position of the organs, but with a certain difference of effect."—*Glossology,* p. 127.

The lingual "letters *l* and *r*; which, however, do not form a pair, the articulating action in the one being *very different from* the action in the other."—*Ibid.* p. 138. In the same page, " That *articulations so close* as those of *l* and *r* should pass into each other is not surprising."

" Although all the European languages employ this articulation, and generally express it by a single letter (either the Latin *r* or the Greek *ρ*), they vary much in the smoothness or roughness of the sound, &c."—*Ibid.* p. 139.

" It is sometimes difficult to decide whether the sound is to be considered as a modification of *r*, or a combination of it with a guttural articulation." —Page 140.

" But though the smoothness of the sound *l* contrasts remarkably with the roughness of the sound *r*, yet the relation of both to the peculiar action of the tongue renders the substitution of one for the other most frequent. Hence *Molly* from *Mary, Hal* from *Harry ;* hence the practice called in Germany *lallen* ; . . . . and hence, too, the common habit of children, when they find a difficulty in pronouncing the harsher sound, of recurring to the softer as a substitute."—Page 141.

Ben Jonson, according to Walker, made a distinction between " the rough and a smooth *r ;*" however, in English, the phonic difference is not indicated in the graphic system—*e.g.,* *r* in *roll,* and *r* in *directly.**

Two are to be found in French, in the words *diriger* and *beurre ;* in the latter word, a distinction is made by doubling the letter. It would appear that the Armenian alphabet " has two different characters, *rra* and *re;* the former expressing the

---

* We often hear children say *didectly,* and *dilectly.*

rougher, the latter the smoother sound of this articulation."[*]
From the tables of Dr. Lepsius we learn that one African language, the Susu, has both *r* and *rh*; and that among Asiatic languages only the Albanian and Hindustáni have both a rough and a smooth *r*.[†] No doubt, numerous other instances could be found, as, for example, the Sechwana, which I have yet to show contains both forms of *r*, is represented in the same tables as having only *one*. The fact of its relative position among other consonants, in a universal classification of the elements of articulation, never yet having been decided, will perhaps account for one form being overlooked in a few languages by some students. I have preferred to call the whole series linguals.[‡]

NOTE.—It will be observed that I have for the present excluded from the *second division* of this series all the consonants *s, z ; θ, δ ;*[§] *f, v ; sh* and *zh ;*[||] which have usually been called fricative or continuous, and always been disposed into pairs of correlative quantities, *fortis* and *lenis*, on the supposition that the affinity between the instances of each pair is analogous to that between *t* and *d*, or *k* and *g*. It will, however, be found in the sequel, that they are nevertheless included in the lingual series (with the exception of *f* and *v*), but by a very different classification, based upon the phonology of this "barbarous" language. It is worthy of remark, that these several " pairs"[¶] of consonants — called *fricatives* " from their sound being determined by friction," or *continuous* " because this friction is not interrupted by any closing of the organs;" and again, by others, *sibilants*—have also been denominated *semi-vowels*, " as agreeing . . . . in presenting only a partial obstruction to the passage of the vocalised breath ;" *but this has never, till recently, been the case with the gutturals, of which we have, in the last section,*

---

[*] Glossology, Sir J. Stoddart, p. 139. In Lepsius's Tables, indicated by r and r.

[†] In Hindustáni there are three *r*'s, viz., *r*, *rh*, and *r ;* the third, from descriptions, would appear to be a *vocalised* form of the second.

[‡] *δ, r, э, v, λ, ρ, σ*, are called linguals by Buttmann.

[§] As to θ and δ of Lepsius, = *th* in *thin* and *thine* respectively, these elements do not exist in Sechwana, but are referred to in Section v., Ch. iii.

[||] For the positions of *s* and *z* in the series, see Chapter v. ; for those of *sh* and *zh*, see Part III. of this work.

[¶] As they are usually supposed to be.

treated.* *L, r,* and *n,* were also, as before stated, formerly included among the semi-vowels, by those who found in their " humming and hissing" "a transition to the vowels; and, in a quotation in the sequel, it will be seen that the two former are regarded by **Dr. Lepsius** as partaking of the nature of *fricatives.* From the above remarks it would appear that even the terms *fricative* and *lingual* are, in accordance with the views stated in the preceding chapter, but synonymes in most of the instances in this series of consonants.

In the above table, *t* and *d* form the only pair of correlative consonants; their correlation is universally admitted and proved, as will be seen by an appeal to some of the usual facts in Sechwana. I shall now attempt to show from these facts that an entirely different arrangement of the other members of the lingual series than that in vogue, is required by the inferences one feels compelled to draw from them. There may be an appearance of presumption in this ; but when a man takes his stand upon the firm ground of induction, he ventures less than by expressing any bold anticipation. Moreover, I may have something to dread in a charge of hasty generalisation. Be this as it may, I shall have the satisfaction of having attempted to supply some of the materials of a natural phonic system, to which some more comprehensive and discerning mind may be enabled, by my humble example, to add much that is new, and to construct a better whole.

Under the *First Division* of the LINGUAL SERIES the data of the Sechwana present a slight irregularity in respect to the pair *t* and *d,* but the mutation of the latter to the former is sufficiently distinct and in keeping with all the instances of other consonants.

---

* According to a preceding quotation from Dr. Lepsius, the essential distinction between these gutturals and the above three fricative pairs " consists in the friction of the breath being formed and heard at the *teeth*" in the latter.—See *Standard Alphabet,* p. 45. The only other pair also considered to be fricatives—namely, *f* and *v,* could have been included with the three pairs, so that the gutturals are exceptions to them all, and their classification together, on this ground, is perfectly anomalous.

Almost the only verb with initial d or nd, as daea, commutes this consonant into t or nt in the examples :—

nDaea, (strike,) ntèò.*†

But we find also that initial *l*, and a faintly tremulous *r*,‡ are similarly commutable with the same letter *t*, in every similar instance of inflection, but *t* itself remains immutable. The examples are—

Rila,	(smear)	tilo,	itila,	ntila.
Leta,	(watch)	tetò,	iteta,	nteta.
Tena,	(disgust)	tenò,	itena,	ntena.

The inference from these particulars is, that the two elements indicated by l, r are, as well as d, *lenes* forms of t, and the latter their corresponding *fortis ;* therefore, both are *simple " explodents."* If the mutative process in the Sechwana has any principle in it at all, the element *l*, and one of the two forms of *r* which Dr. Lepsius has included under the heading *ancipites*, are thus referred to their proper places in a phonetic table as both *" explodent"* *linguals*, and both *lenes*. There can be very little doubt that the three *lenes* consonants *l*, *r¹*, and *d*, are strictly allied. In the earliest publications of the missionaries, we find them using *d*, *dl*,§ where they now use *l* and *r*,‖ so that they appear to have

---

* This diacritical mark, attached to the *e* as *è*, is arbitrary, in order to indicate the equivalent of the French *e* in *Mère.*

† The examples in which the verb is preceded by the object-particles are irregular with respect to *ndaea*—viz., *ititaea* and *ntitaea.* They are, however, regular with respect to *ritaea* (strike), which is most common in the Serolofi.

‡ In the absence of a settled letter, I shall, for the purposes of this section, indicate this consonant by *r¹.*

§ See *Sir George Grey's Library, South African Languages* p. 137.

‖ Some missionaries, though aware of the peculiarity of the consonant, give it, in pronouncing the word, the decidedly tremulous articulation of a rough *r.*

hesitated between four ways of indicating it in the new literature of the same people.

Molimo (God, impersonal). *Liyồ* (food).

Morimo   „   „   *Dliyo* „

Modimo „   „

To those arguing on a physiological basis, this fact ought to savour of a proof that the articulation of the said three consonants is effected by the same organs of the voice.*

The distinct articulation of *d*, as I have implied, rarely occurs in the language. *Daea* is the only instance in which it takes any other vowel than *i* after it, and, in this case, it is generally enunciated with a faint sound of *n* preceding it. In the other few instances, as well as certain pronouns, it occurs in the form of a " palatal"; that is, with a superadded *y* or *i*, as *Dya* (eat), *Dyaha* (cleanse), *Dyala* (sow).†

The well-known consonant *l* is constant before any other vowel than *i* and *u*, and frequently it is perceptible even before these; but that which I have for the present indicated by *r¹*, as above described, seems peculiar to these two vowels, and forms only one of two elements which have been indicated in the literature of some missionaries by the common letter *r*. This consonant (*r¹*) almost defies description. To say that it is an indistinctly tremulous *r*, or something between a rough *r* and a *d*, would convey only a slight approximation to the nature of it. The Greek ρ, in κριβανος and κορω, which were also written κλιβανος and κολω, the Latin *r* in *meridies*, for *medidies*, and the Sanskrit *r* in *rōman* for *lōman*, indicated, no doubt, the identical consonant. If it occurs before other vowels than *i* and *u*,

---

* I cannot divest myself of the idea that, in the Sechwana, the set of *lenes* forms of *t* is incomplete; that the elementary forms of the consonants *th* in *thin* (θ), and also *s* in the words *parts*, *parks*, *harps*, also pertain to it. I shall revert to the subject in Section v., Ch. iii.

† All written by the missionaries without a *d*, but this element preceding the *y* cannot be mistaken.

it will require the ear of a native well practised in observing differences of articulation to detect it. I am not aware that any European has hitherto been able to do so in the Sechwana, in which it must surely exist.

Dr. Bleek, in speaking of the Sechwana "dialects," says of this consonant—

"There is frequently r found in one dialect where the other has *l*, and *vice versâ;* and, in general, one is justified to consider r in these dialects as a sort of floating letter, and rather intermediate between *l* and *r*, than a decided r sound."—*Sir George Grey's Library, South African Languages,* p. 135.

Now, as to either of these consonants being peculiar to different dialects in certain instances, I rather think this is a mistake; for both are found in most, if not all, dialects, and are convertible, as in the particle *ri* (or *li*), which is repeatedly pronounced both ways in the same sentence; but in many cases they appear to be constant, as in *mocweri (a spring of water)*, from *cwêla*—and in the analogous forms.* The value of the above remark further depends upon what Dr. Bleek considers " *a decided* r *sound.*" That r is decidedly " *a floating letter,*" the places of the two generally acknowledged forms of which have never hitherto been found in a phonetic scale, is unquestionable, or they would not be included by Dr. Lepsius under the head of *ancipites!* I shall avail myself of another quotation from the latter distinguished authority, corroborating these remarks:—

"The sounds *l* and *r* † participate of both qualities (explosive and fricative),

---

* Some remarks on the convertible nature of *r* and *l*, in Kaffir, may be seen in " *Corr. S. A. A. B. Society,*" p. 104. Mr. Appleyard evidently writes without any allusion to two *r*'s, and it may be as well to state the probability that that which the Kaffir substitutes for *l* is equivalent to r^1 described in the text. It is nevertheless possible that the Kaffirs substitute the aspirate r^2 (described in the sequel), for even among the Bechwana the children educated by the missionaries are actually changing the pronunciation of r^1 in *morimo* to the aspirate r^2, or its *vocalised* form, by imitating their teachers.

† There being no diacritical mark, the reader is in doubt which *r* is meant, though it is probably intended for the smooth consonant.

being continuous, and at the same time formed by a contact which is vibrating in *r*, and partial in *l.*"—*Standard Alphabet*, p. 30.

If we take the Sechwana as a guide, this dubiousness will be removed. These two consonants are admitted by Dr. Lepsius to be ' *explodents*,' as well as fricatives. I have already shown, in the preceding chapter, that some fricatives, or, as they have been otherwise called, *semi-vowels*, may be simple "explodents," and others aspirate "explodents." The Sechwana goes still further : it points to their position in the former set, and gives us their quantity in the pair—viz., that they are both (together with *d*) lenes forms of the consonant *t*. I hope to show, in the sequel, that the lingual series has also a corresponding aspirate form.

I cannot here forego the following valuable remarks on the subject of certain forms of articulation, supposed to be peculiar to the Sanscrit; for, when resolved into their elements, one of these coincides remarkably with another I have just attempted to describe as occurring in this "barbarous" but extraordinary language :—

" In the Sanscrit system there are several sounds reckoned among simple vowels which should rather, perhaps, be considered as combinations of one or more liquid consonants with a vowel. Thus, Sir W. Jones describes *rï*, the seventh letter of the vowel series, as '*a sound peculiar to the Sanscrit language, formed by a gentle vibration of the tongue preceding our third vowel* i, *pronounced very short*,' as '*in the second syllable of* merrily.' The next to this is '*the same complex sound considerably lengthened* (rēĕ),' and then follow two others, *lrī* and *lrī*, which he describes as '*short and long triphthongs, peculiar to the Sanscrit language.*' "—*Glossology, by Sir John Stoddart*, p. 80.

If we regard these articulations properly—that is, the lingual consonants, independently of the vowels affixed to them—the former will be found to resemble very closely the element above described, which I have indicated by *r*¹. Indeed, the *r* "in the second syllable of *merrily*" is perhaps the fittest which could be chosen to represent as exactly as possible the Sechwana consonant. It will not be surprising if it should be proved that two such closely allied lingual consonants as *r* and *l* have thus been reckoned among the *vowel* sounds by the Sanscrit grammarians, inasmuch as they have frequently been classed as *semi-vowels* by some of our own grammarians, and by Dr. Lepsius, in a preceding quotation, as partaking of the nature of *fricatives;* for, as I have proved, this cannot be denied of any vowels, all of which are in the strictest sense of the word also *continuous.*

Under the *Second Division* of the LINGUAL SERIES, we find the Sechwana presents the following data :—

Initial **r** (as indicated in the literature of the missionaries) is also commuted into *aspirate* **t** (*t* or *t-h*) in the inflected forms; *e.g.* :—

Roga (curse), thogo, ithoga, nthoga.

Again, Initial *aspirate* **t** (*t,* written by the missionaries *th*) remains immutable; *e.g.* :—

Thiba (prevent), thibo, ithiba, nthiba.

The inference which follows is, that the **r** in this case, which is a rustling or strongly tremulous consonant* (and which I shall, for the purposes of this section, indicate by **r^a** in contradistinction from the other), is one of the *lenes* forms of *aspirate* **t** or **th**, and that this (**th**) is the correlative *fortis ;* that, therefore, they form the pair of *aspirate* " *explodents*," corresponding with the simple "explodents" just described.

Of this same element, **Dr. Bleek** (at page 135), in allusion to tho

---

* Dr. Bleek, on the Sechwana, writes : "It has a sound, *r*, which is of peculiar harshness, being pronounced deep in the mouth."—*Sir G. Grey's Library, South African Languages*, p. 113. This definition conveys the idea of a guttural *r*, whereas that evidently meant is an *r* accompanied with an aspirate by which (the physiologist would say) a greater rustling of the tip of the tongue is produced.

differences between the Serolofi and Setlhapifi* dialects, writes: "As regards the pronunciation of the words, the main difference between the two dialects appears to be that, in certain words, a kind of soft *r* sound is peculiar to the *Serolong*, instead of the *h* found in the Sehlapi. *E.g.*, the Barolong say *tiro* (work), for the Sehlapi *tiho.*"— *Sir G. Grey's Library, South African Languages*, p. 135.

It is well known that all the Sechwana dialects (if such they are to be called) have both *h* and *r²*. In the example given by this able linguist, of one tribe having *tirò*, and the other *tihò*, the former is derived from *lira*, or *rira* (to work), and the latter from *riha* (same meaning). In both cases the initial consonant is pronounced as *l* at one time, and as *r¹* at another, by the same person in every tribe, whether indicated as *l* or *r* in the literature of the missionaries in any tribe. The Barolofi say both *rira* and *lira*. As to tihò and tirò, it is to be questioned whether the difference is dialectical. I have shown that, according to the genius of the language, *l* and *r* are both *lenes*, and hope yet to show that *h* and *r²* are also both convertible in the set of *lenes* aspirates, according to a rule which obtains in the language ; so that the difference between the latter couple is, in one respect, precisely analogous to that of the former. It is a very common thing for one to hear the Batlhwaro say *ga re itse* (we do not know), as well as *ga he itse*.

The fact of the letter **r** representing both the smooth and the rough "explodent," not only in the writings of the missionaries, but also in the English graphic system itself, has somewhat interfered with the formation of correct notions as to its real nature. As

---

* Some writers treating on South African dialects are prone to a most inveterate mistake—viz., that the publications of the London Missionary Society at Kuruman are in the *Setlhapin* dialect. It will perhaps suffice to say, that this (if intentional on the part of some who, undoubtedly, have displayed a little rivalry towards this Society—See *Standard Alphabet*, p. 6, and *Corres. S. A. A. B. Society*, pp. 9, 118) is equivalent to a slur upon the genuineness of the standard its missionaries have produced of a *sacred literature* of the Sechwana language, which they have spent some forty years in acquiring, among the people of several tribes, far in advance of the Batlhapin, not only in traditional seniority, but also in purity of diction— not omitting the Barolofi. Surely it must be known to such writers, that the Batlhapin are a people whose language has been deteriorating, by reason of their close intercourse with Koranna Hottentots, for a century or more ; and is utterly disregarded by even such missionaries as have resided in their territory for the last forty years. A large portion of this is occupied by two sections of the Bahurutse, the most ancient tribe in the nation—viz., the *Batlhwaro* and *Bachwen*.

I have said, the rule which generally obtains is that before the vowels *i* and *u;* the consonants *l* and *r* are convertible.* Both *l* and an *r* may be found (in the missionary literature) before all the other vowels without any interchange—that is, in situations in which we cannot replace one by means of the other; the only exception really appears to be before *i* and *u.*

It is therefore a matter of importance that, though writers upon a physiological basis have failed to specify the difference between the two forms of *r* in such a way as to leave no doubt as to their position in a phonetic table, the simple commutation of *r* into *th* in the Sechwana language, not only before the vowels *a, e,* and *o,* but also before *i* and *u* (as in *Rita, thitò; Rima, thimò*), should have led to the conclusion that *r* has a form separate and distinguishable by the ear from that in *Rila, tilò; Riba, tibò,* and above indicated by r^1. Practice has further enabled some persons to detect the difference at first hearing.† The result is, that we are satisfied as to the existence of *r* *in*convertible to *l* before the vowels *i* and *u;* and this I have attempted to show is one of the *lenes* forms of *aspirate* t (*t'* or *th*). As an example among many of the proficiency which may be arrived at, I give the following words with identical vowel sounds, but different meanings:—

Moriri (a worker), from lira (tirò), ⎫ containing both simple and
(Or Morihi) „ „ riha (tihò) ⎭ aspirate *r.*
Moriri (a smearer), „ rila (tilò) containing *two* simple *r's.*
Moriri (hair) „ ? containing *two* aspirate *r's.*

---

* Among others, under the head of Modifications of Initial Consonants, Dr. Bleek has the following :—

  l ....becomes *t.*
  r (before *i* and *u*) .... „ *t.*
  r (before *a, e, o*) .... „ *th.*

In which cases the two letters are intended to indicate the same consonant. —*Sir George Grey's Library, South African Languages*, p. 104.

† The two words ruta (*teach*), and ruta (*conceal*), are additional examples ; the latter, which I detected only a few months ago, is as little known to some missionaries as the former is frequently used by them.

I trust that this beautiful example of the nice shades or differences of articulation, which I have thus shown may be discovered by another mode of investigation than a recourse to the physiology of the human voice, will be satisfactory to those interested in the study of universal phonetics.

The fact of both *r*'s being *lenes* in different divisions, will perhaps account for the failure of physiology in helping us out of our difficulties, as it would scarcely have been practicable to arrive at the difference between the two forms by any experiments on the action of the vocal organs. This could not be otherwise in the absence of unmistakeable *rudimentary* principles, such as I believe I have proved the phonic system of this language to contain.

Under the *Nasals*, the n corresponding with these consonants is all that requires to be added to this series, and I am thus enabled to present the following classification of the linguals, as suggested by the Sechwana :—

	Simple "*Explodents.*"		Aspirate "*Explodents.*"		
	fortis.	lenis.	fortis.	lenis.	Nasals.
Linguals		1			
	t	d	tʻ		n
		r		rʻ	

§ III. The Labial Series.

1st Division.		2nd Division.		Nasals.
fortis.	lenis.	fortis.	lenis.	
p	b	—	—	m

In respect to the labials, the Sechwana proves the correctness of the views generally held as to the nature of the affinity existing between the smooth " explodents" *p* and *b*, the former being unchangeable in the initial inflexions of the verb, and the latter changeable to *p.* The following examples will suffice in illustration :—

Pitla, (rub) **pitlō, ipitla, mpitla.**

Bala, (count) **palo, ipala, mpala.**

Upon the principle assumed at the outset, **p** is thus decided to be *fortis,* and **b** its corresponding *lenis* form.

Under the *Second Division* of this Series, the facts afforded by the language present something anomalous to that principle. *Ph* (*p̆*), which remains immutable in such examples as

Phunya, (pierce) **phunyō, iphunya, mphunya.**

instead of following the analogy of the other aspirated consonants, is commuted from *h* in those of

Hisa, (burn, *T*ʳ) **phisho, iphisa, mphisa.**

and is therefore *fortis.*

But to infer from this, upon that principle, that **h** is the lenis form of aspirate **p** (*ph*), would immediately suggest the existence of a flaw in the system, and invalidate preceding inferences.

It is, however, remarkable, and for my purpose rather opportune, that this is the only case among the simple consonants which is not strictly constant. The changes of *g'* to *k',* of *r'* to *t',* of *d, l,* and *r,* to *t,* and of *b* to *p,* are exceptionless ; but this cannot be said of that of *h* to *p',* for we occasionally find *h* also commutable to *k'.*

Note.—It is worthy of remark, that the latter commutation occurs only in some of those cases in which *h* precedes the vowel *u,* and *not also* before *i,* as in the case of the lenis (smooth explodent) *r.*

1. Sometimes both forms are found, but with different meanings ; *e.g* —

$$huma \text{ (become rich)} \begin{cases} phum\grave{o} \text{ (becoming rich)} \\ khum\grave{o} \text{ (wealth)} \end{cases}$$

2. Sometimes both forms with the same meanings ; *e.g.*—

$$hula \text{ (graze)} \begin{cases} ph\grave{u}l\grave{o} \text{ (grazing)} \\ kh\grave{u}l\grave{o} \quad , \end{cases}$$

3. In the case of the object-particle preceding, we find :

humisa becoming *ikhumisa.*

hurisa „ *iphurisa.*

Though there are a few instances of *h* being commutable into *k*‚ I am not as yet aware of any instance of initial *h* being changed to *t.* The subject of the commutation of the three simple aspirates may thus be explained at one view :—

Initial *h* changing to *th* (*t*') in no instance.

„ „ *kh* (*k*')in a very few instances before *u.*

„ „ *ph* (*p*') in the great majority of instances.

I make no allusion to *f* (even though it is an analogous instance) which prevails in the Sesuto. This is, in a strict sense of the word, a mongrel dialect, which owes the incongruous position it maintains as a *leading dialect* of the Sechwana very much to the circumstance of its having been reduced to writing and critically cultivated by the " accomplished French missionaries," and perhaps also to the notoriety of the Basuto nation. My illustrations of a phonic system, however imperfect, if only correct so far as they go, are intended to be gathered from the *pure* Sechwana dialects alone. The following quotation will serve to show that some examples from Sesuto are likely to be decidedly foreign to the scope of my inductions. " The Kaffir *f* is generally retained in the Sesuto, and the Kaffir *p* becomes *f* in the Sesuto; whilst the *more western dialects,* in which *f* is *lost,** have commuted this letter in both cases into *h.*" (*See p.* 116, *Sir George Grey's Library, African Languages.*) The remarks about to be adduced in the text will show that " *the western dialects*" probably never had an *f* to lose, and that *h* has rather been altered by usage from *bh,* both these forms existing in the pure dialects. This is, moreover, proved by the existence of the initial inflexions *ph*—, *iph*—, *mph*—.

If it should be shown that the change to *kh* is merely euphonic, inasmuch as it precedes the vowel *u,* it will then be practicable to explain the diversity in the following instances:—*Mahura* (Sehurutse), *Mabhura* (Sekwena), *Makhura* (Seganano), *Mafura* (Sesuto.)†

I have already shown that the lenis form of the aspirate lingual *th* (*t*'), viz., *r*‚ is also convertible to *h,* the latter being used

---

* The italics are my own.

† Since the above was in type, it has been suggested to me, by the Rev. J. Fredoux, of the Paris Missionary Society, that the euphonical modifi- cation may be produced analogously to that of *ila, kilò,* by the apposition of *k* to the *spiritus asper,* as in *huma, khumo,* which appears to me to be the best mode of accounting for the exceptions. The ancient example, οὐχ ὕπεστιν, is a precedent, for it would have amounted to the same if the χ had been attached to the ὕ, instead of χ to the particle οὐ in the Greek graphic system.

frequently for the former by people of the same tribe. This is the same with g' the lenis form of kh, for we often hear *hae* for *gae*, &c. This tendency to pronounce the pure aspirate as if there were no simple "explodent" *lenis* attached, in the cases of both r' and g' would suggest the probability that some form analogous to these two consonants may be found corresponding to the simple "explodent" b; and, to conclude that this must be *aspirate b* would only be natural. But inference is anticipated by a legitimate fact which comes to my assistance, in maintaining the consistency of the peculiar phonic principles of the language. Among some tribes—viz., the Baroloñ and the Bakwena, the h is generally* pronounced like bh in the word *hobhouse*, with the *ho* dropped; *e.g.*, *sebhuba* for *sehuba*, *mabhura* for *mahura*, *bhèla* for *hèla*, which has been mistaken by some writers for f† and v.‡ Whether one native pronounce it *bhèla*, and another *hèla*, and a third *wèla*, the corresponding noun is always pronounced *phèlò*, and the verb with the object particles *iphèla*, *mphèla*.§

I can only account for the fact of h in some dialects being almost identified in general use with the consonant bh, in others by the conclusion above stated, that the tendency is to use the pure aspirate in place of the lenis form of the aspirate "explodent;" but the difficulty is to show why this should be the case with bh especially, and to such an extent as nearly to lead to the inference

---

* I say generally, for it has only just occurred to me to set on foot an examination as to whether natives using bh ever employ the aspirate h alone in certain cases as a normal form.

† Mr. Archbell. *See Sir George Grey's Library, S. A. Languages,* p. 137, &c.

‡ Mr. Pelissier. *Ibid,* p. 116, *Note.*

§ The apparent commutation of h to *tsh* (-*ch*), *e.g.*, *gauhe* to *gauchwanyane* (or, as the missionaries write it, *gaucuanyane*), referred to at page 115 of the same work, will thus be accounted for by the fact of this adverb being pronounced *gaubhe* by some tribes. I have heard an individual of the Bañwaketse tribe pronounce this consonant w' in the same word *gauhe*, or *gaubhe*, i.e., *gauw'e*, in which the aspirate is retained, and the labial consonant is altered to the labial "semivowel."

that *h* is absolutely the lenis form of *ph*($\overset{\centerdot}{p}$). But for the exception of *h* becoming *kh* (k^{c}), I should have been inclined to doubt the stability of the principle assumed; as it is, the occurrence of *bh*, in the form of a legitimate instance, really seems to add confirmation to it. Though I am not sure that a physiologist would be able to set one right on being asked to account for the fact, it is possible the following, suggested by the perusal of an able author, will amount to an explanation—viz., that in pronouncing *b*, its consonantal element cannot be perceived till the lips have been re-opened,* and that to pronounce *h* it is necessary to open the lips more or less, especially in the case of its occurring as an initial without any preceding utterance; so that there appears to be an organic connexion between the two.

Note.—It may be as well to append a corollary to the above, that as the tendency in the Sechwana is to use the pure aspirate for the lenis form of the aspirated " explodent," viz., *h* for either $\overset{\centerdot}{g}$, r^{c} or $b^{c}_{,}$ a degree of uncertainty may in some cases present itself on the student meeting roots with initials in *h*, inasmuch as the normal form of the initial may be either of the above three consonants (*lenes* aspirates)—*e.g.*, *huma*, which is commuted into *khumò*, as well as *phumò*, may possibly be found to have an allied form in *ǧuma* and *r'uma*, as well as *bhuma* (*b'uma*), with the same signification.

Including the *Nasal* consonant *m* which the language contains, the following is the classification of labials resulting from the above analysis:—

	Simple "Explodents."		Aspirate "Explodents."		
	fortis.	lenis.	fortis.	lenis.	Nasals.
Labials	p	b	p^{c}	b^{c}	m

Note.—So far as I am aware, *b'* is the only instance of a *lenis* aspirate-mute in the language; *d'* and *ǧ*, so prevalent in Oriental tongues, have not as yet occurred to me, though the Bishop of Natal appears to think they are in the Zulu. The occurrence of at least one form is nevertheless highly satisfactory; as the reasoning employed on it may be applicable to the rest.

---

* *Glossology. Sir John Stoddart*, p. 136.

CHAPTER III.
ANALYSIS OF OTHER CONSONANTS.

EXAMINATION INTO THE POWERS OF THE REMAINING LETTERS IN THE GENERAL ALPHABET OF DR. LEPSIUS.—THE CLASSIFICATION OF SUCH AS ARE REALLY ELEMENTS, AND OF OTHERS THAT MAY BE SUGGESTED BY THEM UPON PRINCIPLES RESULTING FROM ANALYSIS IN PRECEDING CHAPTER.

THE train of facts in the Sechwana, in respect of the *simple* consonants, having been brought to a close, it now devolves upon me to deduce from other sources such conclusions as may be of assistance in arriving at the probable position, in a synthetic view, of the few foreign to that language. This will involve an examination into the real nature of the *spiritus asper*, and also of what are sometimes called vocalized forms of consonants. It is first necessary for me to satisfy the reader, as well as myself, of what, among the large number of remaining letters, are really consonantal elements or simple articulations; and, in order to do so the more effectually, I have, for his convenience, extracted from Dr. Lepsius's work the Table of

CONSONANTS OF THE GENERAL ALPHABET.

	Explosive or Dividuæ.			*Fricativæ or Continuæ*			*Ancipites*
	fortis.	lenis.	nasalis.	fortis.	lenis.	semivoc.	
I. *Faucales*	;	,		h' h			
II. *Gutturales*	k ꟴ	g	ṅ	χ̇	χ̇ (γ)		i̥
III. *Palatales*	k'	g'	n'	χ̌	ž	y	l'
IV. *Cerebrales* (Indicæ)	ṭ	ḍ	ṇ	ṣ	ẓ		r̤]
V. *Linguales* (Arabicæ)	ṯ	ḏ	n	s	z		r l
VI. *Dentales*	t	d	n	{ s̆ / s ; θ‘	z ; θ' (ð)		r l
VII. *Labiales*	p	b	m	f	v	w	

NOTE.—The letter *s*, though in the language, is included in this section on account of its doubtful nature; and the *spiritus*, also, on account of their falling under the "faucales" of Dr. Lepsius.

The letters in bold type are those I have been able to account for by the analysis in the three preceding sections; all the rest will now be considered, in the descending order of the several series, in the form of interpolated notes. Those in italics (including θ' and θ') are what I attempt, in this section, to prove to have elementary forms.

§ I. The "Faucales" of Lepsius.

Explosivæ.		*Fricativæ.*	
fortis.	lenis.	fortis.	lenis.
;	,	h‘	h

I cannot do better than give the reader, who will, I trust, have the patience to accompany me in what may appear to be a long digression, a table of these so-called consonants, as variously indicated by the different grammarians of the several languages in which they are said to occur.*

The confusion in which the subject of these elements is involved is so great, that he will require to follow the writer with almost as much attention as the latter has bestowed in attempting to reconcile the conflicting opinions of different authors. Scarcely one of these has entered upon this intricate subject without confounding the pure (pectoral) breathings with their consonantal modifications (especially the *gutturals*, or "tongue-root" letters), or, in other words, the functions of the "upper or articulating" organs with those of the "lower organs," the careful distinction between which we owe to Sir John Stoddart, and which it is necessary to maintain in order to reason at all clearly upon the subject.

---

* These I have abstracted, as in other instances, from Dr. Lepsius's comparative alphabets.

The members of the whole Arabic series are indicated in the "Missionary Alphabet," of Professor Max Müller. (*See Tableaux, p.* xci.) as follows:—

'h, ('h); h, h‘ | ,
1   2   3   4   5

But he calls the second (not the *spiritus lenis*, as does Dr. Lepsius, but) "*the primitive and unmodified breathing*," or simple "*liquid semi-vowel.*" He gives a fifth element, viz., the "primitive breathing," marked by the *Hamzeh* ‿ and makes *this* the equivalent to the *spiritus lenis*.

Moreover, he makes the 1st and 3rd (viz., ع and ح) both gutturals breathings.

According to Dr. Lepsius, the two pairs are respectively *explodent* and *fricative*. According to Professor Müller, both pairs are *flatus* (i.e., fricatives) and none are explodents.

When philological Doctors are compelled to differ so much as to the powers of archaic letters, it seems rather an unfair mode of inquiry to drag in

Asiatic Languages.	Explosivæ.		Fricativæ.		Remarks.
Hebrew ....*l.*	ע	א	ה		
Arabic—					
Ancient Graph. ...		ﺝ	ﺡ -ﺍ		
Smith & Robinson. }	,	/	ḥ	h	
Actual Pronunc.... }					
Persian—					
M. M. Ibrahim ...	,	,	ḥ	h	
Sanscrit, *anc. gr.* ...			ṙ	ː	
Bopp			h	h·	
H. H. Wilson......			h	h	An h is placed among
Bengáli—					the fricative gutturals.
G. C. Haughton ...					The fortis explodent is
Zend, *anc. gr.*..........	ẇ	ꭩ	◡		stated, in **Lepsius's** con-
Burnouf	q	g	h		fronting alphabet, to be
Bopp	kh	...	h		equivalent to his q.
Brockhaus	q	...	h		
Armenian, *anc. gr* ...			ς (J)		
Petermann			hˁ	h	
Actual Pronunc....					
Georgian—					
Rosen	q		h		
Albanian—					
J. G. v. Hahn......			h		
Hindustáni—					
W. Yates...........	ᛨ	...	h	h	
Gilchrist	...	...	hh	h	
H. H. Wilson......	âi	a	h	h	

these at all from such tongues as Arabic, Hebrew, &c., as equivalents, in illustration of existing articulations; and only serves to bewilder. The confusion which perplexes a student, in examining Professor Müller's system, consists:

1st. In his making no distinction between the *spiritus* and their guttural modifications, *e.g.*, ן and Ɛ, are called in his Tables a *liquida* and *flatus lenis* respectively, and placed under the gutturals. Elsewhere, the former is called simply the "*liquid* semi-vowel," or "an "unmodified flatus," or "a primitive and unmodified breathing," or "a pure breathing without even a guttural modification " (!)—terms very suitable and definitive ; and the latter, a similar element, "differing in definition, but identical in pronunciation."

2nd. In his adding another term, viz., *flatus*, inclusive of all the instances which are classed under both Dr. Lepsius's *fricativæ* and *explodent-faucals.*

	Explosivæ.		Fricativæ.		Remarks.
Malayan—					
J. Crawfurd	(a)	(a)	(h)	h	
Javanese—					
J. Crawfurd	a		·		
Turkish—					
A. Jaubert	...	...	h	h	
Chinese—					
Rev. J. Gough ... ⎫			h*	h	
Rev. T. M'Clatchie ⎭					
S. Endlicher			h	h	
AFRICAN LANGUAGES.					Mr. Tindall tells us no-
Hottentot—					thing about two forms.
Appleyard			x	h	Both he and Mr. Knudsen
Galla—					have an *h*.
Tutschek			h		
Bega—					
Lepsius	ʼ			h	Five other African al-
Abyssinian, Geˌez—					phabets are represented as
Ludolph	...	...	h	h	having one *h*; in twelve
Ditto, Amhara—					additional cases the *h* is
Isenberg	ʼ	ʼ	h	h	included in the guttural .series.

The above is certainly a most formidable array of instances and authorities. In the case of

   8 languages, 11 authorities give 4 members of the series.

1	,,	4	,,	3	,,	,,
5	,,	10	,,	2	,,	,,
2	,,	2	,,	1	,,	,,
5	,,	5	,,	1	,,	,,

1. *Explosivæ.*—But if the reader will take the trouble to cast his eye
over the various signs intended to indicate these so-called faucal elements,
he will feel bound to come to the conclusion that, at least under the *explosivæ,* they are of a very heterogeneous character. In some cases,
the members of each pair are represented by the vowels *ǎt, a; a, a;* in
others, by letters usually employed for gutturals *kh, g;* in several instances
by the mark of the *spiritus lenis;* in two by the *spiritus asper;* and in others
by signs approximating to a *hyphen.* In three cases, the *fortis* explodent is
represented by the letter *q,* which we otherwise find suspended by the
learned philologer in a rather doubtful position between the gutturals and
these faucals. Of course, without a reference to the works of the authorities
themselves, as to the nature of the elements their letters are intended to
indicate—or what would be more valuable, access to the actual pronunciation—it is a most difficult matter to enter into a proper analysis of their

relations. At all events, the dissimilarity of the signs employed by them must be regarded as an index to the fact of a want of unanimity on the subject of their real nature.

In the absence of such desiderata, I append the following descriptions of the "*explodent faucals*" by **Dr. Lepsius**, confronted with those of some of their equivalents by another able authority.

(1) Arabic ﺍ, Hebrew א, Greek *spiritus 'lenis.*

Lᴇɴɪs-*explodent-faucal* (of Lepsius.) (ʼ)

"By closing the throat, and then opening it, to pronounce a vowel, we produce the slight explosive sound which, in the Eastern languages, is marked separately, but not in the European, except in the Greek. We perceive it distinctly between two vowels which, following each other, are pronounced separately, as in the Italian *sarà 'a casa*, the English *go 'over*, the German *see'adler*; or even after consonants, when trying to distinguish, in German, *mein 'eid* (my oath), from *meineid* (perjury), or *Fisch-'art* (fish species), from *Fischart* (a name). We indicate this sound, when necessary, by the mark ʼ, like the Greeks."
—*Standard Alphabet, Lepsius*, p. 59.

"Among the *gutturals*, א is the lightest, a scarcely audible breathing from the lungs, the *spiritus lenis* of the Greeks; similar to ה, but softer. Even before a vowel it is almost lost upon the ear (אָמַר, ámar), like the *h* in the French *habit, homme* (or Eng. *hour*). After a vowel it is often not heard at all, except in connexion with the preceding vowel sound, with which it combines its own (מָצָא, mâtsâ)."*—Gesenius's Hebrew Grammar (14th Edition) by Rödiger, translated by Davies.* 1846. p. 15.

At the end of a word * * * * long *a* was represented by ה, and *sometimes by* א. *These two letters stood also for long* e *and* o."

---

* "Dr. Lee gives to the Hebrew *alif* the consonantal power of our unaspirated *h*, as in *humble, hour*, &c."—*Glossology, Sir J. Stoddart*, p. 128.

Dr. Latham describes *alef* as equivalent to "a vowel or a breathing."—*English Language*, vol. ii., p. 88.

Dr. Duff writes:—" ﺍ Alif, when beginning a word or syllable, is reckoned by Oriental grammarians a very slight aspirate, like *h* in *hour*. But its chief purpose is to subserve the expression of short or long vowels."—*App. of the Rom. Alph. to the Languages of India, by Monier Williams, M.A.,* p. 88.

Dr. Forbes, in reference to the law of the Arabian grammarians "that no word or syllable can begin with a vowel," writes, "therefore to represent what we call an initial vowel . . . they employ the letter ﺍ, Alif, as a fulcrum for the vowel. We have already stated that they consider the ﺍ as a very weak aspirate or *spiritus lenis*; hence its presence supports the theory, at least to the eye, if not to the ear."—(*Hindustāni Grammar*, p. 17.) " *Alif*,

Arabic ع, Hebrew ע, Fortis-*explodent-faucal* (of Lepsius). (:)

" The soft sound just described can be pronounced hard by a stronger explosion at the same point of the throat. Thus arises the sound which the Arabs write ع. We find it expressed by scholars generally by placing a diacritical sign over the following vowels:—a', à, á, ă, å; sometimes below, .. This method would suppose, from the analogy of all systems of writing, that the ع were only an indication of a change in the vowel. It is, however, a full consonant, preceding the vowel. We indicate it, therefore, with regard to its affinity to the soft sound, by doubling the spiritus lenis, :."—*Ibid.*

" ע is nearly related to א, and is a sound peculiar to the organs of the Shemitish race. Its hardest sound is that of a *g*, slightly rattled in the throat, as עֲמֹרָה, LXX., Γόμορρα . . . .; it is elsewhere, like א, a gentle breathing, as in עֵלִי, ʿHλί ... In the mouth of the Arabian, the first often strikes the ear like a soft guttural *r*, the second as a sort of vowel sound like *a*. The best representation we could give of it in our letters would be *gh* or *rg*, as אַרְבַּע, something like *arbagh*, עֲמֹרָה *rga mora*."—*Ibid.*

The above quotations add confirmation to my supposition above expressed, regarding the indefinite character of the elements intended to be represented by the signs : of **Dr. Lepsius,** and the host of equivalents in the form of other diverse signs and letters. The Hebrew א : = to the former of these new signs or the *spiritus lenis*) is generally regarded as a " hiatus

not beginning a word or syllable, forms a sound like our *a* in *war*, or *au* in *haul*."—(*Ibid.* p. 7.)

According to Wallin (cited by Max Müller, " *Proposals*," &c., p. 29) the Arabic grammarians look upon the و as a liquid semi-vowel, distinct from the ١. The latter writer adds (p. lxviii.) " where the Arabic ١ is used for this purpose (the Greek *spiritus lenis*) it is marked by the Hamzeh ٔ so that this archaic letter, as stated by Max Müller, really seems intended to represent " the primitive and unmodified breathing" of which the *spiritus asper* and *lenis* in Greek are modifications. Again, " Arab grammarians . . . consider that a long *a* consists of the short *a* . . . the pectoral semi-vowel (١)"—*Ibid.* p. xlvi.

* Professor Müller makes ع " the sonant representative" (p. xxviii.) of غ (which we shall have to notice under the head of Dr. Lepsius's *fricativæ*); " but identical in pronunciation " to the *liquid semi-vowel*—by which he appears to mean either the Elif or the Elif Hamzatum (p. lxiii.)—but surely the latter, as it is a *lenis* (spiritus) breathing ; for the former, according to his own phraseology, is an " unmodified breathing." But he makes א an element " more pectoral and less modified " than ע, thus reversing the powers of the Hebrew letters which Dr. Lepsius makes the equivalents of the Arabic ١ and ع respectively.—*Ibid.*

occasioned by the disappearance of a consonant." Again, by the above writer, who would nevertheless call it a consonant, this is *virtually* described (if one may judge by his examples), as the articulation or element which always accompanies the lengthening of a vowel—*i.e.*, its *long* quantity.* Again, it is described as equivalent to *h* in some French and English words, *homme, hour,* &c., in which the letter is absolutely silent, and therefore only another mark for the above *hiatus.* This "hiatus" does not designate any known sound ; but, in another ancient dialect, the Greek, "under the name of the *spiritus lenis* . . signified the absence of a letter, and became a negative sign in grammatical algebra." An able writer in the Encyclopedia Britannica† says further respecting this superfluous letter— " We should wonder the more that a people so intelligent as the Greeks should have fallen into such an error, if, as far as we know, Lanzi had not been the first to expose it. His *reductio ad absurdum* of the *spiritus lenis* has not hitherto received the attention which its acuteness merits." Again, it "is only a mark that the E begins another word, as in the example ΚΑΙΕΓΩ, which is equivalent to ΚΑΙ ΕΓΩ, the sign ⌐ being equal to the space between the two words " . . . . . If we consider the *spiritus lenis* in this point of view, the inventors of it will be exculpated from the absurdity of which Lanzi sought to convict them, and it will attach to those grammarians only who retained the mark after the practice of leaving a space at the end of each word became prevalent. In corroboration of this view, I append another quotation from the learned **Buttmann.**‡ " Both *spiritus* are distinct letters in other languages ; the *lenis* is the *alef* or *elif* of the Orientals. . . . Every vowel uttered without a consonant, and,

---

* To be satisfied of this, it is only necessary for the reader to examine all the above examples—" Italian *sara 'a casa,* English *go 'over,* &c., &c." The same remark applies to the examples *blacking* and *black ink* of Professor Müller, of which he says : " In *blacking,* the vowel *i* is introduced by the second half of the preceding *k ;* in *black ink,* the *i* is ushered in by the spiritus lenis."—(*Proposals,* p. xxviii.) But can it be denied that in the former case the *i* is without accent, or *short*—in the latter with it, or *long ?* Had he said the long *i* in *ink* consisted " of the short *i* + the palatal liquid (s)" (p. xlvi.), it would have been more consistent with his principle of explaining the power of the English vowels by those of archaic letters like the *spiritus lenis.* Does the learned Professor not rather mean that the power of *i* in the English *ink* is to be explained by an *abstract whispered element* (call it accent, the long quantity, or anything you please) of which the ancient " pectoral semi-vowel " ( ), the " palatal liquid " (s), and the " labial liquid " (,) are only analogous modifications in respect to the vowels *a, i,* and *u* respectively ?—*See same page.*

† Eighth Edit., vol. ii., p. 613.

‡ *Larger Greek Grammar,* p. 14.

consequently, every vowel which is to he pronounced distinctly and separately from the preceding letter, is actually introduced by a slight audible aspiration, which the ancients had greater occasion to make in their writing, *as they did not separate their words.'*

Dr. Forbes, in speaking of "the Hamza," as it occurs in Hindustáni, in which it is a substitute for the Elif, writes:—" Practically speaking, it may be considered as our hyphen, which serves to separate two vowels, as in the words *co-ordinate* and *re-iterate.*"—*(Grammar*, p. 17.*)*

However, it is evident, from all the preceding quotations, in both the text and the footnotes, that most of the writers to whom I have had access, except Professor **Max Müller** and **Wallin,** whom he cites, have confounded the ‖ Elif with the ‖ Elif Hamzatum, in calling the former the *spiritus lenis*, whereas this is the equivalent of the latter element; the former, according to them, indicating properly the primitive and unmodified breathing which necessarily precedes an initial vowel, and the latter being *one of the two* " modifications of that initial breathing." A little light is shed on this fact by the remark of **Dr. Forbes** (*Ibid.* p. 17), that " the sound of the mark *Hamza*, according to the Arabian grammarians, differs in some degree from the letter ‖, . . . but in Hindustani this distinction is overlooked." According to **Wallin** (cited by **Müller**), " ‖ *is a liquid semi-vowel, distinct from the* ‖." This " liquid semi-vowel," says Müller, "is heard at the end of a long *a*, as *y* and *w* are heard at the end of a long *i* and *u*." In fact, as we may judge from preceding quotations, one of its principal objects is to subserve the expression of *long* vowels. By enlarging on the subject of this " unmodified breathing," it is evident I should be encroaching on the materials which are to form the second part of this work on the VOWELS; but, in order to approximate to some correct conclusion, it seems necessary to dispel the confusion occasioned by misapprehension of the powers of the above two archaic letters.

Opportunely for my purpose, **Dr. J. Müller,** the able physiologist, most minutely describes the *breathing* inherent in vowels. He writes— "All vowels can be expressed *in a whisper,* without vocal tone." These he calls *mute vowels,* and adds—" But the sound of the vowels, *even when mute*, has its source in the glottis, *though the vocal chords are not thrown into the vibrations necessary for the production of voice;* and seems to be produced by the passage of the air between the relaxed vocal chords."—*Elements of Physiology*, p. 1046.

Now an important question arises. Does the *whispering* cease immediately the vocal chords are thrown into sonorous vibrations?* Whether

---

* At page 1051, he seems to think so of "the aspiration *h*;" but this, we must bear in mind, is one of the modifications of the *breathing*.

it does or does not, does there not remain a *breathing* in the former case
only initial (? and terminal), in the latter both initial and continuous (? and
terminal)? And are we by this breathing, or a lengthened form of it, in
each case to understand the Elif?* If so, in what does its so called modification, the *spiritus lenis*, consist? Professor **Max Müller** gives up the
solution of this in apparent despair. He says (p. lxviii.), "practically it
seems impossible to make a distinction between the liquid semi-vowel and
the spiritus lenis on any point of articulation anterior to the palatal."
Therefore it will not be presumptuous for me to suggest the query—Is the
kamzeh not a symbol indicating the *vocalisation* of the "mute-vowel?" It
is remarkable that all the ꝇenes forms of the *fricatives* of Dr. **Lepsius**
(viz., χ̕ z̃, z, θ' v), and of the *flatus* of Professor **Müller** (viz., z̲, z,
zh, v), are also considered sonants, or *vocalised*. Why not apply the same
analogy to the *spiritus lenis*, or Elif hamzatum, and call it a vocalised
modification of the Elif? Moreover, ع is called by **Max Müller** a
sonant, and Dr. **Forbes** considers the hamseh "somewhat akin to ع,
which its shape (∾) would seem to warrant"† (p. 17); therefore it is also
probably a *sonant*. If, then, ı is the "unmodified breathing" lengthened,
and ع is a sonant, is not ˜ı = ı + ع; viz., the same *breathing* + *voice*.
It is remarkable that these two letters were only applicable to *vowels*. The
probability then is, that both the ı and the ع were elements accessory to a
"mute vowel," one implying *long quantity*, the other *voice*. Apparently, a
ludicrous solution; but that at which one is compelled to arrive by the
assistance of mere archæological data. For me to say the Elif hamzatum
˜ı is equal to ˜ı + ع is only more unsophistical, but surely not more
paradoxical than the following indefinite conclusions of Professor **Max
Müller**:—

(1). It "may be true in theory, but is of no practical importance," to
say that ı is distinct from ˜ı.—(P. xxix.)

(2). "The delicate sound of the guttural liquid semi-vowel [ı] is in reality
the same as the guttural flatus lenis [ع̇, and both categories may therefore
be represented by one sign."—(P. lxviii.) Again, "the flatus lenis cannot

---

* In either case we may also ask the question as to the *terminal* breath.

† Dr. Forbes says that ع, like the ı, is "a weak aspirate, but the place of
utterance of ع is in the lower muscles of the throat;" but are we to understand that these are relaxed, or so extended as to allow of *vibration!* "It
is," says Shakespear, cited by Dr. Duff, "one of the guttural letters, being
formed in the lower part of the throat. Its sound has been compared to
the voice of a calf for its mother, or to that of a person making some painful
exertion."—*Original Papers, &c., by Monier Williams*, p. 83.

be distinguished in pronunciation from the guttural liquid,* and there can be no objection to marking both by the same sign."—(P. xxix.)

If the "flatus lenis," and the "liquid semi-vowel," "require different representative types" in these *dental* and *labial* modifications, which Professor Müller admits (p. lxviii.), why not also in their *guttural* modifications, and especially in their "*unmodified*" (or elementary) forms? Why, in the latter cases, should they be regarded as sounds "differing in definition, but identical in pronunciation" (p. lxviii.), and in the former different in pronunciation? for in all cases the modifications are consonantal, and two different elements are modified.

Since archaic letters are inevitably dragged in by devotees to "historical orthography" to illustrate supposed equivalents in living tongues, it seems necessary that men should arrive at some understanding as to their specific powers before venturing to classify them. Throughout this treatise I have to do, fundamentally, with elements *objectively true;* and to reduce these to subjective principles, which are of course theoretical truths, but only axiomatical in proportion to the copiousness of the inductions by which they are evolved. The same process cannot be followed in the matter of these archæological instances, till they are known to be equivalents of standard objective examples.

The preceding remarks all tend to show that the element intended to be indicated by the latter of the above two signs , (or ƪ), amounts to no more than an ordinary breathing inseparable from the pronunciation of any initial vowel (or it may indicate the *lengthening* of a "mute vowel"), and cannot therefore be called a consonant. That which is called its *fortis* form (ε), in the second couple of above confronting quotations, is scarcely distinguishable from a soft aspirate, and is probably only the elementary form, of which the Arabic sonant ε is a guttural (consonantal) modification ; that is, an approximation to the vocalised form of the pure aspirate (*spiritus asper*) without the consonantal element of a guttural attached, and which I think occurs in the Sechwana, in *hae* for *gae*, *hòna* for *gona*, &c., examples not unlike Γομόῤῥα and Αμαλεκ; but it is considered by Dr. Lepsius a harder form of the above "breathing," caused "by a stronger explosion at the same point of the throat," and of this his digraph (ᵓ) is intended to be the exponent—with what propriety will be shown in the sequel.

2. *Fricativæ.*—It will be seen, in the preceding table, that, under the so-called fricatives (which I have previously shown, in respect of the gutturals, to be aspirates), these members of the *faucal* series are more uniformly indicated by the usual marks of the *spiritus asper*, or this letter with a diacritical mark—viz., *hh*, *h* or *ḫ*, *ḥ*, *ẖ*, &c. As in the preceding

---

* By this is meant the "liquid semi-vowel."

case, it will be as well to confront **Dr. Lepsius's** description of these sounds with the opinions of other able writers.

Arabic ح, ٨; Hebrew ה; hʿ, h, (of **Lepsius**.)

The Hebrew letter ה is described by **Gesenius** to be, before a vowel, "exactly equal to our *h (spiritus asper)*." The Arabic ٨, which the same able scholar (and Professor **Müller** since) make the equivalent of this Hebrew letter, is considered by **Dr. Lepsius** the same as the *lenis* h of his system, his description of which is anything but clear, but which we have a right to conclude must also be intended for the *spiritus asper*, or "the common h,"* inasmuch as "the effect of the Latin orthography upon this letter was to fix it as the sign of the so-called aspirate.† Since, by all **Dr. Lepsius's** *other lenes* fricatives (viz., χʹ, z̄, z, z, θʹ, and v), may be understood sonants, or *vocalised* consonants, and the Arabic ٨ (his *h*) is a *lenis* fricative, it must with him consequently also be a *vocalised* element; but he elsewhere calls it an "unvocalised strong fricative," an inconsistency arising from his confounding (like most writers) the "breathings" with "unmodified consonants."

The other fricative member of the faucal series—viz., the *fortis*, or *hʿ* of **Dr. Lepsius**, is stated by him to be equivalent to the Arabic consonant ح, which, again, **Gesenius** makes equivalent to the softer of "the two grades of sound" of ה, while the Hebrew was a living language. This Hebrew letter the latter author considers to have been "the hardest of the *guttural* sounds." "It is," he adds, "a guttural *ch,* as uttered by the Swiss, resembling the Spanish *x* and *j*." But the *hʿ* of **Dr. Lepsius** is distinctly described by himself thus:—"Not the common *h*, but a stronger aspiration, which requires a greater contraction of the faucal point, and is distinguished by the Arabs from the simple *h.*"‡ This element, which is indicated by

---

* It is remarkable that, in his detailed description of the *faucals,* any distinctive remarks as to the position or nature of the *asper* appear to be inadvertently avoided. First it is called an "unvocalised strong fricative," as which it must only differ in *degree,* and not in *quantity,* from ح: in the general tableau (p. 46), it is placed midway between the position of the *lenis* (which is vacant), and the *fortis hʿ* (ح); in the alphabetic series (p. 48), it is distinctly classed as a "*fortis* fricative;" again, in the tables of the different languages, it is placed in the vertical series of "*lenes* fricatives."

† "*The English Language,*" vol. ii., p. 103. 4th Edition.

‡ "*Standard Alphabet,*" p. 39. Professor Max Müller calls it (ح) a *guttural-flatus-asper.* He says, the difference between it (ح) and ح̇ "arises from the *higher* or *lower* position of the *point of contact* by which these consonants are formed in a Semitic *throat* [the italics are substituted] (p. lxx.), forgetting Sir John Stoddart's rule, that consonantal articulations are confined to the "upper organs." Elsewhere he says, "the ح is formed so low in the throat, that here a contact and explosion would be impossible"

Smith and Robinson, as well as Gilchrist, by the letter ḥ, is only described by the latter able Orientalist as "rather a harsher aspiration" than the other h, and "peculiar to the Arabic alphabet, but in Hindoostan pronounced just as the simple breathing *hu*."* Again, it is usually laid down as a postulate in orthoepy, that "no aspirate can be doubled." If the *h* of Dr. Lepsius (lenis-fricative-faucal) is only another mark of the *spiritus asper* (ʿ), as I have shown, ח in the Hebrew, and א in the Arabic (which he himself regards as ancient equivalents of that mark), to be, upon the authority of Gesenius and Rodiger, such a thing as an aspirate aspirate, which *hʿ* of course indicates, must be an absurdity; so that, if there be any peculiarity in the nature (or, I may say, quantity) of the element he has attempted to describe, there must be wanting only a more definitive description of it, and a more consistent letter to represent it.

In the above examination of the so-called *faucals*, it will be observed that I have endeavoured to explain away the *explosivæ* altogether, by attempting to show that the *lenis* form , (ﺀ),† is only the well-known *spiritus lenis*, and the *fortis* ; (ع)‡ probably a component part of that *spiritus;* in fact, that I deny altogether to the series a division of explodents, in contradistinction from another, whether called "fricatives" or aspirate.

I am aware that I have only proved my point by displaying to the reader

---

(p. xxviii.); therefore it cannot be a *consonant.* Again, " the ح is formed higher in the *throat* (!), and occasions, it is said, a friction between the root of the tongue and the lowest part of the palate." (*Ibid.*) The fact of the matter is, the former ع is a " breathing" confined to the " lower organs," the latter to the " upper organs;" the former a *strong breathing* unmodified by any consonant—the latter a strong breathing modified by a *guttural* consonant, forming a " liquid aspirate," or " flatus," or " fricative" consonant, as different writers may choose to call the *same* element; so that Dr. Lepsius's definition of it is decidedly more concise and satisfactory.

* *British Indian Monitor*, vol. i., p. 47.

† The following is from Professor Müller :—" This *spiritus lenis* is the Hamzeh of the Arabs. . . . The Hamzeh cannot be called an explosive letter. Its sound is produced by the opening of the larynx ; but there is no previous effort to close the larynx, which alone could be said to give it an explosive character."—*Proposals*, p. xxviii.

‡ According to Max Müller, it (ع) bears the same relation to ع, as the *spiritus lenis* ﺀ [which I have above suggested includes it], does to the *spiritus asper* (א). The same writer says, " there is no tenuis corresponding to ع as little as to א (p xxviii.) ; therefore, if ع and ﺀ are not *tenues*, which Dr. Lepsius decidedly makes them, what are they ?

the confusion which exists on the subject among eminent scholars, who
have given their undivided attention to either ancient graphic systems
wanting in the "living traditional pronunciation,' or to the cumbrous
alphabets of Oriental literature, abounding in redundant letters; but I hope
in the sequel to sustain this proof by an argument of a more tangible
character.

It will, moreover, be observed that I have, so far as regards the "*fricativæ,* tacitly admitted that the strong aspirate which **Dr. Lepsius** has
attempted to describe may possibly prove to be only another quantitive
form of the *spiritus asper,* or letter *h,* which is classed by him as the *lenis*
form under his *faucales.*

Nature of the SPIRITUS.

It is evident that the whole of the above classification of the
so-called *faucal* series into four members, under the two general
divisions of *explodent* and *fricative,* is based upon the assumption
that *h* is a consonant; for if a consonant, it must be one member
of a series of sounds which are "explodent;" and to those who
are determined to maintain that it is one, it will be difficult
to present any plausible argument to the contrary.

I had previously shown, of all the other consonants (except
the *two* yet to be noticed in the sequel), that the so-called
fricatives, as well as explodents, have aspirate forms; and that,
in the case of the gutturals, the term *fricative* of later writers, and
the more common one, *aspirate,* are merely synonymes; therefore there is a perfect right to assume, that if the *faucal* series,
with its four members, is a legitimate organical class of the
elements of articulation, it must, like all the rest, either have
a separate and additional aspirate division, or, as *in the case of the
gutturals,* what Dr. Lepsius calls its fricative forms are merely pure
aspirates. The above examination of the "*faucales*" has brought
me to the latter conclusion; but, at the same time, I trust I
have succeeded in showing that, though Dr. Lepsius has not
alluded to the *spiritus asper* in his detailed description of the

several members of this series, his arrangement of them into two divisions is resolvable into the expression that *there is an "explodent" form of the spiritus asper*, from which I must dissent.

This brings me to perhaps the most conclusive of all arguments on the subject. When we find such extraordinary consonants as the four *Naman* clicks* performing an important part in the distinctions between the roots of a language—*e. g.*, ca (sharp), *v*a (to slaughter), *q*a (to spread), *x*a (to wash),† we need not be surprised at elements as strange being discovered in other languages; and, moreover, when the peculiar mobility of the tongue is taken into account, it is immediately suggested that any unusual variety of them is more likely to be classed under the lingual series than any other—*e. g.*, what are called Naman clicks, or "Arabic linguals," or "Indian cerebrals," whatever points in common they may possess to allow of a secondary classification, could not be otherwise disposed of in an organical arrangement of the consonants. One has heard of the *f* in the language of a Mexican tribe being "purely labial, the teeth taking no part in it," and of the same description applying to its sonant form *v* in the language of Greenland. In all such examples of labials, linguals, or gutturals, in their mute or liquid forms, the consonantal element, or fact of a contact between two organs, is immediately perceptible; but when we are told of a series of elements, such as the "faucales," formed " behind the guttural point, immediately at the larynx," without the pale of what Sir John Stoddart has distinguished as "the

---

* In place of any remarks of my own in corroboration, I prefer to quote the following :—" The clicks ought properly to be classed among the consonants, for although they are by themselves distinct articulations, yet they cannot be considered complete sounds without the aid of a vowel."— *Grammar and Vocabulary of the Namaqua Hottentot Language, by H. Tindall,* p. 13.

† Ibid.

upper or articulating organs,"* there is an inclination to doubt the validity of the facts upon which it is established.

Taking for granted that no one will deny all simple consonants to be formed by a contact, complete or partial, of two organs, and, consequently, by a momentary stoppage of the breath to the extent of that contact, it follows that the "faucal" series, unless its members can be proved to be formed by a contact of two organs, cannot be included among the consonants. The " *contraction* of the fauces," to which the formation of these elements is attributed, does not surely produce an effect similar to that of a *contact.*

If, however, in the classification of this series, the gutturals have been confounded with the ordinary breathings, or the spiritus, or forcible breathings, of which the descriptions of the "faucales" bear evident marks, it is only what might be expected after the terms have been so often confounded.

It is now necessary to come to an understanding as to the real nature of the *spiritus asper.* I have before stated, in an attempt to improve upon the definition of Dr. Lepsius, that the " *aspirates*" are those elements, either vowels or consonants, which are pronounced with a simple but *forcible* emission of the breath; and the result of the preceding inquiry into the "faucal" series is, that the *spiritus asper*, in apposition with these vocal or consonantal elements, is not a consonant, but merely a *forcible breathing;* and, moreover, that it is a distinct element by no means " inherent in every consonant," and decidedly something more independent in its nature than a mere " increase" of the ordinary breath which accompanies the utterance of every

---

* " Sanscrit grammarians sometimes regard *h* as formed in the chest (urasya), while they distinguish the other gutturals by the name of tongue-root letters (jihvāmūlīya)."—" *Proposals,*" &c., by *Max Müller, M.A.,* p. xxxiv. This amounts virtually to Sir John Stoddart's distinction, who, had he made such a statement, would no doubt have omitted the word " other."

vowel or consonant—*e. g.*, the formulæ $t + h, d + h, h + a,$ $t + h + a,$ represent combinations of different elements, among which that of *h* can be uttered independently of either of the others, and the others independently of it.

At present, I have only to do with this element in its application to consonants, both mute and liquid, as, for the purposes of analysis, included under the head of "*Explodents.*"

NOTE.—I have employed this word ("explodents") throughout the work as synonymous with *consonants*, particularly in reference to all elements formed by a contact of two organs, and a necessary withdrawal of that contact, principally because it is applied by most authors to only *some* consonants, and not to others, which, besides the essential character just described, have the peculiarity of being *liquid*. Not only **Dr. Lepsius,** but **Dr. Latham** also, confines the term *explosive* to the former, and *continuous* to the latter ; but the words "*valvular,*" and "*imperfectly valvular,*" are decidedly more satisfactory, and suggest that the terms *explosive* and *imperfectly explosive* would convey similar meanings, but by no means so definitive. Of the former he says—" The action is *perfectly* valvular— *i.e.,* the breath is absolutely or wholly arrested as long as the parts remain" in contact. Of the latter, " The air escapes even while the parts . . . . are in contact. The action is valvular, but only *imperfectly* so."—(*The English Language,* vol. i., p. lviii.) It is, however, difficult to say why the old terms "*mute*" and "*liquid*" should be superseded. See the quotation from Dr. Lepsius, on "the sounds *r* and *l*," usually called liquids. This learned writer's remarks on them, in a general sense, are surely applicable to all *imperfectly valvular* elements.*

I am here glad to avail myself again of the opinions of Dr. J. Müller, the eminent physiologist, viz., his application of "the mute † sound of the whisper," as he terms it, not only to the *vowels* as we have noticed, but also to the *consonants.* He writes—

"A main error in many of the attempts at classification of the articulate

---

* Dr J. Müller also, I find, calls *r* and *l*, as well as *s, sh, ch,* and *f,* "sounds developed by the valve-like application of different parts of the mouth to each other."—*Physiology.* p. 1048.

† Here the sense of the word "mute" must be somewhat restricted, meaning *suppressed, silent.* Whereas, when we apply the term generally to a consonant, it means the momentary absence of either sound or breath, caused by a complete closure of two organs.

sounds, has been the failing to pay sufficient attention to the circumstance of its being possible to form them *without vocal tone, as in whispering;* while to recognise the essential properties of the articulate sounds, we must first examine them as they are produced *in whispering,* and then investigate which of them can also be uttered in a modified character, *conjoined with vocal tone."—Physiology,* p. 1045. (The italics are substituted.)

Now, the whole tenor of this work is intended to show that the main error of classification has rather been the failing to detect the *essential property* of all consonants, viz., that they are formed by a *contact, whether partial or complete,* of two organs. True, some of them (viz., *k, p, t, g,* &c.) *are* " only of momentary duration," and others (viz., *l, r, s, f,* &c.) *"can be* prolonged *ad libitum,"* according to the complete or partial " occlusion of the faucal passage ;" but the learned Doctor seems to have forgotten that the latter *can* also *be* uttered so as to be of " momentary duration ;" in fact, that, like the (ancient) tenues, the " sibilants," or " semi-vowels," or " fricativæ," or " flatus," (as they have been variously called,) have also *tenues forms,* and can therefore all be uttered in a *whisper.*

I am therefore justified in concluding that it is not only the " absolutely mute consonants with strepitus explosions," viz., *k, g, t, d,* &c., that " may, by aspiration, be completely changed to other sounds," but also the *tenues* forms of the liquids *r* and *l,* and such other elements as I hope to prove are their analogues. It is only the ordinary breathing which accompanies articulation in whispering; and this is proved by the fact that it is quite practicable to introduce or withdraw the *spiritus,* as a distinct element, in whispering, just as in vocalised speech. In the utterance of the *tenues* no more than the ordinary breath is required ; but in order to aspirate them the *spiritus* is called into operation. Both *mutes and liquids* can be uttered in a whisper, that is, their *tenues* form ; but both will also allow a distinct and *forcible aspiration* of any of these elements *in whispering*, viz., a *spiritus* additive to the *ordinary breathing* required in the utterance of " whispered speech," *e.g.* :—

Simple Explodents.	*Aspirate Explodents.*
ORDINARY BREATHING (=whispering and CONTACT (partial or complete)	Same elements $\big\}$ + SPIRITUS.

Now in the classification of the *simple consonants*, as suggested by the phonology of the Sechwana language, we have the binary quantities of *fortis* and *lenis*, the general but unsatisfactory distinction between which terms has been touched upon in the first Chapter. It is only necessary for the reader to conceive of the organs being exactly in the position required for the enunciation of any element, to enable him to apprehend the result of a forcible aspiration of the breath in every instance.

In the case of the *fortes*, in which the contact of the organs is simply perfect or complete, and the withdrawal of the contact (or explosion) sudden, the application of the spiritus is simultaneous and equally short and sudden with the withdrawal.

In the case of the *lenes*, the contact being more than complete, in fact, amounting to a pressure,* and therefore proportionably (though imperceptibly) longer, the amount of interrupted air exploded on the withdrawal of the contact is necessarily greater

---

* It is supposed by some that by this greater compression of the organs, and stronger interruption of the breath, a tension of the lower organs is caused, and an utterance approaching to vocality, whence arises the term *sonant* introduced by some authors, in contradistinction from *surd* (for the *fortes*). Dr. Latham describes it thus :—In the case of *b, v, d,* &c., " over and above the action of the parts within the mouth, there has been an action of the larynx, an action by means of which the column of air that, in the case of *p, f, t,* &c., was ordinary breath, was thrown into certain vibrations—made *sonant,* so to say."—(*The English Language,* vol. i., p. lviii.) It should, however, not be forgotten, that in the classification of consonants we have nothing to do with *vowels* or *sounds,* but only with *contacts* and their modifications, by the addition of either the *spiritus* or the element of *vocalisation,* which latter I have yet to notice.

and softer;* the application of the *spiritus* is correspondingly less sudden and softer. In the case of some *lenes*, however, this interrupted breath or air has a tendency to escape, on account of the contact, though complete at certain points, allowing of its permeation at others; in such cases, the application of the *spiritus* completely modifies the nature of the liquid, or "imperfectly valvular" element, and makes it an *aspirated liquid*, or *continuous* consonant.

It is remarkable that the distinction drawn by Dr. Lepsius between the common "aspirates" and the so-called fricatives, is exactly applicable to that above suggested as existing between the aspirated forms of the "valvular" and "*imperfectly* valvular" *lenes* consonants. He writes—"The aspirate can follow the explosion; not accompany it through, as it does the friction of the fricatives." He shortly after says, "the *spiritus* unites itself more closely with the explosive letters than any other consonants."† These "other consonants" are of course his "fricatives," or "imperfectly valvular" elements, some of which I have already proved to have both liquid (or tenues) and continuous (or aspirate) forms.

Are there Binary or Quantitive Forms of the Spiritus ?

I have before remarked that the analysis of the Sechwana consonants, in the second Chapter, afforded a legitimate proof of all consonants being either simple or aspirate "explodents;" and it must now be manifest to the reader, that the subsequent examination of the "faucales" contains no proof whatever that the

---

* *E.g.*,"The muscles of the tongue, aided perhaps by the co-operating action of those of the pharynx, strike the palate more quickly, and on a narrower point, in producing the articulation *k ;* but more slowly, and over a larger space, in producing *g.*"—(*Glossology,* Sir J. Stoddart, p. 132.) According to Professor Müller, "a kind of breathing" continues "after the first contact has taken place."—*Proposals,* p. xxv.

† *Standard Alphabet,* p. 49.

more *forcible* breathing, or *spiritus*, is capable of subdivision
under similar heads; but the train of the foregoing remarks
would seem to imply that it will, at all events, allow of binary
or quantitive forms, as distinct elements, additive to the strictly
simple consonants, fortes or lenes. However probable I may
consider this, it would be impossible to answer the question by
means of any data from the Sechwana.

NOTE.—It may not be out of place here to remark that, in the event of a
proof being found of the propriety of applying the idea of binary quantities
to the *spiritus* itself, which we must bear in mind is additive to both
consonants and vowels, there would be verified the analogy I have already
supposed to exist, in its applicability (quantitively) to both the former and
the latter.

There is decidedly something apparently stronger in the
spiritus accompanying *k*ʻ, *t*ʻ, *p*ʻ, than in *g*ʻ, *d*ʻ, *b*ʻ; but the *fortis* nature
of the consonantal elements in the former example, and the *lenis*
in the latter, are likely to mislead. Still there can be no doubt
that in both cases the *spiritus* are produced by the same disposition of the lower organs. The following quotation seems to
shed some light on the subject.

" According to the Sanscrit grammarians, if we begin to pronounce the
tenuis, but, in place of stopping it abruptly, allow it to come out with what
they call the corresponding 'wind' (flatus, wrongly called sibilans), we
produce the *aspirata*, as a modified tenuis, not as a double consonant.
This, however, is admissible for the tenuis aspirata only, and not for the
media aspirata. Other grammarians, therefore, maintain that all mediæ
aspiratæ are formed by pronouncing the mediæ with a final 'h, the flatus
lenis being considered identical with the spiritus; and they insist on this
principally because the aspirated mediæ could not be said to merge into,
or terminate by, a hard sibilant."*—*Proposals, &c., by Max Müller, M.A.,*
p. xxxii.

Therefore, in the following page, Professor Müller writes—

" In Sanskrit no scholar could ever take *kh* for *k* + *h*, because the latter
combination of sounds is grammatically† impossible."

---

* Or rather *flatus* (to be in keeping with his own nomenclature).
† Perhaps the word *phonetically* is here meant.

In these quotations there seems implied the fact that the
spiritus accompanying the *fortes k, t, p,* is different in kind from
that in the lenes *g, d, b;* and therefore the conclusion that it
must exist in binary quantities.

If binary forms be found to exist, judging by analogy of the
combinations in which it occurs, the lenis form will not unlikely
prove to be our common *h,* as in *house* (the Arabic ﻩ, or ancient
"*spiritus asper*"); and the fortis is as likely to be that (the
Arabic ع) which is described by Dr. Lepsius as formed by a
sudden "contraction of the faucal point," and as a sudden
emission of the breath, of which it is easy to form an idea by a
little experimenting on the aspirate consonants. At all events,
the subject is one worthy of investigation.

Note.—In the event of quantitation being admitted in the case of the
spiritus, and the above conjectures proving correct, of course this would lead to
the abrogation of a nomenclature which has been rendered sacredly conventional and classical by long prescription—*e.g.,*

	Spiritus.*	
Old Nomenclature.........	Arabic ع	Asper.
New „	*fortis (h)*	*lenis (ʼ)*

So that what has always been called the "*spiritus asper*" would really be
the **spiritus lenis,** and the Arabic ع the **spiritus fortis.** The
utterance of such paradoxical notions makes one inclined to wince under
the mere thought of the prospective lashes of some critic, which must
inevitably follow the literary temerity of any writer. At all events, I trust
that the unequivocal expression of my speculations will not subject me to
a castigation, any more than the high-sounding term *explodent* and *fricative*
faucales, indulged in by another infinitely more able author, in reference
to the *spiritus.*

---

* This does not include the ancient "*spiritus lenis,*" which will be again
referred to in the sequel as a *third* form of the *spiritus.*

The " Spiritus" influenced by the Position of the Long Quantity, or Syllabic Accent.

After what has preceded on the nature of this element of speech, the reader, who is disposed to consider the matter in an impartial manner, will no doubt allow that it is of far more importance than some able writers are willing to allow it. Dr. Lepsius says of it—

" It is of so little weight, that it does not make the preceding syllable long."—*Standard Alphabet*, p. 40.

Zumpt—

" It is only an aspiration; it is not considered as a vowel, and therefore, when joined with a consonant, it does not lengthen the preceding syllable."—*Latin Grammar. Trans. by Schmitz*, p. 4.

Professor Ramsay—

" It exercises no influence whatever on the quantity of words, either taken by themselves or when combined with others, in the formation of a verse."—*Latin Prosody*, p. 16.

Dr. Latham—

" When air passes through *both* the mouth (or nostrils) and the larynx simply as so much ordinary breath, the result is the sound expressed by *h*. . . . It is simply so much ordinary breath expired."—*The English Language*, vol. i., p. lvii.

But it appears never to have entered into a part of the inquiries of philologers as to whether the "spiritus asper" is influenced by the *position of the long quantity* (or syllabic accent); therefore the important part it plays in the apparent modifications of certain consonants, to which it is attached, has hitherto been overlooked. I have already shown that the terms *strong* and *weak,* in common with a host of others, have been applied by different writers to distinguish the difference between the *fortes* and *lenes* quantities of each element; that such binary quantities exist, and that of either of these there may be *stronger* and *weaker* forms: but there is no doubt that these terms have often been employed in the former signification, when they could really only be explained in the latter—*e. g.,*

" In German, **Adelung** distinguishes a strong aspiration *(hauch)* at the beginning of a word, as in *hábe*, have; and a weaker in the middle of a word, as in *géhen*, to go."*

He does not seem to have perceived that in the former case the vowel to which the *spiritus* is attached is *long*, and in the latter short. In the same manner we say *uphóld* and *shépherd*, or *vehément* and *véhicle*, but the *spiritus* is only weak in the latter instance of either couple, because the accent is not on the syllable to which it is attached as in the former.† In both cases of the English examples the quantity of the consonants is the same, but the forcible breathing, or spiritus, is modified.

I am not aware that any previous writer has taken this view of the subject; but the Sechwana phonology, which abounds in aspirates, and forms the basis of inquiry, bears out the truth of my conclusions in innumerable examples, of which the following are only a few :—

Léha (pay)   *Lehíle* (have paid)
P'út'a (gather)   *P'ut'íle* (have gathered)
P'ap'áma (quiver)   *K'ok'óla* (retail scandal), &c.

In all which cases the *spiritus* is undoubtedly stronger where it occurs on the accented syllable.‡

Note.—It is not unlikely it will yet be shown that it is not its *position* relatively to certain combinations of consonants which makes a preceding syllable long, but rather the *position of the long quantity* which affects such combinations§ of consonants. This proved, it will be easy to ascertain the primitive monosyllabic nature of all tongues. To refresh the memory of the student who is prompted by this remark to reflect a moment upon the

---

* *Wörterb*, vol. i., p. 1319, *cited by Sir J. Stoddart.*

† Tho few cases such as *honest*, *humble*, &c., do not fall under consideration, because in them the *h* is absolutely *silent*.

‡ At the same time, it is not requisite to indicate this distinction by means of any orthographical expedients ; it is only as well to know them, to enable us to guard against a habit of " hair-splitting," and discriminating too much.

§ In ancient prosody, this is especially to be noticed in the case of *positio debilis*, where, except in the case of the preceding vowel being naturally long, as *salūbris*, or the *muta cum liquida*, belong to different syllables, as *abluo*, the succeeding syllable, is as likely to be long as the preceding one.

various ways in which, according to the modern rules of ancient prosody, a *position* may be formed (as it is usual to express it), I append the rules:— 1. "When a syllable ends in two or three consonants, as in *ex, est, mens, stirps.*—2. When the first syllable ends in a consonant, and the second begins with one, as in *ille, arma, mentis, innova.*—3. When the first syllable of *the same word* ends in a vowel, and the one syllable following begins with two consonants"* (excepting in the case of the *positio debilis*), as *antus, factus*—4. In the case of *i* and *v, consonants* (= y and w) when preceded by another consonant†—*abies, aries; lingua, equus.*

A proper examination of the point above suggested (as well as into the nature of liquids and their continuous forms) will no doubt also shed some light on "a subject of keen controversy among metrical scholars," viz., the quantity of a short final vowel before a word beginning with sc (=sk), sp, st.

Vocalisation of some Consonants, viz., r and l, &c. Therefore, of the Spiritus. *Of the* guttural *provisionally indicated by* g² (*German guttural* ch).

There is another form of the *spiritus,* the consideration of which suggests the examination of a separate element that plays an important part in the modification of some simple consonants viz., *vocalisation.* This element has been variously denominated "the obscure vowel," "the indistinct vowel sound," and "the slight and scarcely distinct vowel sound."

NOTE.—These terms are sometimes applied to certain unaccented forms of all the vowels, as in *German,* lieben; *English,* velvet; *Italian,* ventura; *French,* tenir, &c.; but I shall reserve the consideration of this view of the subject for the second part of the present work, on the **Vowels.**

But the element to which I particularly refer is that concisely described by Dr. J. Müller as follows:—

"A peculiar murmuring sound accompanies several consonants, which does not resemble any of the vowels. This kind of intonating can be produced either with the mouth open or with it closed, the nasal passage being in the latter case open."—*Physiology,* p. 1050.

---

* *Zumpt's Latin Grammar,* by Dr. Schmitz, p. 20.   † Ibid., note, p. 3.

It is not a *vowel*, though invariably considered one. Till a better term can be found, perhaps it may be called either the " *indistinct vowel element*," or the " element of *vocalisation*."

According to Dr. Lepsius, in a quotation of which I have already availed myself—

" This vowel is inherent in all soft *fricative* consonants, as well as in the first part of the *nasal explosive*; whence all these letters, as z, n, m, appear sometimes as forming syllables. It assumes the strongest resonance, as may be easily explained on physiological grounds, in combination with r and l, which, as is well known, appear in Sanscrit as r and l, with all the qualities of the other vowels."—*Stand. Alph.*, p. 27.

Dr. Latham writes—

" It is an essential condition in the formation of a vowel sound, that the passage of the breath be *parietal*. In the sound of the *l'* in *lo* (isolated from its vowel), the sound is as continuous as it is with the *a* in *fate*. Between, however, the consonant *l* and the vowel *a* there is this difference—with *a*, the passage of the breath is wholly uninterrupted; with *l*, the tongue is applied to the palate, breaking, arresting, or *partially* interrupting the passage of the breath."—*The English Language.*

The generic nature of *l*, as a simple (unmodified) liquid, or " pure *explodent*,"* is, by both writers, entirely lost sight of; one of its accessory or modified forms or specific natures, as a *continuous* consonant, is all that is attributed to it—viz., that it is a *vocalised* consonant. It is decidedly a mistake to suppose that *l* and *r*, and their analogues, are essentially vocalised; as well might they be considered essentially aspirated consonants. It is well to bear in mind that they are, like the other *lenes*, *g*, *d*, and *b*, essentially simple " explodents;" it is only from the fact of their allowing a simultaneous and partial emission of the breath that they are *liquid*, and *may be* continuous. Viewed strictly as simple " explodents" (liquids), we have nothing to do

---

* Dr. J. Müller says, " Kempelen classes the consonants *l*, m, n, and *r*, among the vocalised sounds, but they are certainly not always so; they are heard distinctly as true mute sounds in the vocalised (intonated) speech."— *Physiology*, p. 1051. He uses the word *mute* here in the sense applicable to *k*, *g*, &c. My word " *explodent*" refers only to *contact*, *partial* as well as *complete*, and includes *liquids*; therefore more suitable.

with their continuous nature—*i.e.*, the continuousness of the ordinary breath required in their enunciation, but alone with the operation of two organs, with the *contact* or articulation of which its escape is simultaneous and equally momentary. Viewed as continuous consonants, we have to do with the prolation of the breath alone, (*i.e.* the *spiritus*) or the "vocal element," whenever accompanying it. In the former case we have to do with the contact so far as it is merely momentary, and from the circumstance of the action of the organs being to a certain extent "imperfectly valvular," also *liquid;* in the latter case, with the contact so far as this is prolonged, by a continued exertion of the breath in the form of a "fricative," or "flatus," or by the vocal element, which implies continuity of breath. In either case, the consonantal or " explodent," or unmodified liquid nature is not perceived until the organs in contact have been detached; but it is only in the latter that the continuous element is perceptible, for the passage of the escaping and continued breath is as much as in the case of any vowel *parietal*—*i.e.*, "the tongue" (in whatever position), "the cheeks, and the lips, are the walls of the oral passage," and therefore the consonant is capable of being *vocalised.*

But, in every instance, it is the *breathing* which may be vocalised; moreover, in order thereto, the breathing must be *continuous*; therefore, vocalisation would seem to imply an excess of breath beyond the ordinary breathing required in the enunciation of any simple "explodent;" that is to say, an extra exertion of the breath, which can be called by no other name than aspirative.* This is tantamount to saying, that in regard to some *lenes* "explodents," viz., the *liquids*, their continuous† and aspirate forms are identical; in fact, that the letters *l* and *r*, and

---

* In some letters this is more perceptible than in others; *e.g.*, in *r* and *l*, more than in *s*, *th*, and *f*.

† In reference to breath alone.

their analogues yet to be noticed, for example, as pure "explodents," are not accompanied by any extra exertion of the breath, though they may be, if necessary ; but in this case they would become *aspirate liquids*.

In order to test this conjecture, the nature of the rough breathing, or fricative element, viz., the *spiritus*, alone must be considered, as assumed by every consonant, independently of voice. When this element is attached to the *mutes k, g ; t, d; p, b;* its utterance is simultaneous with the separation of the organs in contact, as in *k, g,* &c. ; when attached to the *liquids* (properly so called, viz., *r* and *l,* and their analogues), its duration is simultaneous with that of the contact of the organs, as well as their separation ; and the longer the duration, the greater the exertion of the breath, amounting to an aspiration, which forms a continuous element in the consonant, the " explodent" nature of which latter is not perceived till the organs are detached.

But the *spiritus* is not the only continuous element which may be assumed by a liquid consonant; therefore the term "continuous," as at present used, is ambiguous. It may mean, also, the " vowel element" above noticed ; so that, to be continuous, a liquid consonant may be either *aspirated* or *vocalised,* and vocalisation is probably only aspiration, modified by an accessory element, viz., the "*murmuring sound*" described by Dr. J. Müller.

When this " vowel element" is attached to the simple "explodents," it merely strengthens the explosion, while it occasions a slight hiatus,* except that in the case of the *lenes g, d, b,* the intensity and comparative prolongation of the contact causes, by the same effort of the organs, only an approach to vocality. When attached to the liquids *r, l,* and their analogues, vocalisation of

---

* It is not unreasonable to expect the occurrence of such a consonant; for, in the Hottentot language, a hiatus is sometimes perceptible between a *click* and the succeeding vowel.

these is the result: "the friction (of the breathing, however strong*) ceases to be audible, and only the vowel element is heard" in combination with the "explodent" element. The three forms of *r* and *l*, according to which all their analogues can be classified, are now as follows:—

	Simp. Exp. (or Liquid.)	Asp. Exp.	Vocalized Exp. (or Continuous.)
Lingual......	l	l᷉	i̥
	r	r᷉	r̥†

I trust that what precedes will amount to a proof that aspiration is essential to vocalisation, or the utterance of the "vowel element" (murmuring sound) attached to some consonants. At all events, unless some proof be alleged, the necessity for two scales of vocalised consonants (simple and aspirate) cannot be obviated. The Sechwana language affords only one instance of a proof, which may not, however, be considered satisfactory to some of my readers. I have already thoroughly explained the nature of the two *r*'s in this language—viz., the simple (not continuous) "explodent" r^1, and the aspirate (continuous) r^2, or otherwise *r* and *r᷉*; but it is remarkable that it is only the latter which becomes vocalised—*e.g.*, one sometimes hears *rèma* (hew), in which case continuous breath accompanies the contact of the organs forming *r*, and at other times *r̥èma*, in which the breathing is inaudible, and a buzzing sound, arising from vibration of the tip of the tongue and the exertion of the voice, accompanies the contact. The *r* is in this word aspirated, and in the verbal noun is changed to aspirate *t* (*t᷉*), which will perhaps, on the ground stated above, account for the modification; but I am not

* Part in parenthesis interpolated. The quotation is from Lepsius.

† Among European scholars, the vocalisation of a consonant is usually indicated by means of a circular dot below the letter, thus—*l̥, r̥*. I trust it will not betray any desire to differ with those who have introduced it, to suggest that it be placed at the top, as is usually the practice of pointing in European graphic systems not formed upon Oriental models.

aware of any instance in the language in which a liquid "simple explodent" becomes vocalised, except in that of a word like *morimo*, as pronounced by native children imitating their European teachers, who invariably vocalise the letter.

NOTE.—The above cited instances in the Sechwana would seem to suggest that both *aspiration* and *vocalisation* are accessory elements, not in the slightest degree affecting the quantity of the consonant which assumes them. But as I have, under a preceding head, shown that the *spiritus*, or any aspirated consonant, is affected by the syllabic accent, or quantity of any particular vowel of a word, it may possibly be found to affect the vocalisation also.

Inasmuch as the free emission of the breath is necessary to the enunciation of a vowel, and those " explodent" consonants which allow of a partial escape of the breath may be vocalised, one would think that the *spiritus*, which is nothing more than a forcible emission of the breath, and a continuous element "uttered with the whole oral canal open," must also allow of being vocalised; in fact, that it is just as possible to vocalise the aspirate as it is to aspirate a vowel.

NOTE.—There must, at this point, occur to the reader some glimmerings of a proof of what I have above suggested—viz., that the *spiritus* has two quantities, and this will become more evident as I proceed ; for if it is only some *lenes* consonants that can be vocalized, and also the *spiritus*, it may be inferred that it is the *lenis* form of the latter.

Since the other " soft (*lenes*) fricatives" of Dr. Lepsius are all vocalised forms, and in his classification *h* is a soft fricative, and he admits (p. 39) that there is a vocalised faucal, why not have inserted this at the head of its fricative analogues? In other words, if " this vowel (element) is inherent in all soft *fricative* consonants," and *h* (ˣ) is a soft fricative, it must, to use his own mystical phraseology, also be inherent in *h*.

NOTE.—In coincidence with Professor **Max Müller**, he admits the *guttural* consonant ̣ɛ (his *guttural lenis*-fricative) to be the vocalised form of the *guttural* consonant ̇ɔ (his *guttural fortis*-fricative); but again, the former linguist calls the simple breathing ɛ the vocalised form (" sonant representative," p. xxviii.) of the simple but stronger breathing $\mathcal{c}$. Now these are both *"faucales"* of **Dr. Lepsius,** and the $\mathcal{E}$ is one of his *explodents;* therefore in his view it *cannot* be vocalised. If there is a vocalised *spiritus,* and the simple semi-vowel of Professor **Müller** is nothing more than a vocalised breathing, it is not improbable that $\mathcal{E}$, or the Elif hamzatum $\tilde{?}$ may prove to be it; in this case it would be the " sonant representative," not of $\mathcal{c}$, but of $\aleph$.

The series would then stand thus :—

	Spiritus.	
fortis.	*lenis* (¹).	*lenis* (²), *or vocal.*
$\mathcal{c}$ (*h*)	$\aleph$ (‘)	$\sim$ (’)

The above is a conclusion rather different from that of Dr. J. Müller, who writes—

" The only continuous consonant (?) which cannot be pronounced in combination with a vocal sound is the aspirate *h.* The aspiration of the *h* ceases immediately that the vocal chords are thrown into sonorous vibrations."—*Physiology,* p. 1051.

As to the former part of this quotation, I have already endeavoured to show that *h* is neither a consonant nor a vowel but a strong *breathing* modification of either. The latter part is equivalent to Dr. Lepsius's words describing the " *lenes* fricatives," *z, v,* &c., of which he says " the *breathing* ceases to be audible, and only the vowel element is heard." Dr. Müller may mean by *h* a forcible breathing, and Dr. Lepsius, by the word *breathing*, the ordinary measure of breath required in the utterance of any consonant; so that they may refer to different degrees of one element, to which their equivocal descriptions are equally applicable. Dr. Müller also classes *z* and *v* (and also certain forms of *r* and *l*) as vocalised consonants, and it seems difficult to conceive why he should not allow also that there is a vocalised form of *h.*

Note.—There is, for example, a striking difference between the three opening monosyllables, *o,* ‘*o,* and °*o,* in the line

$\left.\begin{array}{l} \text{O} \\ \text{‘O} \\ \text{”O} \end{array}\right\}$ every one that thirsteth, &c.—*Isaiah* lv.

The *ordinary breathing* is requisite to the enunciation of every consonant or vowel (of which *O* in the above line would, if correct, be an example); were it not, we should not be able to *whisper.* The operation of the "*wind-chest*," or *trachea,* is steady and without effort,.even during the intonated* speech, when the breathing is inaudible till any, either mute or liquid, articulations are modified by the *spiritus,* when it requires effort, and the muscles are called into play. The *spiritus,* whatever the disposition of the articulating organs, is distinctly audible when attached to either vowels or consonants, not only in the "whispered" but also in the intonated speech, *till it itself is vocalised,* when (I admit) the *spiritus* is apparently suppressed. However, it is not really suppressed; but, doubtless, before it reaches the oral canal, part of its force is spent in keeping the vocal ligaments in a state of vibration, and, before escaping with the voice from the mouth, the two together probably cause a resonance in the cavity of the mouth, formed by any particular disposition of the organs, whether guttural, lingual, or labial. To borrow the expression of Dr. Müller in describing certain nasals, "the cavity of the mouth forms a blind diverticulum" in the case of every articulation when vocalised. A proof that the spiritus still accompanies the voice is that, whatever the disposition of the articulating organs, when vocalised, they undergo vibrations. So that there may be some truth in my inference that the spiritus is necessary to vocalisation; but it must be distinctly understood that by the latter term I do not mean intonation.

Dr. Lepsius regards *z, v, θ'* (in *th*is), and *z* (*zh*), as vocalised consonants, since they are the *lenes* forms of *s, f, θ* (in *th*ink), and *š* (*sh*). As will be seen in the sequel—though it is to be shown

---

* I use this term instead of Dr. Müller's, which unfortunately clashes with the sense in which the word *vocalise* is here used.

that they are not *lenes** forms of *s*, &c.—there is nothing in the Sechwana to disprove that they are vocalised forms.

I shall proceed to notice the vocalised form of one of those consonants that have already passed under analysis, which appears to be the subject of unsettled notions. Inasmuch as the above-mentioned vocalised elements are by Dr. Lepsius regarded as analogues of the Danish *g* (=χ' in his system, the softer form of *ch* in *lachen* = $\overset{\iota}{\chi}$), it must in his view also be the vocalised element in the *guttural* series of liquids. As these kindred or cognate elements, *ch* ($\overset{\iota}{\chi}$), and γ (χ'), are by him regarded as the equivalents, respectively, of those indicated by *kh* and *gh* in the Hindustáni of Gilchrist, I cannot do better than describe the latter consonant in the words of this distinguished Orientalist :—

" *Kh* is the rough guttural *k*, pronounced in the very act of hawking up phlegm from the throat, which becomes tremulous and ruffled, while the root of the tongue is with it forming the sound required. This letter is familiar enough to the Scottish and other northern nations, but very troublesome to the English, &c."—*British Indian Monitor*, vol. i., p. 12.

There can be very little doubt that the consonant above described ($\dot{\zeta}$) is the *ch* in the Scotch *loch*, that is, equivalent to *ch* in German *lachen*—viz., the $\overset{\iota}{\chi}$ of Lepsius.† Of the other ($\dot{\varepsilon}$), Dr. Gilchrist writes :—

"*Gh* is * * * * the guttural Northumberland *r*, heard in the act of gargling the throat with water."—*Ibid*. p. 12.

In this description Dr. Duff coincides with him.

Elsewhere he writes of both elements :—

"The true discriminative articulation of *kh* and *gh* depends on ruffling the throat in a particular manner, while prolating *k* and *g* respectively."—*Ibid*. p. 20.

It must be evident to the reader that, in quantity, the articu-

---

* *I.e.*, related to *s*, as *t* to *d*.

† Dr. Forbes says—" $\dot{\zeta}$ has a sound like *ch* in the word *loch*, as pronounced by the Scotch and Irish, or the final *ch* in the German words *schach* and *buch*."—*Hindust. Grammar*, p. 5.

lations arc identical, but that the former is aspirated, and the latter a vocalised liquid.*

Though Dr. Gilchrist has most distinctly stated that the consonant indicated by his digraph *gh* is the Northumberland *burr*, or *r*, the latter sound is separately included in Dr. Lepsius's system as *r̤*, or the *guttural r*. Now Professor Max Müller writes :—

" The English and the German *r* become mostly guttural, while on the other hand the Semitic guttural flatus lenis fricatus . . (غ) takes frequently the sound of a guttural *r*. It might be advisable to distinguish between a guttural and a lingual *r*; but most organs can only pronounce either the one or the other, and the two therefore seldom co-exist in the same dialect."—*Proposals*, p. xl.

But he elsewhere calls غ " the sonant representative" of ح (p. xxviii). The majority of writers concur in making the Oriental غ an element as nearly as possible equivalent to what is often called " the guttural *r*" or *burr* of some dialects. Among others, Silvestré de Sacy as cited by Garnett. The latter able linguist himself says of it, " the sound meant for *r* has no lingual vibration at all, but becomes a deep guttural . . . almost exactly corresponding to the Arabic غ *ghain.*"† If so, it is not only advisable but absolutely necessary to distinguish between it as a *guttural* sonant (vocalised guttural) and any lingual sonant,

---

* Dr. Forbes says—" غ has a sound somewhat like *g* in the German word *sagen*. About the banks of the Tweed, the natives sound what they fancy to be the letter *r*, very like the Eastern غ." —*Hind. Gram.* Professor Müller makes the *g* in German *tage* the sonant corresponding to the German guttural *ch* in *loch* (which latter, however, he considers the equivalent of the Arabic ح already referred to as a different element from خ); but Germans, whom I have tried in this country, differ so in pronouncing the *g* in *tage*, that it cannot fairly be taken as a type. If this letter, as known to Professor Müller, is equal to the *g* in *sagen*, and this again approximates at all to the *g* in Cape Dutch *dagen*, which is only a very mild form of the " guttural *r*," or Northumberland burr, it is very probable that these are all examples of variations which " exist only in degree."

† *Philological Essays*, p. 253.

viz., between $\dot{r}$ and what I shall provisionally indicate by $\dot{y}'$—in my orthographical nomenclature a letter bearing the same relation to $\dot{g}^2$ as $\dot{r}$ to $\dot{r}$.

I have thus attempted to show the "guttural r" to be the vocalised element in the guttural series; at all events, it is requisite that I should account for the nature of the Danish g, which I propose to attempt in the sequel. The Danish g (γ or χ') is in the same system, but I think erroneously, represented as the equivalent of Dr. Gilchrist's digraph gh (Arabic غ).

The Nasals and their Vocalisation.

It is under the head of *vocalisation* that it becomes me to take into consideration the subject of the *nasal consonants*, properly so called. *M* and *n* have always been regarded as analogues of *l* and *r*—that is, as *liquid* consonants or semi-vowels. Though to this day schoolboys are so taught, and an authority like Dr. Latham classes them as such, they are by linguists of the Continent, and others,* classed separately as nasal consonants, and as analogues of *ng* in English *king*, or German *enge*. Again, just as *m* and *n* have by long prescription been considered liquid consonants, the element usually indicated by *ng* in the same two examples has been exclusively pronounced the *nasal n*. So recently as 1855, the above able writer gives the public the following conclusive remarks on the subject of this element, which he considers the "English representative" of a *class*, but does not acquaint his reader with a single additional instance of other members of this class :—

"The nasal sounds are *vowels*, so far as the actions that form them are *parietal*.

"They are also *vowels* in some of their other properties—*e.g.*, they can form syllables by themselves. In the Chinese, such syllables actually exist, constituting monosyllabic words.

---

* Among the rest, Sir J. Stoddart. "In Hebrew, Greek, &c., it [*n*] is (as I think improperly) reckoned among the *liquids*."—*Glossology*, p. 142.

"They are not, however, *vowels*, in respect to their power of combining with other sounds—*e.g.*, *b-ng* is not a syllable in the way that *ba* or *bo* is one.

"Nevertheless, the nasal sounds are essentially *vowels*, though whether it may be convenient to call them so is another question. The details of their mechanism and classification have yet to be studied, and, as they are rare in our own language,* it is not likely that any Englishman will be the successful investigator. The French and the Portuguese have the best means of studying them. Neither have the muscles of the *nares* and soft palate been examined, with any view towards the phonesis of what we have called the nasal passage.

"Nevertheless, the *ng* in *king* is more of a vowel than aught else."— *The English Language*, 4th Ed., vol. i., p. lvi.

The following abstract from the valuable tables of Dr. Lepsius will show that what is properly called a class of *nasal vowels* has, probably, been confounded with this imaginary plurality of *nasal sounds* so called, of which the single example of *ng* in *king* is considered by Dr. Latham the " English representative."

TABLE OF " NASALS."

	Vowels.					Consonants Gutt.
Standard of Lepsius	ā	ē	ī	ō	ū	ṅ
Hottentot—						
Knudsen	å	ė	i	ȯ	ů	
Wallmann	â	ê	î	ô	û	ng
Sanscrit—						
Bopp....................	aṅ	eṅ, &c.				n
Wilson	aṇ	eṇ, &c.				ṇ
Bengáli—						
Haughton..............	ong					ng
Zend—						
Bournouf	ã	ṅ				ng
Bopp.....................	aṅ	n				ṇ
Brockhaus	ã	ñ				ń
Albanian—						
Hahn	aν	εν, &c.				ν
Hindustáni—						
Yates	aṇ, &c.					
Gilchrist {1796	añ					
{1806	ṇ					ng
Wilson	aṇ					
Chinese—						
Eindlicher	an	en, &c.				,

* This cannot, therefore, include *m* and *n*, which prevail in the English language.

Now, under the *Hottentot,* to my own knowledge, there can be no mistake as to the existence of the *nasal vowels,* whether written by Mr. Knudsen å, ĕ, &c. ; by Mr. Wallmann, or, more recently, Mr. Tindall, as â, ê, &c. ; or by Dr. Lepsius as ã, ẽ, &c. ; but whether the guttural *consonant ng* exists in the language I think there is some doubt.* Mr. Knudsen and Mr. Wallmann, on the statement of Dr. Lepsius, both write it, but I have not succeeded in finding that this is supported by the authority of Mr. Tindall. It is remarkable that in such an example as †*caṅgha* (smoky), where the lingual *n* occurs before the liquid guttural *gh* (German *ch*), it remains a lingual; that is, it does not become *cang-gh,* or, as Dr. Lepsius would write it, *caṅχa.* In his Grammar he speaks of " a *final vowel,* which appears to have the ringing sound of *ing,* as in *ring, sing,* &c. ; but which is not sounded with sufficient distinctness to warrant our adopting the same orthography as in English." He, however, suggests that it will require Dr. Lepsius's "*ṅ*" to meet this case—not, perhaps, aware that this pointed letter is intended to be confined to the English or German articulation, as indicated by the digraph *ng* in *ing,* or *enge.*

It is not improbable that the same confusion which exists as to the fact of the consonantal articulation *ng,* and the nasalized vowels *â, ê,* &c., both being found in the Hottentot, also prevails among some of the linguists quoted in the above table, in respect to the nasals to which they allude. I have placed at the head of this table Dr. Lepsius's standard *nasal vowels,* and classed under them what he considers as their equivalents in the writings of those linguists. With the same view the instances

---

* Since writing the above, I have heard it in the Grikwa (impure Hottentot) expression, *ta eibe qong* (don't go just yet), in which *q* represents the " cerebral" click.

† This letter here represents a click.

are shown in which, according to them, the guttural *nasal consonant* is found in some of the same languages.

Of these, the Hottentot is said to have that consonant; but this has just been questioned in the preceding remarks. Again, the *Hindustáni* is represented as not having it, whereas Dr. Gilchrist* gives it in such words as *hongeeṇ* (will be), *Gunge* (O Ganges!). In fact, no better example could be produced of the manner in which correct views of the phonical nature of elements have been sacrificed to these graphic differences. But in the former word occurs also his "nasal *ṅ*;" this he describes as equivalent to that in the French word *bon*, which, of course, an Englishman, to be in keeping with his own graphic system, would have to write *bong*.† Here we find a fresh source of confusion. It is evident that Dr. Gilchrist's *ṇ* (or *ñ* of 1796) is not the nasal *vowel*, as which it is classed by Dr. Lepsius, but the proper nasal consonant *ng* in *king* (*ṅ* of the "Standard Alphabet"); for there is surely no distinction between *ng* in *king*, and that in *long* or *bong* (Fr. *bon*).

To help myself, as well as the reader, out of this confusion, I shall quote Dr. Gilchrist's description of the letter *n* in Hindustáni:—

"*n*, as a nasal before *j*, *k*, *g*, and *t*, or *d*, requires no particular mark, sounding exactly like our own letters *nj*, *ng*, *nk*, *nt*, &c. in *change*, *rung*, *sunk*, *want*, &c., but elsewhere it is the French nasal when marked *ṇ*. Preceding the labials it becomes, as in most languages, *m*."—*British Indian Monitor*, vol. i., p. 9.

---

* See *British Indian Monitor*, vol. i.

† Unless a Frenchman nasalizes the vowel, as he doubtless does in some instances; but this would not alter the consonant. The vowel is also modified, and requires a separate diacritical mark—thus (French) *sãṅ* (to borrow Dr. Lepsius's orthography). Perhaps it is in allusion to such an instance that Dr. J. Müller says, rather arbitrarily, "the *ng* of the French language is formed still deeper in the throat!" (p. 1048.) He afterwards (p. 1052) refers to the frequent use in French of these three consonants, but especially *ng*, "in constant combination with vowel sounds of nasal timbre, to the exclusion of other vowels not of nasal character." However, I observe the *n* in *bon* (French) is given also by Max Müller as the equivalent of *ng* in *sing* (English).

Now, in the following combinations—

nj   nk   ng   nt   nd,

the *n, separated from the post positive letter in each case,* is in *nj,* lingual; in *nk* and *ng,* guttural; in *nt* and *nd* lingual.

The example = *nj* in *change,* would be called by **Max Müller,** and many other Oriental linguists, a *palatal,* as in his examples *inch, injure;* but he does not deny, and I question whether any of them would, that the tongue is the active agent in the formation of the palatals so-called, as well as in the linguals. Besides the three common organical classes of consonants, Professor **Müller** has two others—viz., *palatals* and *linguals* (wrongly called *cerebrals,* but, he says, properly *cacuminals),* which he calls modifications of *gutturals* and *dentals* respectively. Merely to preserve analogy or consistency in a tableau, or, may be, in deference to Para Brahma himself, these must, forsooth, have their *nasal* exponents. Professor **Lepsius,** besides these, has a third additional class—viz., the *linguales* (Arabicæ), to which he applies the same principle of a forced analogy.— See his Table, " *Consonants of the General Alphabet.*"

To his fourth additional class, the *faucales* (I. in his Table) of which, as consonants even theoretically true, I have attempted to show the absurdity, he fortunately has no *nasal exponent.* A plausible law seems to have been snatched at in every case—viz., that " the peculiar character of a nasal is determined by the consonant immediately following."—(See *Haughton's Reasons for so many Indian Nasals, cited by Monier Williams,* p. 81.) As it was maintained by the Sanskrit or Arabian grammarians that there are differences in the consonants, and inferred that there must be *nasal exponents* corresponding to these differences, it seems to be expected by modern Sanskrit scholars that what was considered at least theoretically true in Arya-âvarta, or at Mecca, will probably turn out to be practically true at Timbuktu, or in Bushmanland. However, leaving the so-called nasals of the Sanskrit and Arabic linguals to their respective sections, I shall here only refer to the so-called *palatal-nasal.* In addition to the above law, which I admit to be true in the majority of instances, but not in all, another seems to have been long in vogue to pervert the notions of the linguist in respect to this imaginary element—viz., that a palatal is a *simple consonant.* Were it one, I admit there would be some reasonableness in seeking a *nasal* exponent for the series; but emphatically deny that *any* palatal is a simple consonant. By going thoroughly, *i.e.,* inductively, into the subject here, I should be anticipating the matter of the third integral portion of this work, as well as a part of the following section. Reference to a single example, which I cull from Professor **Müller** himself, will suffice. He says—" What we call a palatal *n* is generally not a simple but a compound nasal, and should be written *ny*" (p. lxvii.) Why, then, include it at all in a series of simple consonants? It must be evident to the reader that it is not the *n* that is palatal, but the *combination ny*, which is a *palatal* analogue of *dy* or *ky*, or any other letter or combination of letters with a superadded *y*, and that *my* and *ɉy* are articulations quite as palatal as *ny*. In fact, combination of a peculiar kind (not of consonants alone) is essential to palatalization. Again, as is well known, the three common nasals *m*, *n*, and *ng*, exist by themselves, *i.e.*, independently of any other consonant; whereas Professor **Müller** himself says elsewhere, in treating of the *palatals*, " the nasal, again, hardly exists by itself, but only if followed by palatals" (p. xxxvii.); therefore it ought at once and for ever to be omitted from the table of simple consonants.*

In reference to some of these *palatals*, **Dr. J. Müller**, the eminent physiologist, says—" The *j*, soft *g*, and *ch* of the English language are also compound sounds. The *j* and the *g* being pronounced like the French *j* in ' jamais,' preceded by *d*; the *ch* like *t* followed by *sh*," (p. 1052). In fact, the *initial* of most palatal " sounds" can be resolved into a common *lingual*, of which there is a *nasal* exponent ready to hand, without resorting to either the Devanagari or Arabic for any of their superfluous letters.

Now, if guttural in *nk* and *ng*, it must, independently of the post positive consonants *k* and *g*, be equivalent to the nasal consonant *ng* in question. I have shown the French *n*, in some cases, to be a consonant = *ng* in *king*, or German *enge*. Assuming this digraph to indicate this nasal consonant, *rung* would be correctly written, but *sunk* would require to be written *sung-k*; therefore, in the above examples of Dr. Gilchrist, *hongeen* and *gunge*, these would be written *-hong-geeng* and *gung-ge*; so that his French *ṇ* and his *n* preceding any gutturals are identical elements. If his nasal *ṇ* (or *añ*) were a vowel, and his *ng* = to the same digraph in the word *king*, Dr. Lepsius would write the above two words *hoñĩ*; but if his *ng* were = to *ng-g*, the same linguist would write the word *hongĩ*.

---

* In the face of these facts, the learned Professor does not make the simple guttural-nasal *ng* a *base letter* as common with *m* and *n*, but gives this favoured place to the so-called palatal nasal *ny* (French *signe*), and actually calls *ng* a " modification of the second degree" (!)—*See Table*, p. xci.

The conclusion to which we must come is, that in the above table we have a medley of instances, culled indiscriminately from the works of several authors, in which the three separate elements—(1) *ă*, the (mean) *nasal vowel;* (2) *n̊*, the *nasal guttural consonant;* and (3) the latter combined with the kindred guttural *g, i.e., n̊-g,* require to be distinguished;* that is, some of the instances will, perhaps, on proper examination, be found equivalent to *n̊g*, in which the kindred letter *g* is distinctly enunciated, as in the word *English;* some, to *n̊* (or *ng* in *king*, German *enge*, French *n* in *bon*) alone, without the kindred element; and some as real vowels, the pure and indisputable forms of which are to be found in the Hottentot (a living member of the Egyptian family of languages) and Chinese.

If it is by these dissimilar examples that we are to understand the *class* of nasals of Dr. Latham, of which he considers the English *ng* (*n̊* of Lepsius) as the representative, I trust that I have proceeded far enough to show the impropriety of such a classification, and that this element is rather a distinct member of another set of nasal consonants, viz., the analogue (guttural) of the lingual *n* and the labial *m;* a statement which admits of abundant proof in what follows.

Dr. Latham writes:—

" We cannot close the nostrils, as we can the lips, by the action of their own muscles. Neither is there such an organ as the tongue in the nose. If there were, we might form as many sounds through that organ as we do through our mouth. As it is, however, all that we can do with a column of air passing through the nostrils, *is to narrow its line of exit by contracting the passage.*† The nasal and palatal muscles allow us to do so. They allow us to bring the walls of the nasal cavity a little nearer each other, or to separate them a little farther from each other. They do not, however, allow us to close the passage altogether," &c.—*The English Language.*

---

* I have, for the purpose of this distinction, made use of letters in the " *Standard Alphabet*" of Lepsius.

† The italics are mine.

The above appears to explain exactly the nature of the nasal action in the formation of the narisonant *vowels*. There is no *contact* of organs in the faucal passage, this being only more or less narrowed, as in the case of any ordinary vowels; the nasalization of the vowel is caused entirely by a change in the compass of the nasal passage, whereas with the nasal *consonants m, n,* and *ŋ*,* there is a contact of organs in the faucal passage and a perfect closure of the same, but no change in the nasal passage.

Just as *n* and *m* are formed, respectively, by the tongue with the palate, and by the lips alone, so *ŋ* (*ng*) is formed by the contact of the same organs required in the formation of its kindred forms *k* and *g*;† so far they are simple "explodents." They differ from the other liquid consonants, *l, r,* &c., in that they are all *mutes*; that is, the faucal passage is closed by the contact of the organs ‡—the action of these organs is "perfectly valvular" —their closure is complete. Nevertheless, they are analogous to

---

* In order to avoid as much as possible the use of diacritical marks in distinguishing the *simple* consonants or elements, I shall in future employ this letter in place of either the Sechwana *ñ*, the *ɪ* of Lepsius, or the digraph *ng*. I believe it was introduced by Pitman in England, and I have observed that Mr. Appleyard and Mr. Grout, both able linguists, have suggested the use of it in a general South African alphabet. As the original character of the nasal is often determined by that of the simple consonant immediately following, it is supposed by some linguists that it "requires no modificatory sign;" but the rule is not universal, *e g.,* the nasal above referred to in Hottentot *cangha,* Sechwana *siŋtle,* and in Zulu words, *-mnandi, -mtoti, -nwana,* without their prefixes, show examples to the contrary; but when the two accessory elements of aspiration and vocalisation are taken into account, as requiring diacritical expedients to mark them, the importance of being particular in giving each its fixed letter cannot be overrated. Two of the above Zulu examples, I suspect, ought to be written *m̊nandi, m̊toti,* or in any way that will show the *m* to be vocalised.

† That is, in the words of Dr. J. Müller, "by the application of the dorsum of the tongue to the posterior part of the palate."

‡ This is admitted by Professor Müller (p. xxx.), and by Dr. J. Müller; but, strange to say, the latter nevertheless denies that *m* is a labial consonant" (p. 1047). See, in self-contradiction, his remark on Kempelen, already quoted, p. 81, in which he calls it a " *true mute sound.*"

H

the kindred faucal consonants (liquids), in that while there is a contact of the same organs the breathing or vocalisation finds a way of escape. In the case of the liquids, it escapes according to the position of the organs in imperfect contact; in the case of the nasals, it is withheld and "retroverted" to the nasal aperture,* which undergoes no alteration. Like the liquids, they must then, necessarily, admit of vocalisation as well as aspiration. We have thus presented the three possible forms of each organic series.

	Simp.	Asp.	Vocal.
Guttural	g̱	ġ̱	g̱̊
Lingual	n	ṅ	n̊
Labial	m	ṁ	m̊

These all abound in the Sechwana language, with the exception of the aspirate forms, of which there are a few, but they do not just occur to me. The following words, similarly arranged, will suffice as examples:—

ɲ *ata* (a sheaf)   ɲ̊*he* (a species of ground-squirrel)
nala (loiter)   n̊*tsa* (prodúce)
matla (gallop)   *tsam̊a* (a walking-stick)

NOTE.—(1). The object-particles *m*, *n*, and ɲ (= me) of verbs are invariably vocalised in the Sechwana language, *e.g.*, m̊*pona*, n̊*nama*, ɲ̊*khatla*.

(2.) In the case of the prefix *mo* being attached to the initial cognate element *b*, which by synaeresis† becomes m̊, *e.g.*, *mobala* (colour), is always pronounced m̊*ala*; *mobutla* (hare), is always m̊*utla*.

---

* Dr. J. Müller thus describes them:—" In the pronunciation of all the three consonants of this order, the cavity of the mouth forms a blind diverticulum of greater or less length from the throat and nasal canal. This diverticulum is largest during the utterance of *m*, smallest when *ng* is being pronounced (p. 1047). I have already copied this phraseology in describing the formation of the other vocalised liquids *l*, *r*, &c., without at the time noticing, what I now observe, that the vocalised nasals are in this respect also analogues of those (proper) vocalised liquids."

† It is probable that the initials n̊ and ɲ̊ are in some instances

(3.) In all cases like *mohago* (road-food), becoming *ṁhago ; mo henya* (conquer him), becoming *ṁo henya ;* but in examples such as the latter the words are pronounced both ways. In this language these three nasal consonants form initials independently of any other consonants—*ɲ ata, nasa, mothu.*

§ II. The "Palatales" (of Lepsius) and the Letter "q."

Next in order in the above General Alphabet of **Dr. Lepsius,** we find the letter *q,* and (omitting the mute gutturals which have been fully under consideration) a series answering to the gutturals, but with a diacritical mark attached to distinguish them. Professor **Müller** also says—" Palatals are modifications of gutturals, and therefore the most natural course would be to express them by the guttural series, adding . . any . . sign to indicate their modified value" (p. lxi.)* Though acknowledged to be compound sounds in the pronunciation of Europeans, **Dr. Lepsius,** with an over-scrupulous regard for the *graphic* element in the sacred Davanagári writing of the Indians, must, forsooth, pronounce them to be simple sounds,

---

analogously formed. See *Kellic* permutations referred to in sequel (Sec. ii. ch. iv.) The above is perhaps the phonical process called *eclipsis* by " the Irish grammarians," *e.g., mbaile* (town), pronounced *maile. — See Garnett,* p. 81.

* The palatals are indicated by the gutturals *k, kh, g,* &c., modified thus—

> By Professor Lepsius ... ... *k′ kh′ g′* &c.
> „ „ Müller ... ... *k kh g* &c.

With regard to the flatus or fricative form of these palatals, Dr. Lepsius adheres to his graphical rule by borrowing the Greek letters thus—χ̆, χ″ ; but Professor Müller wanders from his own by introducing the sibilants *s* and *z* italicised. The following is a list of some of the " sounds" commonly comprehended under the term palatals :—

> { *ch* in English *church,* German *rutschen,* Italian *ceci.*
> { *j* in English *join.*

> { *sh* in English *sharp,* French *ch* in *chose,* German *sch* in *scharf.*
> { *j & g* in French *joli, genou,* English *s* in *vision.*

> { *ch* in German *ich.*
> { *g* „ *könig.*
> { *g* „ *taglich.*

> *gn* in French *besogne,* &c., &c., &c., (= *ny.*)

Its imperfection will account for the amount of unsuccessful speculation on the subject of these " sounds."

because in that system represented by simple signs. "This is, moreover," he says, "proved by their not rendering the preceding syllable long, and by the possibility of doubling them." Professor **Müller**, in other words, says—"All (the French *tch*, the Italian *c*, and the Russian Ч), even the German *tsch*, are meant to express simple consonants, which, with the exception of the tenuis aspirata in Sanskrit, would not make a preceding short vowel long" (p. lxi.)* I have already alluded to this subject in the preceding section, in attempting to show that there is no such element as a separate palatal *nasal*, and shall therefore not attempt to anticipate by more than a few remarks here, what will be fully treated on in its proper place.

Just as "the name of χ (chi) connects it with the vowel *i*" in the minds of such as have given more attention to graphic differences, so the letter *q*, from its Hebrew and Greek names *qof* and *koppa*, seems to be connected with the vowel *o ;* but it is necessary to disabuse the mind of the "syllabic power" originally attached to such letters, and resolve them into their elements. The former is merely an instance of a *guttural* being prefixed to the prepositive vowel of a palatal diphthong, and the latter (in later orthography) of the guttural *k* being attached to that of a labial diphthong. On this account, neither they, nor any analogous syllabic combinations,† can be said to fall under a classification either of the *simple* or compound consonants, and are, therefore, reserved for the third part of this treatise. Professor **Müller** again says—"Although, therefore, we are forced to admit the palatals, as a separate class, side by side with the gutturals, because most languages retain both sets, and use them for distinct etymological and grammatical purposes, still it will be well to remember that the palatals are more nearly related to the gutturals than to any other class, and that in most languages the two are still interchangeable" (p. xxxvi.) It is to be hoped that before the writer has time to disprove this phonetical tenet, of which some European linguists seem so tenacious, they will anticipate the numberless proofs to the contrary which he hopes to produce from a barbaric dialect—viz., that "palatals" are as much modifications of both *dentals* and *labials* as of gutturals, and that they are in no instances *simple* consonants.

---

* He, however, elsewhere says—"Frequently the pronunciation of the palatals becomes so broad that they seem, and in some cases really are, double consonants." (p. xxxvii.)

† There is very little doubt that all "sounds," called by Dr. Latham "*Unstable Combinations*," fall under these. I find similar "sounds" are called by Professor Müller "*Specific Modifications of Gutturals*."

The Oriental q, *probably the elementary form of the aspirated consonant* خ *(German guttural* ch, *Sechwana* g² *of the preceding analysis.*)

But the element which is intended by Dr. Lepsius to be indicated by *q* is that out of which the modern letter is proved to have grown, viz., the Arabic ﺝ (*káf*), or the Hebrew ק (*qof*), which, according to that learned writer, "is formed at the posterior part of the soft palate." Besides the two languages above mentioned, it occurs in the tables of the *Persian, Hindustáni, Turkish,* and *Malayan,* suspended in a doubtful position between his *faucales* and *gutturales;* and is uniformly represented by the same letter, except by Wilson in the *Hindustáni,* and Smith and Robertson in the *Arabic,* who employ the pointed letter *ḳ,* and Crawfurd in the *Malayan* that of *k.* However, the same letter *q* is used by Burnouf and Brockhaus in the *Zend,* and by Rosen in the *Georgian,* to indicate another element, which is included by Dr. Lepsius under his *faucales;* so that there is still a good deal of uncertainty attached to its nature.* To a local student of South African tongues it is very difficult to form a correct conception of it.

It is, therefore, the more necessary that some discussion should be raised on the subject, as similar elements may occur in those tongues which it will otherwise be a troublesome matter to classify. The Oriental articulation in question is thus minutely described by the learned Dr. Gilchrist, in a work on the *Hindustáni:*—

" *Q,* or our *k,* articulated by raising the root of the tongue simply towards the throat, *which must not be in the smallest degree ruffled,* as in forming *kh,*

---

* Some objection may be urged against the repeated mention in this work of the graphic symbols used by different writers; but I refer to them upon the ground of the probability that every linguist will have chosen a certain letter, or diacritical modification of it, to indicate what he considered an articulation approximating to that which it was usually intended to indicate. In this respect, the tabular abstracts which I have made from the numerous tables of Dr. Lepsius cannot but be valuable.

or *gh*. The *q* may consequently be styled a deep but liquid linqual letter,* produced by clinking the root of the tongue against the throat, so as to cause a sort of nausea. The same sound will be recognised when pouring water in a particular manner from a long-necked guglet, as the liquid decanting may represent the lower part of the tongue acting upon the throat or neck of the vessel in question, *unruffled* by the water gushing from it."— *British Indian Monitor*, vol. i., p. 12.

Again :

"Though *q* be called a guttural, I would rather name it a linqual letter, because its formation is almost entirely owing to the root of the tongue being raised to the roof of the palate or throat, which last is *preserved perfectly unruffled* in this operation, *whence the real difference between* q *and the other gutturals already enumerated.* Water poured in a particular manner from a long-necked guglet, or the hiccup of a man more than half-seas over, will, I believe, yield a sound very near the *q*, which, when duly articulated, has the peculiar property of exciting a nausea in the learner. When followed by *u*, the scholar must never, as in English, change *u* to *w*, but call words like *qulum* (a pen), *qazee* (a judge), *kulum*, *kazee*, never *qwulum*, *qwazee*, &c. ; nor *qeer* (pitch), *queer*, but *keer*, or rather *qeer*, &c., with the lingual *q* above described alone."†—*Ibid.* p. 20.

The above quotations only confirm the fact of the universally acknowledged difficulty of giving a reader an adequate con-

---

* In taking exception to this term, I may as well state that the root of the tongue is called into operation in the formation of all the *gutturals*, and that there is no good reason for not including this element *q* among them.

† The italics are all substituted ; also in the examples throughout the above two quotations.

Dr. Duff considers that the articulation has been happily described by Dr. Gilchrist in the former.—*See " Original Papers," by Monier Williams, M.A.*, p. 79.

Professor Müller, I find, makes little reference to it. At p. xxxv. he calls it " a low guttural," and speaks of its " superlative degree of explosiveness" as " a characteristic peculiarity." In his *Table*, at p. xci., it is called a *guttural tenuissima*, and indicated by *q* as a base letter, or by *K* as a " modification of the second degree." Rather indefinite ! When in Natal, in August, 1861, I examined a Hindoo on the subject of this element. His pronunciation answered to Dr. Gilchrist's description, and confirmed me in the above conclusions. It did not appear to be more explodent in its nature than *l* or *r*, and, so far as I was then able to judge, is certainly not a *mute*. An acquaintance of mine, who spoke Bengáli, considered it was " a sort of liquid guttural."

ception of a consonant by mere verbal description; they will at all events enable us to form a pretty close comparison.

Dr. Forbes says of it:—

" ک bears some resemblance to our *c* hard, in the words *calm, cup ;* with this difference, that the ک is uttered from the lower muscles of the throat."— *Hindust. Grammar,* p. 6.

I have already given Dr. Gilchrist's description of his digraph *kh,* alluded to in both of the above quotations, and shown it to be identical to the *ch* in German *lachen,* or the Sechwana *g* of the missionaries ($\check{g}^2$ of preceding analysis). The learned writer describes the element *q* as only differing from this *kh* in the fact that in its enunciation the organs in contact are *unruffled,* by which may be understood that they undergo no vibration by means of a strong aspiration of the breath. It is evident, from the whole description, that the element intended to be indicated by *q,* is a lenis form of the simple explodent *k*—that is, a liquid modification of *g,* bearing the same relation to this letter as I have proved *r* and *l* do to *d,* and as *ch* (*lachen*), $\check{g}^2$ does to aspirate *g*—viz., $\overset{\iota}{g}$.

Now, in respect to all that has preceded, it must be borne in mind that I have stated my objections to the terms *fricativæ* or *continuæ* merely as generical terms, in contradistinction from *explodents* on the one hand, and *aspirates* on the other. My meaning will, I trust, be apprehended, inasmuch as I have at the outset attempted to show that, in respect to the *gutturals,* the terms fricative and aspirate have been confounded, and to the sibilants, that some of the so-called fricatives are simple "explodents," and the others aspirates. I am not aware of having denied that either word, *fricativæ* or *continuæ,* may be used in a specifical sense, or that it may be introduced consistently into a general classification, in contradistinction from the *mutes.* In fact, the whole of my reasoning goes to prove that this is quite practical, and that it amounts to a necessity, as the following tableau of the results of my operations thus far will clearly show. While I hold that certain elementary forms of *r* and *l*, and those elements that may be proved to be their analogues, are all *simple* (tenues) *liquids*, I admit that all these must also have corresponding *aspirated* forms ("modifications" of the first *kind*), and also *vocalised* forms ("modifications" of the second kind), to both of which the terms *fricativæ* or *continuæ* are not only applicable, but have already been applied, unfortunately, by those who, in hastily leaping at a physiological classification and terminology, ignore demonstration of another kind. To borrow the opinion of Dr. J. Müller, the application of the principles upon which the distinction between *mutes* and *liquids* is founded, has been imperfect (*Physiology*, p. 1045); and so long as men refuse to abide by these principles, it is impossible to arrive at correct results.

		Simp. Exp.		Asp. Exp.	
		fortis.	lenis.	fortis.	lenis.
GUTTURALS ...	Mutes......k		*g*	k^c	g^c
	Liquids ...		*(q?)*		$\overset{.}{g}^z\,(\overset{.}{q}?)$
LINGUALS......	Mutes......t		**d**	t^c	d^c
	Liquids...{		**r**		r^c
			l		l^c

It must be evident to the reader of the above tableau, that if I would maintain consistency in this classification, an element is actually wanting where I have placed the asterisk, that is, a simple liquid "explodent" related to $\overset{.}{g}^z$, as *r* and *l* to r^c and *l* respectively; or to *g*, as *r* and *l* to *d*. It is difficult to conceive of any other position to which to assign the Oriental *q* in

---

* I am aware that, in consequence of *q* being a superfluous letter in the European alphabets, it has been employed in the *Hottentot* as well as the *Kaffir* to indicate one of the clicks; but as it, or the letter from which it was derived, has for ages indicated a guttural sound, it is not improperly employed in the above classification.

question, for it is evidently not an aspirate consonant. If my conclusions prove correct, and the letter q be retained for this peculiar element, in order to preserve analogy in their graphical representation, we shall have another letter prepared to supply the want of one to represent the $\overset{\centerdot}{g}^2$ of my analysis (*ch* in *lachen*, Sechwana g)—viz., $\overset{\centerdot}{q}$.

The foregoing remarks will, no doubt, shed a little light on the following quotation from Mr. Döhne's admirable dictionary of the *Zulu*, and bring the subject of this consonant a little within the range of observation of those whose studies are confined to the South African tongue.

"G is a guttural, and has, in Zulu Kafir, two sounds. The first is the hard sound—*e.g.*, igama, goba, as in English *go, gab; the second is soft*— *e.g.*, gapa, *or a sound between* g *and* k, *or between* g *and* r (*soft*).* The dialectic differences, however, respecting the gutturals, particularly in Natal, render it extremely difficult, if not impossible, to assign to each sound its proper limit, and hence only one character represents them both. Besides, there is no provision made yet for the proper distinction of sounds in the present state of orthography."—*Zulu Kafir Dictionary, letter G*, p. 90.

By the aid of all these quotations, I am led to conjecture that the Oriental q, and the *soft* form of the g of Mr. Döhne, are probably identical consonants; but to proceed beyond conjecture is impossible, without the aid of more satisfactory data than have been collected.

It is very probable that the Danish g (γ or χ' of Lepsius), which I have only heard pronounced by one intelligent *Dane*, is the same element, inasmuch as it is not an aspirate, but a simple liquid articulation, though considered by Dr. Lepsius as the soft form of *ch* (in *lachen*), the $\overset{\centerdot}{q}$ of this arrangement, and called by him a *fortis* fricative. This assumption would only make them both *lenes*, and, judging by the above fragment of a classification suggested by the *Sechwana* phonology, no fricative (or continuous or liquid) consonant can be *hard*.

* The italics are substituted. By the r here must be distinctly understood the arbitrary letter introduced by the missionaries to indicate the Kaffir "*soft guttural*."

The result of the above analysis is, that the Oriental q is probably the simple *guttural liquid* (tenuis); but Professor Müller writes (p. xxvi.), "in truth, a guttural liquid is not to be distinguished from a guttural flatus, except in theory." I have, however, proved the lingual *aspirated liquids* (lingual "flatus") *ŕ* and *l* in Sechwana and Zulu respectively, to have corresponding simple lingual *liquids* in the former language; and the probability is, that there is elsewhere to be found an analogous *guttural* form, to which the three elements above alluded to are very close approximations. The above very learned writer, as I have already shown, confounds simple breathings with their guttural modifications, which will account for his opinion just quoted; but the physiological fact should be borne in mind, that the same disposition of the organs (*i.e.*, partial contact of the dorsum of the tongue with the posterior part of the palate) is required in the enunciation of the *pure guttural liquid* as in that of its *aspirated* form, *ch* in *loch*, and its *vocalised* form, the Arabic غ.

However unsuccessful the reader may consider me in attempting to prove this interesting point, he will no doubt admit that the relations of, or differences between the powers of, the three letters, ڌ Arabic, *g* Danish, and the *soft* Zulu *g* of Döhne, are worthy of further investigation.

§ III. Cerebrales Indicæ (of Lepsius.)

Next in order we find the two series—(1) the *Cerebrales*, said to be peculiar to the *Sanskrit;* and (2) the *Linguales*, pertaining as "exclusively to the *Arabic* and cognate languages," both of which appear to be frequently confounded, but are considered by **Dr. Lepsius** to be "entirely different."

Professor **Müller** says—"It is true that there is a difference between the Sanskrit ट and the Arabic ط. In the former, the tongue is more contracted than in the latter, but both are produced by contact between the tongue, more or less contracted, and the palate. Their difference is so slight, that here again an organ which is able to form the Sanskrit lingual is generally unsuccessful in the formation of the Arabic lingual. In Hindustáni, therefore, where, owing to the mixture of Arabic and Sanskrit words, both letters occur, no difference is made between the two."— *Wilson, Indian Terms*, p. xvi.

This able writer classes them as *first* and *second* *modifications* of the "dentals" (common linguals) *t, d, s, z, &c.* ; and (*in his Table*, p. xci.) indicates the former (except the sibilant *sh* and the liquid *r*) by *italicised* letters, and the latter by *capitals*. It is to be questioned, however, whether these "modifications" (excepting the Sanskrit sibilant *sh*) are intended by him to be analogous to those of the gutturals called *palatals*, as he would appear to make them in his "Missionary Alphabet" by italicising them. He says elsewhere (p. xxxix)—"These linguals vary again in the degree of obtuseness imparted to them in different dialects, a difference which evades graphical representation."

In the absence of the living pronunciation, I shall, as usual, give the reader an abstract of the various modes of indicating these consonants by the able linguists who have given attention to those tongues, so as to enable him to arrive at an approximately correct conception of their peculiarities.

The Series of "Indian Cerebrals" in the Orthographical Systems of different Linguists.

"Standard Alphabet" of Lepsius, used also by him for the *Sanskrit* and *Bega*.........	Explosivæ. fortis.	lenis.	nasals.	Fricativæ. fortis.	lenis.	Ancipites.		Aspiratæ.	
	t	*ḍ*	*ṇ*	*ṛ*		*ṛ*	*l*	*ṭ*	*ḍ*
Sanskrit (*Orient. gr.*)...	ट	ड	ण	ष		र	ळ	ठ	ढ
Bopp	*t*	*d*	*n*	*s*		*r*		*t*	*d*
Wilson	*t*	*d*	*n*	*sh*		*r*		*th*	*dh*
Bengáli :									
Haughton	*t*	*d*	*n*	*sh*		*r*		*th*	*dh*
Zend :									
(*Oriental gr.*)	ᛟ	ᛟ		ᛉ	ᛃ				
(*Lepsius*)	*t*	*d*		*š*	*ž*				
Burnouf	*t*	*t*		*ch*	*j*				
Bopp	*t*			*s*	*sh*				
Brockhaus	*t*			*sh*	*j*				
Hindustáni :									
Yates	*t*	*d*		*sh*	*zh*	*r*			
Gilchrist (1796)	*t*	*d*		*sh*	*zh*	*r*			
(1806)* ...	*t*	*d*		*sh*	*zh*	*r*			
Wilson	*t*	*d*		*sh*	*zh*	*r*			
Malayan :									
Crawfurd	*t·*	*d·*		(*s'*)					
Javanese :									
Crawfurd	*t·*	*d·*							

* British Indian Monitor, vol. i.

Other letters are made to take the place of these consonants, under the *explodents* of the Chinese.

	Explosivæ. fortis. lenis. nasals.			Fricativæ. fortis. lenis.		Ancipites.		Aspiratæ.	
"Standard Alphabet" of Lepsius, used also by him for the *Sanskrit* and *Bega*.........	ṭ	ḍ	ṇ	ṣ̌		ṛ	ḷ	ṭʻ	ḍ
Chinese :									
Revs. J. Gough ...⎫ T.McClatchie⎭	t (ts̀)	d (dz̃)		s̃	z̃			ṫ (ts̃)	
Stephen Endlicher ...	tcʻ	tcʻ		sh	sh			tcʻ	

1. *Explosivæ*—In the comparative table under this head, there is not sufficient variety in the letters used for these articulations to assist one in his conjectures. The following is **Dr. Lepsius's** physiological description of their formation:—" This class . . . is formed by bringing the tip of the tongue backwards, and upwards to the neighbourhood of the palatal point, so as to produce there the explosion or friction.* To our ear, these sounds are nearest to the dentals."—*Standard Alphabet*, p. 44.

Of the same sounds, **Sir John Stoddart** says:—

" The reason of applying the term *cerebral* to any of these letters, I never could discover; nor does **Dr. Lee's** remark render it to me more intelligible. He says of the Hebrew *téth,* ' it should be pronounced with the tip of the tongue against the roof of the mouth, just as our own *t* is, and hence it may be termed *cerebral.*' To the English ear, the sounds expressed by the two Sanskrit series appear scarcely, if at all, distinguishable; but, to the native ear, they are perceptibly different. According to some persons, this arises from a slight lingual vibration in the (so-called) cerebral series, somewhat approaching to the Mexican *tl.*† It is said, however, that the native writers employ the characters of this, but not of the other series,‡ to express the *t* or *d* in English proper names."—*Glossology*, p. 133.

According to **Dr. Gilchrist**, one of the most able authorities quoted, the above articulations, which he indicated in 1796 by t̆, d̆, and in 1806 by ṭ, ḍ,

* This description, as well as Dr. Gilchrist's, in the sequel, does not differ from that of the formation of the cerebral *click* in Hottentot, by Mr. Tindall, p. 12 of his Grammar, before referred to.

† As will be observed in the sequel, this sound is frequent in the *Sechuana*.

‡ There appears to be confusion in this quotation—*i.e.*, the Hebrew *teth* ט, according to scholars, is equivalent to the Arabic lingual ط (not the Sanskrit cerebral); so it is not certain to which series the remarks are intended to apply.

are " formed by conveying the tongue forcibly against the roof of the mouth, while articulating the common dentals *t* and *d* of our own alphabet, in *tub, duck,* &c., which, he continues, are however *softer* than they. Elsewhere he says—" *d, t, r,* require that organ [the tongue] to be curved backwards, and then struck against the roof of the mouth, as in *dull, tub, rub,*" and then further describes them as " a great deal harsher than our English *d, t, r.*"

Professor **Müller** indicates them by *l* and *d* (always italicised), and classes them as *first* modifications of the common European linguals, *t, d.* The same with their aspirate forms.

Both **Dr. Duff** and **Dr. Forbes** concur with **Dr. Gilchrist** in his description of these elements in Hindustáni, excepting that the latter speaks of the tongue being only *well turned up* towards the roof of the mouth in their articulation. They also indicate them by *t* and *d*. All state that *they approximate more closely to the European linguals than do the Arabic elements.* According to the former linguist, the Sanskrit *t* and *d* are of far less (*ten times*) frequent occurrence in Hindustáni than the Arabic linguals *t, d*. According to the latter, Sanskrit *d* is very much akin to Sanskrit *r* (*r* of **Duff**) ; " in the Davanagári, the same letter serves for both, and the same applies to their aspirated forms," *dh* and *rh*.

Notwithstanding the above attempts of able linguists to explain the nature of these two members of this so-called series of consonants, it is a difficult matter to conceive of even an approximation to their " sounds." I have already alluded, under the head of *vocalisation,* to the nature of the articulation produced by an attempt to vocalise the *mute* consonants— viz., that the explosion of the element in each case is strengthened, and a hiatus is caused between it and the following vowel. Some analogous articulation has also been referred to as occurring in the Hottentot language. In the absence of the living pronunciation, it is not easy to explain those in question otherwise. Were they only described as *faucal* utterances, it might be possible to explain them as modifications of lingual consonants, or combinations of these with *liquids;* but the subject is rendered more intricate by the addition of a *nasal* to the series—viz., *n,* in the *Sanskrit, Bega,** and Bengáli.

As the late Professor **Wilson** is one of the authorities quoted in the table, the following remark from **Sir John Stoddart,** on the letter *n,* will enable the reader to make an effort at hair-splitting in English phonology, based upon the *Sanskrit* distinctions :—In the latter (' proper *n*'), indeed, Professor **Hayman Wilson** makes three distinctions (besides the other which he galls guttural)—viz., a *palatal* in *singe,* a *cerebral* in *none,* and a *dental* in *content ;* but I must own that I see no ground for these distinctions in the

---

* An African language.

proper pronunciation of the English language."*—*Glossology*, p. 142. *(See Professor Wilson's " Sanscrit Gram.," p. 5, cited in that work.)*

Professor **Wilson** (cited by **Müller**) has four modifications of the common *n—e.g.*,

Sanskrit Lingual.	(Tamil).	Guttural.	Palatal,
n̤	n̤	n̤	n̤

I have already shown that the *third*, viz., n̤ (= *ɲ* is decidedly a simple consonant, as much as *m* or *n*; and the *fourth* a compound articulation, as much as *my* or *ɲy* would be. To call either of them a *modification* of the common *n* is only a graphical fallacy, arising from the assumption that the sound of a nasal depends on the nature of the consonant which follows it. It is strange that, though the Hindustáni linguals *t* and *d* are borrowed from the Sanskrit, the corresponding Sanskrit lingual nasal (so-called) did not accompany it. As it is, *phonically*, only one, *i.e.*, the common *n* is used in Hindustáni. The probability is that, as a phonic element, it has no existence separate from that of the common *n*, as it is said to occur only in the Sanskrit (and Bengáli); and the former is a dead language, which, according to Professor **Monier Williams**, "was never spoken, and never intended to be spoken in the way it is at present written" (p. 262).

It may perhaps assist the reader in forming his own conclusions, if I add that, besides the *n*'s preceding a guttural, "dental," and labial, respectively, and the "French nasal" in *bon*, all of which have already been considered, **Dr. Gilchrist** gives, in his work on the Hindustáni, frequently quoted above, the following remarks on two additional forms of the letter:—

" n̤ ⎱ The first is peculiar to the Hindoos; the second to the Arabs; still
  n̤ ⎰ both are pronounced like the common *n* in *run, nurse.*"—*Brit. Ind. Mon.*, p. 47.

2. *Fricativæ.*—Under this head (in above table), there is more material for conjecture, assuming the comparative tables of **Dr. Lepsius** to be correct.

It is remarkable that *five* English linguists, and one German, have represented the *fortis* (š of **Lepsius**) by the digraph *sh;* one French writer by *ch,* which in his language is well known to coincide with the above English sound; Bopp by *ṣ*, which, judging by the remarks at p. 34, *Stand. Alph.*, is intended by him to indicate a sound equivalent to "the English *sh*, the

---

* Trusting that the reader will not suspect me of presuming to "abrogate" English orthography, I venture the following remark:—

The *n*'s in the three words here instanced would, upon the principles of his work, be written as follows—*siñge, noñe, content.* In the first example, the "palatal" element is not *n*, but a portion of the combination of sounds following it, which is improperly indicated by *g*. The *n* is only vocalised, as is also the second *n* in *none;* both upon principles to be examined in the sequel.

French *ch*, German *sch ;*" only one writer, Crawfurd, gives it a new letter—viz., *s*. In all the tables of the languages, except the Sanskrit and the Bengáli (the only two in which the so-called lingual *n* is said to occur), these two fricative elements are confronted by **Dr. Lepsius's** exponents *s̆* and *z̄*, not *s* and *z̄* ; so that it must be concluded the *s̆* is also confined to those two languages. It is therefore strange that, while the explodent forms are represented as occurring in so many languages, only the Sanskrit should contain an example of the fricative equivalent *s̆* (**Lepsius**).

Professor **Müller** calls the fortes *s̆* a lingual flatus, and says it " is a sound peculiar to the Sanskrit, and, owing to its hollow guttural pronunciation, it may be expressed there, as it has been hitherto, by *s*, followed by the guttural *h* (*sh*)."—P. lxxi.

Dr. Duff says of it, in Hindustáni " it is pronounced in the same way as *sh* ; and is so marked (*sh*) because it has a distinct letter in the Sanskrit." —" *Original Papers*," by *Monier Williams*, p. 84.

Dr. Lepsius himself, by placing *s̆* in the series in the Bega and Zend, would seem to indicate that it indicates the same sound ; but the following is his description of the difference :—

" When the tongue recedes still further [than in the articulation of *s**], so that behind the upper and lower teeth a greater hollow space remains, this enlarged resounding space produces the sound *s̆*. . . . . The Indian cerebral *s̆*, however, receives, from the peculiar flexion of the tongue, which produces a double cavity in the mouth, a somewhat different expression, indicated by the cerebral point."

As to the *lenis* form, the fact of three English writers representing it by *zh*, and one French writer by *j*, leads to the supposition that the intended element approximates to *z̆* of Lepsius (*zh*, or *s* in *vision*).

So it is really in the Sanskrit and Bengáli that the *fricativæ s̆* and *z̄* belong to the series of sounds confronting them under the head of *explosivæ*. Judging by the examples of the *explodents* in Chinese, to which the common " palatals" *sh* and *zh*, *s̆* and *z̄*, are apparently allied, the probability is that *s̆* and *z̄* also will rather be included among the " palatals," otherwise called the " unstable combinations" of **Dr. Latham.**

3. In respect to the letters under the head of *ancipites* and *aspiratæ*, I shall merely, for the information of the reader, add the following remarks, culled from Dr. Gilchrist's able work :—

(*a*) " The letters *r̤*, *r̤h*, are rather nominal deviations from *d̤*, *d̤h*, than formal characters."—*B. I. Mon.*, p. 23.

(*b*) " *r̤*, *l*, letters peculiar to the Hindoos in form, but exactly of the same power as *r* and *l*."—*Ibid.* p. 47.

Professor **Müller** says—" The liquid is the lingual *r*, produced by a vibration of the curled tongue in which the Italians and Scotch excel, and

---

* Interpolated.

which we find it difficult to imitate," p. xl. The same occurs in Welsh, and is that I have attempted to show is the *vocalised* form, or second modification of the unmodified liquid *r* in Sechwana *morimo.*

In the foregoing observations on the "Indian Cerebrals," it must be evident to the reader that it is only with regard to those under the head of *explosivæ* that any real difficulty is presented, which would lead one to doubt whether they are merely simple modifications of *t.* At all events, no one will deny that it is absolutely requisite that sounds should be resolved into their elements before they can admit of classification.

§ IV. Linguales Arabicæ (of Lepsius).

The following table shows in a compendious form the different modes in which the members of this series have been indicated.

The series of " Arabic Linguals" in the Orthographical Systems of different Linguists.

	Explosivæ.		Fricativæ.		Aspiratæ.
	fortis.	lenis.	fortis.	lenis.	fortis.
"Stand. Alph." of Lepsius ...	t	d	s	z	
Hebrew *equivalents*	ט		ע		
Arabic „	ط	ﺽ	ص	ظ	
Smith and Robinson......	ṭ	ḍ	ṣ	ẓ	
Persian:					
M. M. Ibrahim............	t	z	s	z	
Armenian *equivalents*	Ճ	Ձ			ᒎ
Petermann..................	ṭ	ḍ			ẓ
Hindustáni:					
Yates	t	z	s	z	
Gilchrist, 1796	tw	thw	sw	th	
Wilson	ṭ	ẓ	ṣ	ẓ	
Malayan:					
Crawfurd	(t)	(ll)	(s)	(l')	
Turkish:					
Jaubert	t	z	ϙ	z	
Galla (African):					
Jutschek..................	t	dy	z'	z'	

Other letters are made to take the place of these consonants, under the *explodent* of the

Chinese:					
Revs. J. Gough ....⎱	t (ts)	d (dz)			tʻ (ʦ)
T. McClatchie ...⎰	ṭ	ḍ			ṭ
Stephen Endlicher.........	ts	ts			ts

In the above table, the examples which would lead men to suppose that they are a series of compound sounds, is that they are represented as such by **Gilchrist** in four members, by **Crawfurd** in one, and by **Jutschek** in one.

Dr. Gilchrist elsewhere* remarks of the *explodent* forms—"The Oriental *t, d*, [are] formed with a slight protrusion of the tongue between the teeth. *Tub, duck, do; tube, duke, dew, due*, will convey a tolerable idea of the difference between palatials [Indian cerebrals already noticed] and dentals [Arabic linguals]† in the Eastern tongues, the *t d* of the four last even with us being much softer than in the three first; for, in fact, some people seem to soften the liquified *d* and *t* with us so far as to say *tshube, jook, jew* for *due*, &c. The lisp of children and others will convey a tolerable notion of the very soft dentals *d t* in question, as essential sounds in the Oriental tongues, &c."

Again, he writes‡—" The soft *d, t, r* [Arabic linguals], cannot be softened too much, and the harsh *d, t, r*, can hardly appear enough so, till their opposite natures be sufficiently understood from practice."

Dr. Duff (*Papers by Monier Williams*, p. 80) writes—"It resembles, says Dr. Carey, the Yorkshire pronunciation of *t* in *butter*.§ It also resembles as nearly as possible the soft French dental *t* in *tu*." Of the *d*, " it is formed with the point of the tongue pressed on the roots of the upper teeth, nearly as in *duke, due;* or still more nearly as the French dental *d* in *des*."

Dr. Forbes, also, in the Hindustáni, describes the pronunciation of the *fortis* thus: " Softer and more dental than that of the English *t*, it corresponds with the *t* of the Gaelic dialects, or that of the Italian in the word *sotto*." Of the *lenis d* his description is literally the same.

Professor **Max Müller** considers these elements as modifications of the second degree of the common linguals *t, d, s, z*, and represents them thus—

Tenuissima.	*Flatus Diacrit.*	*Flatus Aspirate.*	*Tenuissima Assil.*
T,	Z̧ ;	Z̧ (*ts*),	T.

From the above descriptions, it seems but reasonable to conclude that the sounds in this series, if not consonantal diphthongs, can only be regarded as those combinations of simple elements which **Dr. Latham** would call "unstable," and which, under the provisional denomination " palatal," I propose to reserve for the third part of this work.

---

* British Indian Monitor, vol. i., p. 10.
† Parts in brackets are interpolated.
‡ British Indian Monitor, vol. i., p. 17.
§ This is not unlike *but-ther.*—See Chap. V.

In respect to both the *Indian cerebrals* and *Arabic linguals*, and I may add the *Namân clicks*, it is very difficult for any European, without hearing the sounds thus indicated, by means of numerous orthographic expedients, to decide whether they are consonantal diphthongs* (*mutæ cum liquidis*), vocalised consonants, or elements combined with the pure "palatals;" but there is nothing in the foregoing analysis to warrant the conclusion that any of them is a simple consonant.

In studying these peculiar consonants, it ought not to be forgotten that they belong to graphic systems which possess " such a superabundance of characters that one sound has often three letters," and in which the *forms* of the letters are " not less liable to change" than the "*powers* of the letters are very absurdly ever varying" in the European systems. In the words of Professor Monier Williams, " what creates the difficulty [in reading them] is, that every letter has four separate forms, according as it is initial, medial, final, or detached; and that groups of three, four, five, or even six letters are shaped exactly alike, being only distinguishable from each other by the number and position of their dots."† In comparing the opinions of the learned on the distinctive natures of such letters, it is difficult to discriminate between those of men, on the one hand, who have studied a language critically—that is, who have had to do with its literature very much in the same way as we, spite of the absence of the living pronunciation, manage to command a knowledge of Greek and Latin; and those, on the other hand, who have acquired it practically, by "condescending to learn the vulgar tongue," as spoken by the bulk of the people. As an instance of the confusion arising from a superfluity of letters being worse confounded by the contrary opinions of learned linguists, I give the following:—

---

* See Chap. III. on Compound Consonants.
† " Original Papers," p. 260.

An interesting writer, in a late journal of literature, commenting unfavourably on a system of " romanising" suggested by Professor **Monier Williams,** *writes*—	*Remarks.*
" He would only give *one h* for the Hindustáni *two ;*	As to the " *two h's,"* I have already given a quotation from the learned Orientalist, **Dr. Gilchrist,** to the effect that they are identical elements in Hindustáni.
" Only *two t's* for the Hindustáni *three ;*	As to the " *three t's,"* the preceding analysis will show how far linguists are at present justified in regarding them as simple consonants, and, till resolved into their elements, it is impossible to distinguish them by any uniform orthographic expedients.
" *One z* for *four z's* in Hindustáni ;	These, viz , *z*, *z̤*, *z̤*, which **Dr. Gilchrist** gives, besides *zh*, he pronounces " merely formal varieties of the self-same sound."
" Only *two s's* (viz., *s* and *sh*) for the Hindustáni *three,* and similarly in other letters "*	These, viz , *s̤* and *s̤* which **Dr. Gilchrist** gives besides *sh*, he pronounces " varieties of simple sounds by different letters."†

Such glaring differences of opinion are of course to be attributed to difference in the modes of acquiring Oriental tongues. Indeed, unanimity cannot be expected to exist between the closet student and the colloquial learner. In the case of the one, the language is presented in written characters to the eye; of the other, in spoken sounds to the ear. Both modes of research may be united, but how seldom is this convenient to men bent on some third occupation.

Sources of Confusion, and the main Obstacles to Uniformity.

(*a*) The nature of the confusion which exists will be more clearly illustrated by an examination of three series of *letters* in the Hindustáni alphabet.

---

* Evangelical Christendom, vol. i., p. 242.
† See British Indian Monitor, p. 47.

(1) The Sanskrit has a set of peculiar linguals (*Linguales Indicæ* of Lepsius.)

(2) The Arabic has also a set of peculiar linguals (*Linguales Arabicæ* of Lepsius*).

(3) Each of these languages, again, has a set corresponding with the common European linguals, *t, d,* &c.

(4) Now the *Graphic System* of the Hindustáni is a composition of the alphabets of both of these languages; *i.e.*, every consonant in either of them is represented *graphically* (that is, however, not to say *phonetically*) by a corresponding *new letter* in Hindustáni.

(5) But, *phonically*, the peculiar Sanskrit linguals are said by linguists to approximate to the common European linguals.

(6) Moreover, *phonically*, the peculiar Arabic linguals are said to be *actually* used by the natives of Hindustan to represent the common European linguals.

(7) Therefore, *phonetically*, the Hindustáni alphabet must be deficient in some consonants, viz., some of the European linguals; and is, after all, rather a sort of artificial or hybrid orthography maintained out of traditional respect or veneration for those more ancient ones of which it is composed.

(8) It seems to be the vain object of modern linguists to preserve these merely *graphical* distinctions in any scheme for a *phonetic* alphabet.

I append the following example among those alluded to:—

		t	d	s	z
Graphical Equivalents adopted by	Lepsius ...	t̲	d̲	s	z
	M. Müller..	T	Z̤	Z	T̤
	Forbes and Duff......	t (we)	z	s	z (we)
ARABIC......	Its peculiar linguals..	ط	ض	ص	ظ
	Its common linguals..	ت	د	س	ز
Graphical Equivalents by	above Linguists	t	d	s	z

Now, according to the descriptions of most linguists the *phonical* equivalents are—

Of the former............	t	d	s	z
	(peculiar)		(*common Europ.*)	
Of the latter	t	d	s	z
	(*common Europ.*)		(*common Europ.*)	

So that the only strange elements are really *t* and *d* of the former; and it is very probable that such an examination of the Sanscrit linguals would have nearly a similar result. Thus, to a legitimate number of phonetical equivalents are added hosts of superfluous graphical equivalents, which must necessarily suggest divergent articulations, and tend to mislead.

The above is a suitable example to show the degree to which the subject has already been complicated by trying to maintain a scrupulous respect for Oriental classifications. It is out of such a jungle of graphical materials that it is necessary for the linguist to extricate himself before he can fall into the plain paths converging to a uniform phonetic alphabet.

(*b*) This very important error, which made the Hindustáni alphabet a mere graphical hodge-podge rather than a phonetic model, must forsooth be followed up by European linguists in the application of one graphic system (the Roman) to two different processes of *transcription* and *transliteration.*

By *transcription* must be understood the employment of certain letters to represent certain articulations and sounds; by *transliteration* that of certain letters (*e.g.,* Roman) to represent certain other letters (Oriental or Hieroglyphic).

The one process, which is that of the principle of a *phonetic* alphabet, would indicate—

A *simple* articulation or sound ....by a *simple* letter.
A *compound* do. ....by a *compound* letter.
A *modification* of either ....by a *modificative mark.*

The other process, however, is proposed to represent—

" Every [Oriental or other] *double letter*, though in pronunciation it may be simple ....} by a *double* letter."

E.g., that anything like the English word *though*, pronounced *tho*, be transliterated to the same number of letters.

"*A single* letter [Oriental or other], although its pronunciation be that of a double letter ......} by a *single* letter."

E.g., that the Sanskrit श्च = *ch* in *church*, consequently a compound articulation, should be represented by *k'* (**Lepsius**), or,by *k* (italicised, of **Müller**); or, *that the Armenian* e *and* o, *which are pronounced* ye *and* we, *be written* e *and* o.

The difficulty which has no doubt given rise to this new process is thus carefully described by Professor Lepsius :—

It " is greatest in those systems of writing, which originating in an earlier period of the language, and fully developed, have been retained unaltered, whilst the pronunciation has undergone a change, as also in those in which several reformations have left their traces. An instance of this kind has already been mentioned in speaking of the Sanscrit palatals. The differences of European orthography have mostly arisen from similar circumstances. Some such difficulties, however, are presented by almost all existing alphabets which are not of modern formation. As the object of a standard transcription is to avoid as much as possible all such incongruity of sound and sign, no other course remains open in such cases than to fix upon a distinct period of the language in question, and to adapt its transcriptions to the different purposes of rendering either the *actual* pronunciation, or the *ancient* one which had been expressed by the alphabet, and which may be deduced from it by linguistic researches."—*Standard Alphabet*, p. 53.

This able linguist chooses the latter alternative, in the words which I have confronted with those of the late Baron de Bunsen on the title-page of this treatise, viz., that " the linguistic scholars will prefer to follow the written system fixed by literature, and to neglect the varying deviations and shades of modern pronunciation." It must, however, be apparent to my intelligent readers, that for Professor Lepsius to ignore the *actual* pronunciation is tantamount to a denial that phonetic philology is " a branch of inductive science" standing " on precisely the same footing as geology, and those other sciences which are 'connected by this bond, that they endeavour to ascend to a past state of things by the aid of the evidence of the present.'"*

Professor Müller, in defence of this process, recently suggested by him, remarks:—

"If we attempted to represent the sounds in transcribing literary languages, we should be unable to tell how, in the original, sounds admitting of several graphic representations were represented. In written languages, therefore, we must rest satisfied with transliterating letters, and not attempt to transcribe sounds."

Again, in other words:—

"If, instead of imitating the letters, we attempted to represent their proper pronunciation at a certain period of history, how should it ·be known, for instance, in transcribing the French of the nineteenth century, whether ' su' stood for ' sou,' halfpenny, or ' sous,' under, or ' soul,' tipsy."†

Now, it cannot be denied that "in historical languages the system of orthography is too important a point to be lost;" but it seems very natural to expect that by mere transliterations, such as that suggested, it is most likely to be lost. And, just as much as " it is a mistake to imagine that in living languages all etymological understanding would be lost if phonetic reforms were introduced,"‡ so it would be equally a mistake to suppose that in archaic literatures all etymological understanding would be lost if the historical orthography were maintained. A reference to the Greek classics will bear me out in this assertion; for in spite of our ignorance of the genuine pronunciations, the etymology of this extraordinary language is to this day a rich field of research, and will be rendered still more interesting in the light shed on its structure by vernacular forms of speech. Professor Lepsius tells us that " the Armenian alphabet has also undergone peculiar alterations of pronunciation, which may be *historically proved ;*" and also speaks of the *ancient* pronunciation of a tongue being deduced from the *actual* one by linguistic researches. In

---

* Dr. Donaldson, Eucy. Brit., vol. xvii., p. 539, citing Whewell.

† Proposals, &c., p. lxxxix.

‡ Ibid.

a similar manner, the difference between Professor Müller's examples, *su* of the present, and *sou, sous,* and *soul* respectively of the past, could be arrived at by comparing French works of the nineteenth century with past historical records of the language. According to this learned philologer himself, historical or antiquated alphabets are objects of archæological research; and I think that under this specification ought to come all Oriental alphabets, most of which have already been reduced to " romanized" forms. Vernacular alphabets, on the other hand, no one will venture to deny, are, elementarily, objects of phonical research. Transliterations may be all very well in the one branch of inquiry, but transcription is certainly the process which is indispensable to the record of phonetical data; therefore the two methods ought to be kept separate. The one scholar ought to persist in writing the Greek ἐγγύς as the Greeks wrote it—the other, if he adopt the Roman alphabet, to write it according to the ear, *engus* or *eggus,* or to any preconcerted standard of letters; but neither of them is justified in transliterating it to arbitrary Roman characters (thus, eggus), in which word the two gutturals are universally agreed to have distinct phonical powers.

The two modes of recording the symbols of speech can be pursued separately, the one rather aiding than detracting from the other. In the one case, the philologer merely places and transposes the dusty specimens of a valuable cabinet, and contents himself with noting the chronological relations of materials collected and successively shifted by his predecessors; in the other case he plods, and observes, and notes as he treads the *situs* of all that his attention is bent upon, while his mind conceives and generalizes, and thus builds up a fabric of positive science, which in its turn becomes a subjective means of fresh and more important acquisitions.

In presuming to write in this strain, I have been actuated

merely by a desire to unveil to those versed in historical philology the difficulties which have occurred to myself at the
threshold of vernacular studies, in endeavouring to overcome
this troublesome subject, and certainly not by any meddlesome
inclination to question the mature opinions of men supposed to
know better.

I trust that what has preceded in this humble treatise will
show the reasonableness of my opinions, viz.—(1) That if Dr.
Lepsius only aims at a standard historical alphabet, his maxim
holds good, and he remains consistent; but, if his aim is a
standard *phonetic* alphabet, he must abandon to the archæologist
the second-hand materials of historical orthography, to consult
him only occasionally and supplementally, and rather look to
the *situs* of all living human speech for the only valid materials
of inductive phonology; and (2) That the compromise suggested
by Professor Müller, between the different modes of recording
historical and phonetical data, would only be another name for
" confusion worse confounded."

§ V. Dentales (of Lepsius).

It is under this series of Dr. Lepsius's classification that we
first meet with a few instances of *simple* consonants foreign to
the Sechwana, and in disposing of which, especially, I shall have
to alternate with a little speculation, the treatment of those
instances found in the language to admit of classification; as I
have already done with regard to the element *q*, under the head
of the *gutturals*.

Inquiry into the Nature of the Letters s *and* z, th (*in* thin) *and*
th (*in* thine); *and the probable Existence of their Elementary*
Forms.

I have elsewhere implied that the consonants *l* and *r*, which
are common in the Sechwana, form only part of a more complete

set of *lenes* elements, the remainder of which do not exist in the language; and the probability that the element *s*,* in the English words *parts, parks, harps,* and the elementary form of *th*† in the word *thin,* which has frequently been indicated by the letter *θ,* upon the supposition that it represented the same consonant in the ancient Greek, both belong to it. It is, however, necessary for us to arrive at a conclusion on this head more satisfactory than such mere conjectures. I am fully aware that this would in any case involve a further conclusion, as in the case of *g* and *k,* that had the said elements *s* and *th* occurred in the language as initials of verbs, they would have been commuted into *t;* that, moreover, like *r* and *l,* they would be expected to have their *aspirated* and *vocalised* forms.

The consonant *s,* as before remarked, seems to be little understood. The letter is chiefly employed in English to represent two different consonants, as in *this* and *these.* It is by some writers regarded as not admitting of classification, and of a peculiar nature; therefore not included under either the *liquids*‡ or the *mutes.*§ Its affinity to *r* seems to be often admitted. Of the Latin language, Zumpt writes—

"*S,* like the Greek *σ,* was pronounced more sharply than with us. . . . .

"In the ancient pronunciation, there must have been a peculiar resemblance between the letters *s* and *r;* since it is mentioned by **Varro**

---

* That is, as a simple consonant, independently of any prepositive element. It abounds in the language in composition with the letter *t,* as in *mocuetsana* (*a fountain*), *morwetsana* (*a damsel*).

† For the purposes of this section, I shall in the text indicate *th* in *thin* by *th*², assuming it to be in *most* cases in English an *aspirated* liquid (continua); the other, in *thine,* by *th*³.

‡ Unless it be shown that this and the term *continuæ* are intended by them to be descriptive of the same instances.

§ It is remarkable that Dr. Latham places under his *aspirate mutes* all those sounds called by Dr. Lepsius *fricative* or *continuous,* except *s* and *z,* which he includes among the *lene mutes;* but upon what principle it would be difficult to say. Much more difficult would it be to account for his placing any *continuous* sounds under the *mutes,* unless by the latter term he means "*explodents,*" in the sense in which I use it throughout this work.

(De Ling. Lat. vii. 6), and others, that formerly—that is, before the Latin language had assumed a fixed form through its literature—*s* was pronounced in many words for which afterwards *r* was substituted, as in *Papisius, Valesius, lases, eso,* &c."—*Latin Gram. by Dr. Schmitz,* p. 6.

It is not improbable that also in the Sechwana *barimo,* and the Suahili *wasimo,* dialectical variations of the same expression, the letters *r* and *s* indicate only analogous elements.*

There is every reason to suppose that th^2 (θ) is related to *s*,† as *l* is to *r*. In one respect, there is a remarkable analogy between the two couples. What is often considered the natural infirmity, or disability of pronouncing *l* instead of the *r*, called in Greek τραυλισμος, and in Latin *balbuties,* is precisely analogous to the substitution of the articulation *th* for *s* in the words "*mith* for *miss, thpell* for *spell,* and the like," by those who are said to lisp, and which was called *sonus blæsus* among the Romans. There can be but little dispute as to *s* and *th* belonging to the *lingual* series; for though they may be both continuous and fricative, or semivocal, in some of their modifications, like *l* and *r*, they are, like these elements, essentially formed by a *contact*‡ of two organs, though not a complete stoppage of the breathing, therefore as much as any consonants *explosive.*

But the main difficulty appears to be in establishing their quantity under the "explodents." Where, but under the *lenes* forms of these linguals, can the two elements in question be

---

* In *mozimo* (-*morimo*), the singular form of this word found among the seaboard tribes of Sofala, the letter *z* indicates perhaps only a vocalised modification of the Sechwana element.

† Dr. J. Müller calls the English *th* a modification of *s* (p. 1049). A writer in "Chambers's Cyclopædia" (1860), under "Alphabet," says:— "The sound of *th* is very nearly allied to that of *s* (witness 'loves or love*th*'); also the pronunciation of a person who li*thpth*," p 169. He suggests that for each pair *l* and *r*, *s* and *th*, one letter would suffice. And I may add, that th^3 is similarly related to *z*. Sir John Stoddart (*p.* 134, *Glossology*) writes—"these two sounds, th^2 and th^3, approximate less nearly to *t* and *d* than to *s* and *z*."

‡ For the *elementary* forms of these consonants I shall, for the purposes of this section, employ the letters th^1 and s^1.

placed? They differ physiologically in no respect whatever from l and r, except the fact that the contact of the *tongue*, in place of with the *palate*, is with the *teeth*; and that while the former may be called, organically, *palatal* linguals, the latter are *dental* linguals. Moreover, admitting that they are liquids, and, what may be inferred from all that precedes, that all liquids are *lenes*, their quantity is explained. It is only by this train of analogical reasoning that I can arrive at their classification as kindred forms of r and l, and therefore as *lenes*. In the event of its appearing unsatisfactory to the reader, I shall at any rate venture to assume it; for it is not till I come to treat of certain combinations of simple consonants that the assumption will be found to bear the test of anything like a legitimate proof.

The set of *lenes* simple " explodent"-linguals thus amounts to five—viz., l, r, d, s^1, and th^1. I have shown that l and r have their corresponding *aspirate* forms; the same must consequently apply to s^1 and th^1. It is easy to form a theoretical conception of the aspirate forms of r and l, even had no objectively true instances of these occurred, by simply supposing a forcible " augmentation of the breathing" in every case, which is well indicated to the eye by the *spiritus asper, e.g., $\dot{r}$, $\dot{l}$;* but the difficulty is to conceive of aspirate forms of s^1 and th^1;* and why? Simply because of the absence of a preconceived notion of these elements, in their *simple " explodent"* forms. This difficulty will remain so long as the fact is lost sight of that all consonants are essentially *" explodent;"* that s^1 and th^1, though liquid consonants, and may be either aspirated or vocalised, are both completely formed by a mere contact of organs, and, as I have shown, with regard to l and r, to say that they are either *continuous* or *sibilant*, or *lisping*, is to say that they are *aspirated*; to say that they are *semivocal*, ought to mean that they are *vocalised*. It would not

---

* Latham denominates the two English forms of th " so-called aspirates," and elsewhere classifies them as " aspirate mutes."

be going too far to say that, in English speech, just as the conventional notions of the simple forms of l and r, which are so
prevalent in it, exclude any notion of the rough forms of these
elements found in other languages;* so the rough forms of s^1
and th^1 (viz., s^2 and th^2), usually called *sibilants* and *lisping*-dentals
respectively, and by others *continuæ* or *fricativæ*, equally prevalent
in it, seem to preclude the formation of correct notions of their
simple *liquid*-" *explodent*" forms. It would be difficult, and almost
impossible, on the mere spur of this suggestion, for myself or
any one to distinguish cases in English phonology of the occurrence of either of these elements s or th in both their simple and
continuous (or aspirate) forms. But, in the Sechwana language,
I have been able to ascertain beyond a doubt that, in the compound examples, *mocwetSana (a spring of water)*, and *natSane*

---

* I have since met with the following remarks of the Rev. Richard
Garnett:—"An Englishman or German is apt to take a limited view of the
subject, because he only allows of one power of the letter l, and naturally
supposes that the same is the case in all other languages."—*Philological
Essays*, p. 249. (See context.) Again—"The same remark is equally
applicable to the other liquids, especially to r. A native of our Southern
counties, accustomed to enunciate this element with a delicate, sometimes
scarcely perceptible vibration, naturally thinks his pronunciation the
standard and only genuine one, and regards every marked deviation from
it as a defect in utterance or a provincial peculiarity."—*Ibid.* p. 254.
Again—"In Welsh, the common soft r is unknown as a primary initial of
words, the aspirate form *rh* being invariably considered as the primitive."—
Ibid. p. 255. Now, this articulation abounds in Sechwana, in both its
aspirated and vocalised forms. I have heard a very intelligent Welsh
missionary so much at home in it, his native sound, that it gave (even
independently of one or two of his native gutturals) a character of unusual
accuracy to his pronunciation, which of course elicited a good deal of
obsequious flattery, of which Bechwanas are so lavish ; but, at the same
time, this led him to misuse the *tenuis*, or simple liquid r, in such words
as *morimo, rusa, rila*. Moreover, the *Welsh l*, as it is usually called, is a
fine instance of the *aspirate l*, also found in the Zulu language, and none
except a Welshman will be inclined to deny it, as I have heard one do,
by alleging that (like the clicks of other " barbarians," Hottentot and Kaffir)
the contact of the tongue with the palate is lateral !

(*a young buffalo*), the instances of *s* are respectively simple and aspirate.* The fact of its being practicable to distinguish such instances of *s* alone in the Sechwana phonology, satisfies me that, could we arrive at them by a similar principle of analytical investigation, success would follow in all instances of both elements. In the Sechwana, neither of the two forms of *r* (*r* and *r̊*) need be left doubtful in any word of the language. I am very sanguine the same remark will soon apply to *s;* and is it unreasonable to suppose that if the language contained the element *th* (*θ*), it would be a mere matter of inductive analysis to distinguish its different forms?

Again: I have shown that *l* and *r* have their corresponding *vocalised* forms. If *s* and *th* are analogues of those elements, the same must apply to them. I have elsewhere stated that the approximation to vocality is stronger in the *aspirate lenes*, inasmuch as vocalisation implies aspiration, which again means something more than the mere momentary action of the breath, required in the sudden collision and separation of two organs; therefore we must look to modifications of the aspirate s^1 and th^1 for their vocalised forms. Now, s^2 and th^2 are commonly supposed to have the same relation to *z* and th^3 (*δ* of Lepsius) respectively as *t* to *d*, *k* to *g*, &c.—viz., that the former are *fortes,* and the latter *lenes;* indeed, as before stated, they are so classed by Dr. Lepsius, Dr. Latham, and most writers. But, upon the principles of this treatise, s^2 and th^2 are analogues of *r̊* and *l̊*, which are *lenes;* therefore they are also *lenes,* and consequently also analogues of *d̊*, *g̊*, *b̊;* but differing from *some* (two) of these organically, and with *all* (three) specifically, in that these are mutes, and they are liquids. They cannot, therefore, have the

---

* A proof is to be found in the fact that, in the former case, *ts* is a euphonical modification of simple r^3 in the noun *mocweri* (r^1); in the latter, of aspirate r^3 in the noun *nari* (r^3).

same relation to z and th^3 (δ) as k to g, and t to d. The forms z and th^3 must then be accounted for in some other way, and is it unreasonable to suppose that they are the vocalised forms of s^2 and th^2? The former of these latter elements I have said exists in both its simple and aspirate forms in the Sechwana language, in such words as *morwetsana (a damsel)*, and *natsane (a young buffalo)*, which examples are a sufficient proof that z is not the simple aspirate form of s, as the words *exhibit, exhort*, in English, in which x is considered a substitute for either ks or gs, would lead one to suppose. It must be evident to any. one who pays a moment's attention to the utterance of either z or th^3, that they are *vocalised* elements; and it cannot be questioned that the affinity between s and z, and th^2 and th^3 (θ and δ of Lepsius), bears a striking resemblance to that existing between $\check{r}$ and $\tilde{r}$. On this point I have the satisfaction of coinciding with Dr. Lepsius, who considers that, in the pronunciation of z and th (his δ), "a vowel sound is produced in the larynx." All the modifications of these two liquid elements will now be indicated as follows:—

s (s^1)   s̗ (s^2)   ṡ (s^3 *or z*)

th (th^1)   t̗h (th^2 in *thin*)   ṫh (th^3 in *thine*)

NOTE.—If there be any truth in the results at which I have arrived, a difficulty is here presented as to the graphical representation of these modifications of the simple "explodent" element. If the mode of employing a diacritical mark, in the form of a small circle, either above or below the letter, be adhered to by learned linguists, who have adopted it in the case of both l and r, to indicate the vocalisation of an element, z must be thrown out, and rendered as superfluous and useless as q is long known to have been. Again, the diagraph th, for the well-known consonants in English, has been considered so objectionable, as to have ancient foreign letters substituted for its two forms—viz , θ and δ; but there is little probability of even these meeting with public favour. Admitting the correctness of my conclusions, it would not be going too far, I think, to suggest that the letter z* be substituted for it; as such an innovation would at all events

---

* I find, as precedents, MM. Ibrahim in the *Persian*, Yates, Gilchrist, and Wilson in the *Hindustáni*, Crawfurd in the *Malayan*, Jaubert in the *Turkish*, Hahn in ihe *Hereró*, all adopt s and z to represent the two English

obviate the necessity of introducing a foreign letter into the Roman
alphabet. The series of modifications would then stand thus :—

$$\underset{\text{z } (th^1)}{\text{s}} \qquad \underset{\dot{\text{z}} (th^2)}{\dot{\text{s}}} \qquad \underset{\overset{\circ}{\text{z}} (th^3)}{\overset{\bullet}{\text{s}}}*$$

But this change would not be admissible in the event of *all* the vocalised
modifications ever being indicated by separate letters, as with *z* and the
letter *v* (still to be considered). The difficulty would then be increased—
viz., to finding *three* simple letters for the vocalised forms of *r, l,* and *q,*
instead of $\dot{r}$, $^{\circ}l$, $\overset{\circ}{q}$, and even *th³*, which, though phonically different from
th², is not graphically distinguished from it in English phonology, not to
mention the vocalised forms $\dot{m}$, $\dot{n}$, and $\overset{\circ}{y}$, already noticed.

I am fully aware that my opinions on the subject of these two
elements and their modifications are not likely to find general
favour, especially as I am unable to produce any objectively
true instances in support of my conclusions. However, whatever of an original character has preceded on the lingual series,
will, I trust, suggest that it is worth the consideration of such
philologers as are too well assured of the importance of the science
of language relatively to that of speech, to deem such a subject
as trivial, or " below the dignity of a philosophical inquiry."

The remaining articulations in Dr. Lepsius' series of dentales—
viz., $\dot{s}$ and $\dot{z}$, usually indicated by *sh* and *zh* (French *ch* and *j*),
and by most writers called *simple* consonants, but unquestionably
" palatals," and, as much as any other instances furnished by
Dr. Latham, " unstable combinations," I reserve for the third
part of this work, as the *Sechwana* and other aboriginal tongues
contain satisfactory proofs of their formation from more than
one element.

---

forms of *th*. Professor Max Müller represents them by *th* and *dh* (or *th*,
dh), or as " second modifications" of these ; thus TH and DH, and frankly
states that he is " at a loss how to mark" the elements (p. lxvi.)

* Professor Müller calls *s* the dental *flatus asper*, which is nothing more
than I have assumed it to be in the letter $\dot{s}$ (*s²*). He says, " the more consistent way of expressing the sonant flatus (*z*, his dental *flatus lenis*),
would be to put a *spiritus lenis* over the *s*," (p. lxx.) I happen only to have
acted upon this by substituting for the *spiritus lenis* the *circular dot* to mark
its *vocalisation*. He, however, retains *z*.

§ VI. LABIALES (OF LEPSIUS).

Under this head Dr. Lepsius's only other simple consonants not yet considered, are those commonly indicated by the letters *f* and *v*, to which it is probable a mode of classification will apply similar to that employed in the case of the linguals above mentioned. Assuming, upon the grounds stated in that case, that *f*, in its continuous and sibilant form, is an aspirate, the lenis form of *ph* (*p*ʿ) it must also have its simple "explodent" form—viz., the lenis form of *p*; and *v*, which Dr. Lepsius admits as containing the indistinct vowel sound, must be its vocalised form, so that it may be represented in its modifications thus—

$$\text{LIQUID} \dots\dots \left\{ \begin{array}{c} dental \\ labial \end{array} \right\} \qquad f \qquad f^{\mathfrak{c}} \qquad f^{\circ}\ (v)^{*}$$

NOTE.—Graphically considered, *v* would thus become superfluous, unless it were decided to substitute it for *f* in all three instances; but as there is an instance of a pure liquid labial in the native languages of Greenland and Mexico (before referred to), its retention for the purpose indicating this would perhaps be considered desirable.

Another element is included by Professor **Müller** among the labials as a *tenuissima*, viz., the Ethiopic pait; but as yet I have met with no description to decide whether it is the tenuis (or simple liquid) form of either *f*, or the so-called Mexican *f*, or whether a liquid at all.

As in the case of some other elements above referred to, it is not till I come to treat of the combinations of these dental-labials

---

* Professor Müller calls *f* the labial *flatus asper.* I have already assumed the common *f* to be an analogue of *s*ʿ, and therefore write it ʿ*f*. He thinks this "soft labial" ought consistently to be written as *f* with a *spiritus lenis.* I have, as in the case of *s*° already adopted °*f*, to express the sonant *v*. He fears, however, we must sacrifice consistency to expediency, and therefore retains *v*.

that any proof will be afforded of their belonging to the class of liquids, *i.e.*, as analogues of *r, l, s,* &c. The *Sechwana* does not contain these elements, and it is only by this analogical mode of viewing them that I find it possible to dispose of them.

CHAPTER IV.
SUMMARY OF PRECEDING ANALYSES.

§ 1. — COMPENDIOUS VIEW OF THE SIMPLE CONSONANTS, AS SUGGESTED BY THE PHONOLOGY OF THE SECHWANA LANGUAGE.

I flatter myself that, in the analysis contained in the second chapter, I have provided all the requisites of a complete induction. The presumption with which I started, upon the basis of a palpable inference from a few facts, has been verified in a detailed and more complete examination. The third chapter was an attempt to supply by speculation—that is, by the assumption of a continuity of principle, or by analogy—other facts in which the Sechwana language appeared to be deficient.

The following is a complete tableau* of the results:—

		FAUCAL.					NASAL.		
		Simple Explodent, or Tenues. fortes. lenes.		Aspirate Expl., or Aspiratæ fortes. lenes.		Voc. lenes.	Ten.	Asp.	Voc.
Gutturales	Mutæ...	k	g	k	g				
	Liquidæ	q		q͗	q͗	ġ	ẏ	ğ	
	Liquidæ..	l		lͨ	l°				
		r		rͨ	r°				
Linguales	Mutæ ...	t	d	tͨ	dͨ		n	ṅ	n̊
	Liquidæ..	s		sͨ	s̊ (z proper)				
		z		z̧ (thin)	z̊ (this)				
Labiales	Liquidæ ...	f		fͨ	f° (v proper)				
	Mutæ	p	b	pͨ	bͨ		m	m	m̊
	Liquidæ ...	v		v̧	v̊				

* Those in bold type occur in the language; the rest, excepting *s*, are foreign to it. Those in italics indicate elements not hitherto, to my knowledge, admitted in any classification.

The above are all the *simple* consonants suggested by the phonology of this language, together with their *aspirated* or *vocalised* forms, or *first* and *second* modifications.

NOTE.—Professor **Max Müller** writes:—"All I insist on is this, that there should be one class of simple or base-letters; that there should be a second and third class of modified letters, expressive of the first and second degrees of modification, as explained in the physiological alphabet." Again, "The three classes of simple and modified letters must be kept distinct." (*Proposals, &c.*, p. lxxiv.) However, it is an open question as to whether the learned Professor has given even a physiological explanation of the nature of his *first* and *second* degrees of modification. His description of these is decidedly indefinite, and they are applicable to only two classes of his consonants, the dentals and the gutturals. When **Dr. Lepsius** uses the acute accent, and Professor **Müller** the italics, to indicate the palatals [thus, for *ch* in *church*, the one writes *k'*, and the other *k* (italicised)] neither of them has given a scientific explanation of what a palatal is. The same with the Sanscrit and Arabic linguals; and though some of either of these may yet be proved to be simple consonants, those able linguists, in the case of the *palatals*, are virtually speaking of combinations of consonants with vowels as modifications. Whereas, before speaking of even simple modifications, they are expected to refer us first to simple consonants, or elements; *e.g.*, in my table above, the gutturals, *k, g, q*; the linguals, *t̓ l, r, d, s, z (th')*; and the labials, *p, b, f*, are all simple consonants or phonetic elements—in fact, *tenues* proper. Again, the gutturals, *k, g, q*; the linguals, *t̓, l̓, r̓*, &c., &c., are *first* modifications by the *spiritus* of both mutes and liquids. Again, *g̓, l̓, r̓, s̓*, &c., are *second* modifications (but only of the liquids) by the element of *vocalization*. These are simple modifications, applicable not only to simple consonants, but also to the *palatals* of the above writers, which, as I have said, are combinations of articulations, not *simple consonants modified, e.g.*, *t*, and *s*, and *y*, are all phonetic *elements* or simple articulations, which, without exception, may be aspirated (1st mod.), and the two latter may also be vocalised (2nd mod.), and thus indicated respectively, *t̓, s̓, y̓, s̓, y̓*;* but the same applies to their combinations (not modifications) usually called *palatals* tsy (=*ch* in *church*), sy (=*sh* in *shall*), sy (=*si* in *vision*). These combinations would be written by Professor **Müller**, *k, s, z* (all italicised); by Professor **Lepsius**, *k', š, ž*, by simple letters, because they consider them simple consonants—modified by a change of the passive organ—from the throat to the palate. With regard to these palatals, Professor **Müller's** principle

---

* As this element ẙ belongs to an analysis of the *vowels*, it is rather premature to indicate it by any arbitrary letter; it is sufficient for me to imply by above that I consider there is a vocalised form of *y*.

of a first modification is based upon a mere assumption that there are modified forms of only *gutturals* and *dentals*; whereas, as before stated, it will be easy to prove that some of them are also analogously modified forms of the *linguals* and *labials*. This very process of modification by the combination of simple articulations is that which has never yet been explained to us. The question has never yet been answered as to what constitutes a " palatal," whether called by one a "palatal," by another a " specific modification," by a third an " unstable combination," or by a fourth a " divergent articulation;" and, of course, it is impossible to arrive at a correct reply, till we first ascertain all the simple articulations. It has been the object of this treatise to arrive at that reply. Such *first* and *second* modifications as those embraced in the above classification, I have attempted to explain in a clear manner, which will, I trust, meet with the concurrence of the reader.

From this it would appear that there are sixteen elements, or *simple* forms of articulation (*tenues*); *thirteen* of which are faucal, and *three* nasal. Of the faucals, seven are *liquids*, leaving the same number of mutes as has always obtained—viz., *six*. The nasals remain as usual, according to the latest authorities—viz., *three*.

NOTE.—If there is any truth in my inferences from the Sechwana, and therefore in this classification, the above table shows the practicability of having a complete scale of *simple* consonants, without the introduction of one foreign letter—viz., by the mere transposition of *z* and *v* for other letters, viz., the English *th*, and the Mexican *liquid-labial*, respectively. It must be borne in mind that I have omitted in the above table all sounds usually called "*palatals*," or any which can be resolved into a simple consonant and a post-positive vowel element, under which may be included both *sh* (Fr. *ch*, Germ. *sch*) and *zh* (Fr. *j*), not to mention the Italian *gl*, or the French *ll*, *mouillé*,-&c.

The result of the preceding analyses may be explained as follows:—

(*a*) All the *faucal* elements are *simple* articulations, formed by the mere contact of two organs, and momentary (partial or complete) interruption of the breath, whether viewed as *liquids* or *mutes*, and therefore essentially "explodents."

(*b*) They all admit of an accessory element, called the *spiritus asper*, and are therefore divisible into simple "explodents" and aspirate "explodents," or, better expressed according to the old nomenclature, *tenues* and *aspiratæ*.   The probability is, that the *spiritus* exists in binary quantities.

(c) They all exist in binary quantities—viz., *pairs*, between which there is an affinity, not only as universally acknowledged to exist between *k* and *g*, *t* and *d*, *p* and *b*, but also between *k*, and a liquid form of *g*, i.e., *q*; between *t*, and several liquid forms of *d*, i.e., *r*, *l*, *s*, and *th*; and between *p*, and a liquid form of *b*, i.e., *f.*   The same remark applies to their *aspirate* forms.*

(d) In the case of all these liquids, the terms *continuous* and *aspirate* are synonymous.

Note.—There is, after all, nothing new in the general arrangement thus suggested by facts of a very original character; for it is but a return to that of the ancients, with the addition of a second vertical set of *aspiratæ* to correspond with the *mediæ* of these systems, or the *lenes* "*explodents*" (*tenues*) of the more recent one.

ANCIENT SYSTEM.

	Tenues.	*Mediæ.*	*Aspiratæ.*
Gutturales	—	—	—
Linguales	—	—	—
Labiales	—	—	—

The only remarkable thing is, that the principle of binary quantities which did not exist in the ancient classification, while it was the turning point of a new one, became at the same time the erring point in the latter, because based on a vulgar view of the correlation existing between certain letters; and that the *liquids* were in both systems excluded from classification.   The error of the ancients arose from ignorance of the binary nature of some elements; their only alternative was to place the *mediæ* (lenes) into an intermediate position with respect to the *tenues* and *aspiratæ*, and to exclude the *liquids*, because they apparently bore no analogy to any of these.   That of the moderns consists in their making certain consonants, partially similar to these mediæ (as *lenes*), but different from them (as *continuæ*), into a separate division, corresponding with one of *mutes*, including both *tenues* and *mediæ*, thus : —

MODERN SYSTEM.

Explosivæ.		*Continuæ.*	
fortes.	lenes.	fortes.	lenes.
(Ancient *Tenues.*)	(Ancient *Mediæ.*)	(*Aspirated Liquids.*)	(*Vocalised Liquids.*)

---

* See *Proposals, &c.*, by Max Müller, p. xxvi., where he remarks :—" Professor Wheatstone's researches prove that a distinguishing mark of the

Thus excluding from the tabular view the *aspirated mutes* (ancient *aspiratæ,*) as merely "*explosive* sounds which are pronounced with a simple but audible breath,* as well as placing the commonly known liquids *r* and *l* under the head of *ancipites*, because apparently both *continuous*† and *explodent* in their nature, and thus altogether leaving doubtful the important fact that they also have *tenues* and *aspirated* forms, and ignoring altogether the probability of there being several consonants analogous to these two.

The more natural classification, suggested by an inquiry into the phonology of the Sechwana, is the following :—

		Tenues.		*Aspiratæ.*	
		fortes.	lenes.	fortes.	lenes.
Gutturales, &c.	*Mutes*	—	—	—	—
	Liquids	—	—	—	—

While it admits the division into *tenues* and *aspiratæ* of the ancient arrangement, instead of the *explosivæ* and *continuæ* of the modern, it at the same time admits the binary quantitative arrangement of the latter under

---

liquid semi-vowels consists in their having no corresponding mutes." My conclusion above, if correct, would seem to prove that they have corresponding mutes.

* Professor Müller calls the aspirated *fortis* a "modified tenuis."

† It is easy to account for *l* and *r* being thus dubiously classified, and alone of all the other liquids considered "exploded" by both Lepsius and Müller, by the fact that the sibilant nature of *s, th, f,* &c., and which has led to their being classified as *continuæ*, is quite accidental to the breathing required in their articulation—*i.e.*, arising from the permeable nature of the set of teeth, and the proximity of the aperture of the mouth; any sibilation in *l* and *r* being stifled by their formation above the aperture. It is, however, remarkable that, conversely, the same fact will account for the "explodent" or simply liquid nature of these analogous elements, *s, th, f,* &c., being lost sight of, and which it is one of the objects of this treatise to uphold.

Professor Müller considers that in the formation of these "sibilants" "*there is no contact at all*, and the breath passes between the two organs without being stopped, still not without giving rise to a *certain friction in passing that point of contact* where guttural, dental and labial consonants are formed."—*Proposals, &c.*, p. xxvi. I leave the reader to test the correctness of this statement, by experimenting on his own organs. His description, I believe, applies only to the formation of the *spiritus,* and the German *ich*, which under the new name of *flatus* he confounds with the liquid *consonants* of the different organs. See preceding note on *l* and *r* (p. 125). What I have aimed at proving is, that these *fricatives* of Lepsius and *flatus* of Müller, viz., Germ. *ch* (gutt.), *s, th, f,* as well as the aspirate form of *r* and *l*—otherwise called *continuous* consonants—are in every case liquid consonants or *spiritus* (or *flatus* or *fricative*).

each head with respect to the *six* mutes; but goes still further, as the reader will presently see, with respect to the *liquids*, which it leads us to suspect are not only more numerous than is usually supposed, but also admit of consistent classification of another nature, under each organic series—viz., that they are all *lenes*, and none *fortis*. Of these liquids, it proves that not only *l* and *r* are both *explodent* and *continuous*, but that, viewed as the former, they are *simple* liquids, and, viewed as *continuæ*, they are *aspirated* liquids; and, moreover, that the same applies to all the elements usually classed under *continuæ*.

(*e*) That *l* and *r*, commonly called *liquids* under the old as well as new arrangement, but, in the latter, shelved under the head of *ancipites*, are probably only two members of a numerous set of analogues—viz., *seven*, including, *one* guttural, *four* linguals, and *two* labials; that they are *tenues*, being *lenes* forms of *t*, and have their corresponding aspirate forms, which again are *lenes* forms of *t'* (aspirate); and it is only in the case of these aspirated liquids that the term *continuous* is at all applicable to consonants.

Note.—I would here remind the reader of these two elements, called *ancipites* by **Dr. Lepsius**, and by him considered as both "*explodent*" (formed by a contact and apertion of organs) and *continuous*, that, by my inferences from the Sechwana, there are *tenues* forms of them both, and also *aspirate* forms, which may occur separately and distinctly. According to the principles of this treatise both are explodent,* whether *tenues* or *aspirate*, but both are continuous only when aspirated.

(*f*) That certain articulations—viz., Germ. gutt. *ch*, Sech. *g*, *s*, *th* (English), and *f* (above indicated by *q̓*, *s̓*, *z̓*, and *f'*), usually regarded as *continuous* consonants, and therefore, in such instances, according to what has preceded, *aspirate* forms—have also their simple "explodent" (elementary liquid) forms (*q*, *s*, *z*, *f*), just as some writers have supposed both *l* and *r* to have, and as has been proved in the second chapter.

(*g*) The probability that both *st*† (in *parts*, *parks*, and *harps*),

---

* Professor Müller, I observe, also admits that in the formation of liquids, among which he includes *r*, *l*, and a guttural '*h*, there is "an approach or a very slight contact between the organs."—*Proposals, &c.*, p. xxv.

† The following occurs in an able American periodical, the *Bibliotheca*

and the English *th* (in *thin*), in their *simple* as well as *aspirate*
"*explodent*" forms (tenues and aspiratæ)—the former of which
are not usually included in phonological classifications—are not
only analogues of the simple and aspirate forms of *r* and *l* respectively, inasmuch as they are all *liquids;* but, moreover,
organically, kindred forms of these two elements, and therefore
also *lenes* forms of *t* and *t'*; and that the correlation usually supposed to exist between them, as indistinctly represented by
the letters *s* and *th* (*thin*), and the other kindred articulations *z*
and *th* (*thine*), is not analogous to that between each of the three
pairs of mutes—*k-g*, *t-d*, *p-b ;* but that these simple and aspirate
forms are both *lenes*, and *z* and *th* (*thine*) *vocalised* modifications
of these *aspirate* forms.

NOTE.—It must have struck the reader that we have no satisfactory
terms by which to express the nature of the distinction between the instances of any pairs in this binary arrangement of consonants, but it is
necessary that we should bear in mind the peculiar nature of those which

---

Sacra, so recently as Oct., 1860 (p. 831), and affords another instance of the usual
loose mode of forming deductions from the physiology of the human voice :—
" *S* is a sui generis sound, which, like the sponge, mediate, as it were,
between a vegetable and an animal, or the bat between birds and quad-
rupeds, occupies a sort of middle ground between a consonant and a vowel,
uniting the characteristics of them both."—*B. W. Dwight.*
This is, of course, only a circumlocutory way of saying it is the only *semi-
vowel* or semi-*consonant*, but the same writer elsewhere calls δ and σ *lingual
or dental aspirates*,) which I have admitted; but only on the principle that
the *continuous* forms are *tenues-liquids* + the *spiritus asper*), and distinguishes
the latter from the *spiritus* as follows :—
" *H* is not so much a consonant as a breathing. It differs from the
sibilant, physiologically, only in being a breathing through the whole open
mouth, with the tongue at rest on its base, and the teeth apart; while the
sibilant is a *breathing* through the teeth, in a nearly closed state, with the
tongue against the upper teeth. *H* and *s* are therefore *both breathings*,
and differ only in the different positions of the tongue and teeth. The
sibilant and aspirate have accordingly au etymological as well as phonetic
parallelism with each other, &c."—*Ibid.* p. 839. (The italics are substituted.)
Whereas, the actual difference may be simply expressed in the following
formula :—*h = spiritus asper.* The sibilant (aspirated or *continuous*) *s* = a
tenuis-liquid (dental lingual) + the spiritus asper.

were called *semi-vowels* under the ancient arrangement, and *continuæ* under
the new, and their similarity, essentially, to all called *liquid-lenes* (whether
simple or aspirate), under that suggested by the Sechwana, and that, in
respect to the *mutes*, the terms *fortis* and *lenis*—*short* and *long*—are perfectly
compatible. When most of the writers who reason upon a physiological
basis admit that the difference between *vowels* and *consonants* consists in the
former being caused by free emissions of both the voice and the breath,
and the latter by the check, interruption, or impediment of the breath, and,
moreover, use such expressions as quickly—slowly, complete—incomplete,
intense—firm, strong—weak, in reference to the degree of closure, contact,
collision, or compression of the articulating organs, it seems strange that
the idea of relative time, which appears to be implied in every antithetical
expression, has not also suggested the terms *short* and *long*, which would
convey, in the case of the consonants, a difference, or a correlation, precisely analogous to that between the vowels; for in all cases the position
of the organs is the same in the respective pairs, whether vowels or consonants. In the case of vowels, proportion of time is distinctly the element
of the difference; in the consonants, it is only less distinctly the element
in the interruption of the breath. At all events, *quantity* is a term quite
as applicable to the binary arrangement of the *pairs* of consonants, as to
that of the vowels.[*] Admitting all this, it must be the more satisfactory
that the terms *lenis* and *long* are quite compatible to express the quantitative
nature of all *liquids*. For instance, it will be immaterial whether we give
the following nomenclature:—

	Tenuis.	*Aspirate.*
Mutes	fortis-lenis	fortis-lenis
Liquids	lenis	lenis
Or *Mutes*	short-long	short-long
Liquids	long	long

In order to enable the reader to compare the terminologies of Professors
Lepsius and **Müller** with that of this treatise in the classification of
the so-called semi-vowels, I arrange them as follows, the vertical columns
showing equivalents:—

Lepsius

Liquids.	*Fricativæ*	or	*Continuæ.*
(Including *r* and *l*.)	fortis	and	lenis.

Merely alludes to continuous forms
of *r* and *l*, and including both.

s	and	*z*
th(in)	„	*th*(is)
ch (Germ. gutt.)	„	غ (Arabic)
f	„	*v*

and the *spiritus* lenis and aspirate.

---

[*] The following will not be out of place here, though intended by the

Max Müller

Liquids.
(Including *r* and *l*,
and '*h*, a breathing.)

Flatus or '*Sibilants.*
asper and lenis.
Not including modifications of *r* and
l, but all the rest of above consonants
in the same order, and the *spiritus.*

Arrangement sug-
gested by the
Sechwana

Liquidæ.

tenues	aspiratæ	voc.
Including simple or elementary forms* of *s, th, f,* Germ. g. *ch,* &c., as well as of *r* and *l* (viz., *s, z, f, q.*)	Including aspirated and vocalized modifications of the simple forms of *r, l,* as well as of *s, th, ch, f,* &c., and consequently all above consonants, viz.:—	

ṡ
ż (th²)
q̇ (Germ. *ch*)
f˙

ṩ (z proper)
ż (th³)
q̊ (Arabic غ)
˚f (v proper)

The pure *spiritus* is classed as a
separate and independent element.

As to quantity, all three divisions are *lenes.*

(*h*) That the elements *m* and *n*, usually called *liquids*, are not properly so in their *tenues* forms; but, so far as regards the organs by the contact of which they are articulated, both they and their analogue ɲ (*ng, n,* of Lepsius) are strictly *mutes.* On the other hand, viewed as nasals, their aspirate and vocalised forms are *liquids.* But they differ from the proper liquids *l, r,* &c., in that, as will be shown in the sequel, these are liquid with *all* other *faucal* consonants, and form the post-positive elements in diphthongal combinations; whereas *m, n,* and ɲ, are only liquid with their cognates *b* or *p, t* or *d,* and *k* or *g,* respectively, and their aspirated or vocalised forms, and generally

learned writer to have quite another application:—"The consonantal, like the vowel, elements of speech, have their different degrees of weight; and their weight is but another name for the amount of their phonetic force, or the density, as it were, of their phonetic substance."—*Dwight, in Bibliotheca Sacra,* p. 272, April, 1860.

* These are the consonants to which I allude as being entirely ignored in classifications.

form the prepositive element in such combinations—*e.g.*, *mp, nk, nt*, &c. ; but these do not form diphthongs. This is only the case when, combined with their cognates, they form the post-positive element, as *pm, tn, kp*.

(*i*) That all the *liquids*, as well as the three *nasals*, and also the *spiritus asper*, admit of another accessory element called *vocalisation*.

Principles at Work in variable Pronunciations.

It is generally supposed that "the exact place of contact" of two organs "can never be fixed with geometrical precision, and that by shifting this point forward or backward certain modifications will arise in the pronunciations of individuals, tribes, and nations."* But this has the appearance of being too general a conclusion; at all events, it requires proof. If correct, it will, I think, apply chiefly to cases in which simple consonantal articulations are compounded with vowel dipthongs, *i.e.*, the numerous forms of the " palatals." It is strange that while only one capacity of hearing is allowed, every shade of pronunciation is ascribed to a different disposition of the organs; and it is frequently forgotten that one element may sound variously to half-a-dozen ears.

It is chiefly in regard to the gutturals that there is a difficulty in identifying the powers of an element in different languages. There is not half so much dispute in respect to the linguals, even though these include as many articulations as the other organical divisions together; and still less about the labials, which on this account are rather arbitrarily pronounced by Professor M. Müller, " the most constant sounds in all dialects,"† whereas it is simply because the mode of their formation is the most palpable to the eye as well as to the ear.

However, I think that the variable pronunciations of different

---

* Proposals, &c., p. xxxiii.   † Ibid.

tribes and individuals is regulated by certain principles, which, if carefully examined, will very much simplify the subject; and which it is necessary for me to sum up in review of the preceding classification suggested by the Sechwana language.

(1) I have referred to the term *quantity*, expressive of the difference between k and g, t and d, &c., and between k, t, &c., and the liquid forms of g and d respectively (viz., q Oriental gutt., and r, l, s, $z(th)$ linguals). The correlation of the former pairs is what has generally been admitted; but that of the latter has, I believe, been first pointed out in this treatise. Both g and q differ from k in quantity.

(2) But between g and q (Oriental), which are both *lenes* relatively to the fortis k, there is another difference arising from some accessory or accidental property in the latter, viz., that of being prolonged in the utterance; the one is a *mute*, and the latter a *liquid*. The same applies to the difference in the linguals between the mute d and the liquids r, l, s, and $z(th)$. In the case of the gutturals, the position of the organs is the same in every instance, but there is a quantitive difference between k and g or q, and a difference in property between g and q, though both of the same quantity.

(3) Again, we find that the mutes k, g, &c., can be pronounced in another very different way, viz., with *first* modification of the *spiritus*, e.g., k or $\dot{g}$. But the Oriental q as a liquid can be pronounced in two other very different ways, viz., with *first* modification of the *spiritus*, as in the Germ. *ch* gutt., or Sechwana g ($\dot{q}$ of my table); and with the *second* modification of the element of *vocalisation* as in the Arabic ﻉ ($\ddot{q}$ of my table). In these two or three modes of pronouncing the same element, the same organs are at the exact place of contact; * but the differ-

---

* If this does not apply similarly to the *linguals*, this is easily accounted for by the greater mobility of the point of the tongue required in the formation of them.

ences consist in the modifications by accessory elements. We have thus—

Difference in *quantity* between *fortis* and *lenis*, *k* and *g* or *q*.

  „   property „ *lenes*   *g* and *q*.

  „   modification „ $\left\{\begin{array}{c}\text{tenues aspirate}\\ \text{and voc.}\end{array}\right\}$ $q, \dot{q}, \overset{\circ}{q}.$

In the case of the gutturals there are thus *seven* articulations formed at one point of contact of the organs, " without shifting this point forward or backward."

Now I have remarked, that "either the fortis or lenis form of any consonant may be enunciated with different degrees of distinctness; but its quantity relatively to that of the other instance of the pair, remains constant." These remarks will apply to any of the *seven* articulations in the above examples. To repeat the useful description by Sir John Stoddart, "It is not to be understood that either the one or the other articulation in each pair does not admit of nice shades and discriminatory touches, as it were, perceptible to some ears and not to others."

It is to such variations of pronunciation that Professor M. Müller gives the appellation of "*Dialectic modifications.*" He writes —

"Where this variety of pronunciation exists only in degree, without affecting the *nature and real character* of a guttural or dental consonant, we need not notice it. Gutturals from a semitic throat have a deeper sound than our own, and some grammarians have made a new class for them by calling them pectoral letters. The guttural flatus asper, as heard in the Swiss *ach*, is deeper, and as it were more pectoral than the usual German *ch*."

Again,

"The Swiss *ch* is, according to Wallin, page 21, the same as the Arabic خ."

Again,

"But though there is a distinction between the *ch* as heard in *loch*, and the خ and ح of the Arabs, as described above, yet it *is not necessary to admit more than one type* of the guttural flatus asper."[*]

---

[*] The italics are mine.

Now, the Arabic ع is, according to Lepsius, the equivalent of the Germ. gutt. *ch*, which cannot therefore differ much from the Swiss *ch*, nor any of these from the Scotch *ch* in *loch*, the Dutch *g* in *dag*, the Sechwana *g*, the Naman *gh* of Tindall, and the Kaffir *r;* every one of which is to be looked upon as a quantitive equivalent of the others, *i.e.*, an *aspirated liquid guttural*, and any of them may be chosen as the type. The same will apply to the tenuis form of this consonant, viz., the *q* (Oriental), which I have suggested has equivalents in the form of the Kaffir *g* and the Danish *g;* also to its vocalized form the Arabic ع the equivalents of which are said to be the Northumberland *burr* and the Hindustáni *gh*. It is the business of the linguist to put these facts to the test, and raise upon them something more solid than mere conjecture.

Throughout these analyses it has been my aim to express my meaning by a uniformity of nomenclature ; but where one has to do with a plurality of systems, this is in a measure impracticable. The terms simple and aspirate "explodent," and some others, have merely been used for the purposes of this investigation ; but, as distinctive terms earlier in use, such as *tenuis* and *aspirate, liquid* and *mute, fortis* and *lenis,* express all that is required, I propose to adhere to these in future, in the treatment of the various forms of compound consonants. Hitherto I have only attempted to classify simple or elementary articulations, and shall in the following section proceed to the consideration of simple consonants in their mutual combinations.

§ II.

On the application of the Nomenclature and Orthography above suggested, to systems of Consonantal Permutations in other Languages.

At the outset of this treatise, I had never given attention to the subject of permutations as existing in other languages. I merely referred to the remarks of Dr. Richardson, commenting on Horne Tooke, as rather crude; and in a foot-note (p. 6) gave a quotation from the *North British Review*, in which the learned writer does not suppose that Grimm's law, with its nine equations, is without a foundation in the history of language, but considers it exaggerated by being run out into a vicious circle. The following is what has met my eye since, and as it is contained in the first Encyclopædia of the day, and professes to give a concise view of all that inductive philology has accomplished in what may be called the science of the "embryogeny" of human speech, I give it at length, especially as it is probable some of my readers will not have the means of referring to that cumbrous but invaluable work.

" Its claim (Philology), however, to rank as a branch of inductive science, does not rest merely on its services in classifying the phenomena and interpreting the facts of language. It has also proved itself able to discover, like other inductive sciences, the general laws which prevail among the phenomena. One of the most important of these general laws is that of the ' transposition of sounds' (*Lautverschiebung*) ; or, as it is sometimes called, ' the law of the interchange of the mutes,' which had been imperfectly indicated by **Rask,** and which **Grimm** demonstrated completely in its application to the Greek (Latin, Sanscrit), the Gothic, and the old High German (*Deutsche Grammatic*, vol. i. pp. 584, sqq.) and which Bopp has extended to the Zend and Lithuanian (*Vergleichende Grammatik*, pp. 78, foll.) The general law is thus stated :—

Labials.

In Greek (Latin, Sanscrit)—
P answers to the Gothic F, and the old High German B or V
B   „   „   P,   „   „   F
F   „   „   B,   „   „   P

Dentals.

In Greek (Latin, Sanscrit)—
T answers to the Gothic TH, and the old High German D
D   „   „   T   „   „   Z
TH   „   „   D   „   „   T

Gutturals.

In Greek (Latin, Sanscrit)—

K answers to the Gothic $\left\{\begin{array}{l}\text{H (init.)}\\\text{G (med.)}\end{array}\right\}$ and old High German G

G   „   „   K   „   „   CH
CH (H) „   „   G   „   „   K

" Or thus :*—

Greek (Latin, Sanscrit.)	*Gothic.*	*Old High German.*
Tenuis.	Aspirate.	Medial.
Medial.	Tenuis.	Aspirate.
Aspirate.	Medial.	Tenuis.

" One example of each interchange will explain the application of this law

	Greek. (*Latin, Sanscrit.*)	*Gothic.* (*Old Norse.*)	*Old High German.*
P, F, V, (B)	Πούς=πόδ-s; *Pes*=*ped-s ; Padas.*	*Fótus,*	*Vuoz.*
B, P, F,	θόρυΒοs; *turba,*	*thaurP,*	*doroF.*
$\left.\begin{array}{l}\text{F}\\\text{PH}\end{array}\right\}$ B, P,	Φηγόs, *Fagus*	*Beyki,*	*Puocha.*
T, TH, D,	ὀδούς=ὀδόνT-s; *dens*=*denT·s , danTas,*	*TunTHus,ZanD.*	
D, T, Z,	ὀΔούs; *Dens ; Dantas,*	*Tunthus,*	*Zand.*
TH, D, T,	θυγατηρ,	*Dauhtar,*	*Tohtar.*
K, $\left\{\begin{array}{l}\text{H}\\\text{G}\end{array}\right\}$ G,	ἰKυρόs, *soCer,*	*SvaiHra, SchwaGer.*	
G, K, CH,	Γίνοs, *Genus,*	*Kuni,*	*CHunni.*
$\left.\begin{array}{l}\text{CH,}\\\text{H,}\end{array}\right\}$ G, K,	Xόρτοs, *Hortus,*	*Gards,*	*Karto.*

---

* This summary, reduced to my nomenclature, would read as follows :—
Fortis mute.   Aspirated liquid.   *Lenis* mute.
Lenis mute.   *Fortis* mute.   Aspirated liquid.
Aspirated liquid.   *Lenis* mute.   *Fortis* mute.

But there is no mention of *tenues liquidæ*, which abound in the European tongues, and the existence of which, in a scale of sounds, it is the object of this work to prove.

" Mr. Winning has pointed out a curious interchange between the Greek
and the Gothic, with regard to the relations established by this law (*Manual
of Comparative Philology*, p. iii). Other modifications require to be introduced; and Dr. Guest attaches so much weight to the exceptions which
he has noticed, that he has arrived at a conviction of ' the general un-
soundness of these celebrated canons' ('On the Elements of Language,
their Arrangements and Accidents.' *Proceedings of the Philological Society*,
vol. iii., p. 180.) The great majority of philologers, however, acquiesce in
the general validity of this theorem of interchange. Bunsen calls it 'one
of the most fertile and triumphant discoveries of philological ethnology'
(*Report of the British Association* for 1847, p. 262); and Max Müller
accepts it as a proof of ' the systematic regularity, the almost absolute
certainty, to which the phonetic laws of different languages can be brought.'
(*Edinburgh Review*, October, 1851, p. 319.)"—ENCYCLOPÆDIA BRITANNICA,
vol. xvii., p. 539.

The above statement of the general law of Rusk, Grimm, and
Bopp, is, after all, the mere record of a very general inference
that certain articulations in one language answer regularly to
those in others, and amounts to a simple synopsis of facts like
that at page 15 of this work, of the permutations in the Sechwana
language, discovered by the missionaries some forty years ago,
though of a different nature. The Indo-European law is based
upon a comparison of cognate dialects, which had lost all ap-
pearances of cognation by reason of historical vicissitudes, and
has been evolved from a mass of heterogeneous materials, which
it has become a subjective means of rendering more accessible
and comprehensible to the efforts of the mind. Its discovery in
the evolution has shed light on that cognation. It amounts to
a mere series of palpable facts, exhibiting the relations of other
facts; but I am not aware that any attempts have been made
to reduce them to abstract laws or principles. The same, to a
certain extent, may be said of the laws of permutation in the
Sechwana. The first missionary who reduced the language to
writing stumbled upon these laws as so many difficulties; but
the more he observed of them and their constancy, the more
easily he made a comprehensive grasp and maintained a firm hold

of his knowledge; and by noting them, in fact made the language more easily acquirable by others; but, till the humble attempt made in this work, I am not aware of any efforts to reduce these palpable laws, as fresh objective facts, to still more abstract subjective principles. One would think that we have to search in such singular phenomena for "a phase of progress, of growth, of history," for a department of science explanatory of both lexicology and syntax.

Moreover, the above general law of what may rather be called comparative or dialectical phonology than phonics, however striking, labours under a disadvantage alluded to throughout this work—viz., that it is necessarily based upon a very copious induction of materials of questionable analogy, culled from both purely historical and purely phonetical facts, in dead and living, archaic and vernacular examples of speech. Therefore the remark of the *North British Reviewer*, that "it has been run out into a vicious circle," seems not without foundation, and it can therefore only be regarded as empirical. The late Richard Garnett, an eminent philologer, considered that the above scale of permutations would "admit of being considerably extended beyond the limits assigned by Grimm and Pott."—P. 254.

Of the two, the scale of permutations laid down by the humble and plodding missionary is by far the more important in a scientific point of view, inasmuch as it is based upon the observation of the "living traditional pronunciation," and that in *one* language. When looked at in this light, what is usually called "Grimm's law" seems at present destitute of value, further than as a subjective means of rendering the relations between the archaic forms of the Greek, Gothic, and old German, and one or two other cognate dialects, more easily accessible for the mind.

Of considerably more importance, and withal more satisfactory than such general speculations, are the following peculiar permutations* in Welsh, inasmuch as they also, like the Sechwana, are gathered from the vernacular pronunciation :—

Gutturals.

Car	(*a kinsman*)	k† fortis	⎫ Tenues mutes.
Ei gar	(*his* „)	*to* g *to* lenis	⎭
Ei char	(*her* „)	*to* q *to* lenis	Aspirate liquid.
Vy nghar	(*my* „)	*to* g̊g *to* lenis	{ Aspirate mute, *with the cognate* nasal *preceding.*

Linguals.

Tad	(*a father*)	t	⎫
Ei dad	(*his* „)	*to* d	⎬ Same mutations.
Ei thad	(*her* „)	*to* ż (*th²*)	⎭
Vy nhad	(*my* „)	*to* nh *to*	{ Simple aspirate (*spiritus*) with the cognate nasal *preceding*, which is *vocalised,probably by absorption with the* d.

Labials.

Pen	(*a head*)	p	⎫
Ei ben	(*his* „)	*to* ḅ	⎬ Same mutations.
Ei phen	(*her* „)	*to* f̣	⎭
Vy mhen	(*my* „)	*to* m̊h	⎱ *As in preceding example, the* b *being probably absorbed in the vocalised nasal.*

The other examples cited are not so regular, but I append the following :—

Gutturals.

Gwas	(*a servant*)	gw	lenis mute.
Ei was	(*his* „)	*to* w	lenis *is lost.*
Vy ngwas	(*my* „)	*to* g̊w	{ lenis *is absorbed in the cognate vocalised nasal.*

Linguals.

Duw	(*a god*)	d	lenis.
Ei dhuw	(*his* „)	*to* ż (*th³*) *to*	lenis vocalised liquid.
Vy nuw	(*my* „)	*to* n̊	{ lenis absorbed in the cognate vocalised nasal.

Labials.

Bara	(*bread*)	b	⎫
Ei bara	(*his* „)	*to* f̊ (*v*)	⎬ Same mutations as in preceding case.
Vy mara	(*my* „)	*to* m	⎭

* These, as they occur in the first column, I have found in Latham's " *Eng. Lang.*," vol. i., p. 327, cited from Prichard ; but I have tested them by the speech of a genuine and intelligent *Welshman.*

† The bold letters in the middle column are those arbitrarily assumed in my tables, and the terms in the third column have reference to my nomenclature.

Of the above "regular mutation of *initial* consonants," called by Garnett the "Celtic process," he states they "are changed into others of the same organ, to denote a diversity of logical or grammatical relation;" and adds, "the entire system is, so far as we know, peculiar to the Celtic tongues, and it exhibits a phenomenon as curious as it is difficult to account for."

On examining the living pronunciation, I ascertained the Keltic process to be strictly regular in the case of the tenues-*fortes* consonants k, t, p, except in one instance. The second example under each consonant is a change to the corresponding *lenis;* the third into the *aspirate liquid* ("fricative" or "flatus"), which is also a *lenis;* the fourth presents an anomaly, in that, in one case (k), the consonant becomes an *aspirate mute,* and in two cases, t and p, the *mute* itself is absorbed in the vocalised nasal preceding—*e.g.*, $\underset{\circ}{\eta}\dot{g}$ (instead of $\dot{y}h$); $\dot{n}h$, $\dot{m}h$.

In the case of the tenues-*lenes* g, d, b, one anomaly occurs only under the guttural. The second example, under the lingual and labial, is a change to the cognate *vocalised liquid*, *i.e.*, $\overset{\circ}{z}$ (th^3), and $°f$ (v), for, by the analogy of these two examples, one would have expected the corresponding articulation under the guttural to have been $\overset{\circ}{q}w$—viz., the *vocalised*-liquid-guttural. Under the lenes, again, the anomaly alluded to under the *fortes* does not hold good, for here one finds the guttural, lingual, and labial, respectively, becoming $\dot{y}$, $\dot{n}$, $\overset{\circ}{m}$.

It is, probably, principally in reference to this peculiar process of permutation that Mr. Garnett writes of the Keltic language—It "appears to be the most ancient, the most singularly constructed, and the most true to its original form of all European tongues." If the greater perfection and constancy of the Sechwana process of permutation be considered in conjunction with its equally remarkable and normal syntactical structure, the same remark will apply to it in comparison with other African languages of the same family.

It is to be expected that a process of permutation in one language must shed some light on that of another, especially if arrived at by the same mode of observation. One case occurs to me at this moment. The Sechwana contains proofs that *t* and *d*, *p* and *b*, are correlatives or pairs, but it fails in data to prove that *k* and *g* are similarly related (see p. 20); whereas, the Keltic examples *kar* to *ei-gar*, *tad* to *ei-dad*, *pen* to *ei-ben*, are conclusive and satisfactory in respect to all three pairs of consonants. It would be difficult to find such a beautiful example in Grimm's law to corroborate any inductions from even the Welsh or Sechwana, and yet the above result, at which we arrive in both these languages, is founded upon what Professor Müller would once,* perhaps, have called " the irregular utterance of savages !"

It is remarkable that, in Sechwana, precisely the same initial permutations, presented in the table of verbs at page 15 of this work, are repeated with great exactness in the formation of plurals in **Li** from nouns in **Lo**, with one or two omissions only, and also, in some cases, a few exceptions in addition to the normal forms.

Mutations.	Singular.	Plural.
b to *p*	Lobopò (*form*)	Lipopò

EXCEPTION.—**ob** to **mp**—*e.g., Loobu* (brack ground), *Limpu.*

---

* 1855. The following, however, written *six* years later, shows less scholastic prejudice in the investigation of truth. " In the science of languages, languages are not treated as a means; language itself becomes the sole object of scientific inquiry. Dialects which have never produced any literature at all, the jargons of savage tribes, the clicks of the Hottentots, and the vocal modulations of the Indo-Chinese, are as important, nay, for the solution of some of our problems, more important, than the poetry of Homer or the prose of Cicero."—*Lectures on the Science of Language, by Max Müller*, p. 23.

Mutations.	Singular.	Plural.
c* immutable	Locwiisa (cuticle side of a skin)	Licwiisa
g to kh (kʼ)	Loǧoñ (ɉ) (wood)	Likhoñ (ɉ)
h to ph (pʼ)	Lohaʔò (fissure)	Liphaʔò
h to kh (kʼ)	Lohibiʔi(umbilicalcord)	Likhihiʔi or Liphihiʔi

NOTE.—*I have already remarked that this mutation is probably euphonical, and was the only exception in the case of the verbs.*

k immutable	Loketla (fragment or chip)	Liketla
kh (kʼ) ,,	Lokhuru (eggshell)	Likharu
l to t	Loleme (tongue)	Liteme
m immutable	Lomati (plank)	Limati
n ,,	Lonaka (horn)	Linaka
ñ (ɉ) ,,	Loɉamu (flank)	Li ɉamu
p ,,	Lopalò (scab, in goats)	Lipalò
ph (pʼ),,	Lophèǫò, (hollow potsherd)	Liphèǫò
r to t		

EXCEPTION.—r to nt—e.g., Lori (cord), Linti

r to th (tʼ)	Loʔole (dust)	Lithole
s to ts	Losika (generation)	Litsika

EXCEPTION.—s to nts—e.g., Losi (eyelash), Lintsi.

sh to c	Loshwaèla (skeleton)	Licwaèla

EXCEPTION.—sh to nc—e.g., Lusho (spoon), Linco.

t immutable	Lotolo (fire steel)	Litolo
th (tʼ) ,,	Lothèka (loin)	Lithèka

EXCEPTION.—th (tʼ) to nth—e.g., Lotha (membrane), Lintha

tl immutable	Lotlowa (net)	Litlowa
tlh (tlʼ),,	Lotlhakoʔe (side)	Litlhakoʔe
ts ,,	Lotsatsa (thin)	Litsatsa
— to k	Loatò, or katò (increase)	Likatò, or maatô

EXCEPTION.— to ny—e.g., Loètò (journey), Linyètò.

But this will not apply to the formation of other plurals, save in a few exceptional cases—*i.e.*, nouns in *Bo*, with plurals in *Ma*; in *Se*, with plurals in *Li*; or in *Mo*, with plurals in *Ba*, *Ma*, or *Me*, as a general and constant rule, form these without a change of the initial.

---

* C of the missionaries, as before stated, equivalent to *ch* in *Charles*.

Under *Se*, we find the exceptions—

l to *t*	Seleru (*beard*)	Literu

$\left.\begin{array}{l} g\ (\dot{q})\ \text{or} \\ h,\ \text{or} \\ bh \end{array}\right\}$ to $\left\{\begin{array}{l} b,\ \text{or} \\ bh \end{array}\right.$ $\left.\begin{array}{l} \text{Sehaqa} \\ \text{Seqaqa} \\ \text{Sebhaqa} \end{array}\right\}$(*beads*) $\left\{\begin{array}{l} \text{Libaqa} \\ \text{Libhaqa} \end{array}\right.$

In the formation of plurals in *Ma*, from nouns in *Le*, there are more variations; but these are only exceptions, which can be confronted with regular forms.

s (prob. *š*) *to* ṙ Lesapò (*bone*) — Maṙapò

Reg. forms :—{ Lesaṙi (night garment) — Masaṙi
Leṙotobolo (dune) — Maṙotobolo

c (prob. *c*) to ṙ Lecoha (*hole*) — Maṙoha

Reg. forms :—{ Leṙothori (drop of rain) — Maṙothori
Leouti (cloud-shadow) — Macuti

c *to* b Lecòqò (*arm*) — Mabòqò

Reg. forms :—{ Lecomane (flock) — Macomane
Lebori (rat) — Mabori

cw *to* dy Lencwè (*stone*) — Madyè

Reg. forms :—{ Ledyè (stone) — Madyè
Lencwi (voice) — Mancwi

ts *to* l Letsatsi (*sun*) — Malatsi

Reg. forms :—{ Letsatsa (squirrel-hole) — Matsatsa
Lelata (female slave) — Malata

ts *to* b Letsèlè (*grain of corn*) — Mabèlè

Reg. forms :—{ Letsela (rag) — Matsela
Lebicò (name) — Mabicò

tsh (*tš*) *to* ṙ Letšama, or } (*cheek*) — Maṙama, or
Lesama } — Masama

Reg. forms :—{ Letsètsè, or (louse-nit) — Matsètsè
Lentsètsè — Mantsètsè

sh (prob.*šy*) *to* ṙ Leshophi (*old site*) — Maṙophi

Reg. forms :— Leshoṙi { (name of a peculiar custom) } Mashoṙi

Among other permutations in Sechwana, we find—

c to r	Cwa (*come out*) *perfect* rule	
		Causative rusa (*Stock, with milk, of a cow before calving*)
l to r	Cwela (*come out towards*)	mocweri (*fountain*)
s to sh (*ˑy*)	Risa (*herd*)	tisho (*herding*)
ts to c	Retsa (*listen*)	theco (*listening*)
ts to s	Tsimo (*garden*)	masimo (*gardens*)

g̱w (*äw*) to **ny**	Ñwaꞑa (*year*)	linyaꞑa (*years*)
b (prob. *bi*) to **dy**	Leba (*look, Tr.*)	ledywa (*pass.*)
h (prob. *hi*) to ẏ (Germ. *ch* in *ich*)	}Ruha (*pay wages*)	ruẏwa (*pass.*)
p (prob. *pi*) to **c**	Hapa (*bind*)	hacwa (*pass.*)
r to **ts**	Mocweri (*fountain*)	mocwetsana (*spring*)
r̈ to **tṣ**	Mariri (*hairy*)	maritshane

All the preceding *regular permutations* are those upon which the principles of this work have been based. The *exceptional forms* (all in bold type) are those other instances of interchanging consonants to which I referred in a note at page 15, and which, together with the following, showing the affinities of the Sechwana and Isi-Zulu, represents pretty nearly the general character of the numerous *irregular* dialectical variations observable in a comparison of all cognate African languages.

*List of Permutations showing the Affinities of the Sechwana and Isi-Zulu Languages.**

Sechwana.	Meaning in both Languages.	Isi-Zulu.	S.	Z.
Atlhola	(*adjudge*)	Ahlola	tl̇	⎫
Dya	(*eat*)	Hla	dy	
Tla	(*come*)	„	tl	
Tatatha†	(*crush or mince with the teeth*)	Hlahlatà	t	
Se ꞑtlè	(*well, beautiful, &c.*)	Isihle	ꞑtl	⎬ hl
Sèba	(*backbite*)	Hleba	s (prob. ṣ)	
Kaboga		Hleboka	k	
Tshèga	(*laugh*)	Hleka	tṣ	
Shepola	(*shorten*)	Hlepola	sh (sẏ)	
Cokotsa	(*rinse out*)	Hlukuhla	{ c (= tsy) ts	⎭
Atlhama	(*open wide*)	Akama	tl̇	⎫
Qanoꞑa		‡Canuka	q	⎬ k
Khalemèla	(*reprove abruptly*)	Kulimela	kh	⎭

---

* All the Zulu examples are from Döhne.

† *Kakatha* is also used with the same meaning.   ‡ The click.

Seçhwana.	Meaning in both Languages.	Isi-Zulu.	S.	Z.
Apara	(become clothed)	Ambată	p	mb
Atla	(kiss)	Anga	tl	} ɳg
Beka	(jerk flesh)	Benga	k	
Itsè	(know)	Azi	ts	
Setlhori	s. (dangerous person) k. (a ghost)	Ihlozi	r	
Tlhwari	(species of snake)	Hlwazi	r'	
Moruti	(shade)	Umtunzi	t	
Ruha	s. (pay wages) z. (reward)	Vuza	h	
Tlala	(become full)	Zala	tl	
Letsha	s. (lagoon) z. (ripple)	Iza	ts'	z
Shuma	s. (breathe hard, or hiss—of a serpent) z. (take by surprise)	Zuma	sh (= sẏ)	
Mosari	(woman)	Umzali	s	
Còna	(themselves)	Zona	c (=tsy)	
Phacèqa	(bespatter)	Baceka	c (= tsy)	
Qama	(milk, v.)	Cama	q'	
Khamèlo	(pail)	Isicamelo	kh	c (click)
Sèba	(slander)	Ceba	s	
Tima	(extinguish)	Cima	t	
Borutu	(dulness)	Ubutuntu	t	nt
Sebata	s. (rag) z. (scar)	Isibanda	t	} nd
Serèthè	(heel)	Isitènde	th (t')	
Khaola	(cut off)	Gaula	kh (k')	} g
Kobò	(mantle)	Gubo	k	
Pitse	(the quagga)	Ibisi	ts	
Marini	s. (the gums) z. (gap of a tooth)	Isisini	r	s
Còma	(speak a strange language)	Soma	c (= tsy)	
Ka moshò†	(to-morrow)	Ngomso	sh (= sy)	

* All the Zulu examples are from Döhne.
† The sh here is often pronounced like fw.

155

Sechwana.	Meaning in both Languages.	Isi-Zulu.	S.	Z.
Phutha	(gather)	Butā	ph	} b
Qopela	(think)	Goboda	p	
Tabola	s. (take a good handful) z. (separate)	Dabula	t	} d
Tona	(male)	Doda	n	
Rumola	(root out)	Domula	r	
Qopola	(think)	Goboda	l	
Shwa	(die)	} Fa	sh (=sy)	
Sha	(burn)		kh	
Khwèla	(spit out)	Fela		
Sesari	(female)	Isifazi	s	
Ñce	(sweet cane)	Imfe	c (= tsy)	
Hitlha	s. (bury) z. (conceal)	Fihla	h	} f
Mothu	s. (person) z. (stranger)	Umfo	th	
Phinya	s. (πέρδομαι) z. (blow the nose)	Finya	ph	
Leru	(cloud)	Ilifu	r	
Ritla	s. (linger) z. (consider)	Zinhla	tl	nhl
Sepèntla	(a lewd female)	Isibanxa	ntl	nx (click)
Literu	(beard)	Idevu	r	
Bula	(open)	Vula	b	} v
ỹku	(sheep)	Mvu	k	
Mophatò	(regular body, or uniform class)	Mhadu	ph	h
Nca	(dog)	Nja	c (= tsy)	j (=dsy)
Hohoma	(boil over)	Pupuma	h	p
Ga we	(once)	Kanye	w	ny
Khèthèla	s.(pay tribute) z.(choose for)	Kétéla	th	} t
Sha	(name, v.)	Ta	sh	
Rata	(love, v.)	Tanda	r˚	
Cola	(get)	Tola	c (= tsy)	
Borutu	(dulness)	Ubutuntu	r	
Dya	(eat)	Tya	d	

Sechwana.	Meaning in both Languages.	Isi-Zulu.	S.	Z.
Hatsi	{ s. (*earth*) { z. (*down*) }	Pänsi	ts	ns
Khucama	{ s. (*fall on the* *knees*) { z. (*crouch*) }	Qotjama	kh	} q (*click*)
Kotama	(*squat*)	Qotama	k	

The above permutations are, however, not all constant, for *s* in the Sechwana often corresponds to *s* in Isi-Zulu, *p* to *p*, *b* to *b*, *l* to *l*, *n* to *n*, and *m* to *m*. This list is a very different one to that given by **Dr. Bleek** (*See p*. 40 *Sir G. Grey's Lib. S.A. Languages*); but that able linguist laboured under a great disadvantage—viz., the absence of any complete dictionary of the Sechwana language—a thing which actually does not exist, except, perhaps, in the manuscripts of two or three individuals. I have had the great privilege of comparing my own copious vocabulary of the Sechwana with the excellent Zulu dictionaries of **Mr. Döhne** and **Bishop Colenso**, which has enabled me to give a more satisfactory summary than has hitherto been published. It is, nevertheless, very far from complete, having been transferred to these pages from a few rough pencil notes on the margins of **Mr. Döhne's** interesting work. I have previously stated the drawbacks to a careful comparison of these two important languages, and in the above list, however precise I have endeavoured to be in representing the powers of the Sechwana articulations, it has been impossible for me to be sure of those in the Isi-Zulu, especially after having met with a few discrepancies between the actual pronunciation and that indicated in the orthography of some missionaries. An asterisk points out every instance in which I believe an aspirate has been lost sight of, though I may be wrong in some instances on verifying them by the actual pronunciation.

The examples of *initial* permutation in the Sechwana, upon which I have based the principles of a new classification, are absolute permutations of either simple consonants, or their simple modifications, or simple combinations, for which there appears to be no other mode of accounting. But, of most of the *exceptional* cases above shown (and of the relations between the Sechwana and the Isi-Zulu) this cannot be said. Such permutations must be accounted for upon principles or analogies of either phonical constructions or phonical corruptions. They show the extent to which one or other of these processes has interfered with the normal forms of speech, and it must be interesting to the European scholar to know that these very processes, which he so delights in observing and describing in the Arian family of languages, are at work in the Sechwana and its cognate barbaric dialects.

Among the permutations showing the former process—viz., that of phonical construction or growth, may be classed the palatals, as they are commonly called, otherwise the "*unstable combinations*"* of Dr. Latham, or the "*specific modifications*"† of Professor Max Müller. The Sechwana abounds in such instances, which may all be traced to combinations of consonants, with a post positive *y* or *w*, though in the root neither of these elements may be perceptible. Such mutations as above, of *p* to *c* (= tsy), *h* to *y*, *b* to *dyw*, *ts* to *c* (= tsy), *s* to *sh* (= sy), are all permutations of this kind.

	Constructive Form.	Pronounced	Written by the Missionaries.
In Hapa (*bind*), the change to the *passive* is	*hapiwa*	*halsywa*	*hacoa*
Ruha (*pay wages*) „	*ruhiwa*	*ruywa*	*rushoa*
Leba (*look*, Tr.) „	*lebiwa*	*ledywa*	*leyoa*

The above analogy, again, would seem to shed some light on the probable existence of an *i* prepositive to the *o*, in the formation of verbal nouns derived from verbs with terminal *sa*.

Retsa (*listen*)   Thecò (*listening*) prob. constructive form, Thetsio
Risa (*herd, of cattle*) Tishò (*herding*)   „   Tisio

" The Neapolitan *echiu*, from *piu*,"‡ is an analogous instance. Another is " presented by the Spanish language, in which the Latin *li* not unfrequently becomes a pure guttural, as in *muger* for *mulier*, and *hoja* for *folium*. Μόλις and μογις exhibit the same species of affinity."§ In Sechwana, for instance, *dyá*‖ is often

---

* Vide " *English Language*," vol. ii., p. 8, &c.
† Vide " *Proposals. &c.*" p. xxxv., &c.
‡ R. Garnett, p. 241.
§ Ibid. p. 251.
‖ Written by the missionaries *ya* and *yoa;* but the *d*, in both cases, though mollified, is distinctly audible.

substituted for *lea,* in the possessive particle of nouns—*e.g.,* *lehuku dya mè* (my word); the same with *dywa* for *boa*—*e.g.,* *bogòbè dywa qàqwe* (his bread). Again, the Sechwana has *syòna* for *seòna,* *tsyòna* for *tseòna.** In cases where the *spiritus* occurs, the combination is less perceptible, and the conjunct articulations have more the *appearance* of a single sound. But, as has been repeatedly implied, a proper investigation of these compound permutations presupposes a thorough analysis of the **vowel system,** and ought to form the subject of the third part of a work of this nature; for it is in all such examples that we have to continue tracing a process of construction, and deriving from this the phonical laws* by which the Sechwana language discloses its own peculiar but natural growth from the common elements of all human speech.

The permutations comprehended under the process of phonetic *corruptions* are of greater variety; and they appear to form that branch upon which the labours of the European philologer are chiefly expended. While those included under the first process are to be found in all their simplicity in barbaric languages, these pertain chiefly to languages whose *accidental* or *material* forms have alternately undergone disintegration and reconstruction by the numerous circumstances attending the vicissitudes of nations; though both processes have been at work in all tongues, as the Sechwana, distinguished by the prevalence of normal forms, and the paucity of exceptions, will alone show.

This subject would of itself supply materials for a whole treatise, but a hasty survey of the different classes of irregular permutations may not be uninteresting to the reader, and will at all events throw light on some apparent anomalies in Sechwana.

1. There are those instances in which the *now conjunct consonants were formerly merely initials of conjunct monosyllables.*

---

* Written by the missionaries *shòna* and *còna* respectively.

The following quotation, from the invaluable and fascinating work of the late Richard Garnett, will clearly illustrate this principle :—

"Even many of the words usually regarded as Sanscrit roots are capable of being resolved into still simpler elements. For instance, the root *i* denotes *to go* (Latin *i-re*, Greek *ιεναι*) ; *ri*, also *to go*, may very possibly be a compound of *ra + i* = *pergere; tri* (to pass), *ta + ri* — q. d., go *thither ; stri*, to strew, or spread, a further formation with the particle *sa*, and so of many others. Our readers will find much ingenious speculation on this subject in Potts' ' Etymologische Forschungen.' We consider many of his conclusions as highly deserving of attention; but we do not feel disposed to agree with him in referring the above prefixes to the Sanscrit *prepositions* in their *present form*, which is evidently not their *primeval* one. We think. for example, that *tri* is probably compounded, not, however, with the preposition *ati*, but with the pronominal or prepositional root *ta*. We freely admit that all this is, in a great measure, conjectural, and requires to be confirmed by a more copious induction from cognate dialects. Could the fact be sufficiently established, it would afford scope for much curious discussion respecting the formation of language, and might perhaps serve as a clue in tracing the affinities of tongues commonly supposed to be entirely unconnected. It is scarcely possible for two languages to be more unlike than Sanscrit and Chinese, but it is by no means improbable that both were at a very early period much in the same condition, and partly composed of the same elements. Both consist of monosyllabic *roots ;* and a few more pronouns and particles, employed copiously in the connexion and composition of words, might have made the latter not unlike the former, But while the component elements of Greek and Sanscrit have, as it were, crystallised into beautiful forms, Chinese, as an oral language, has remained perfectly stationary, and is still, as it was 3000 years ago, ' arena sine calce.'" —*Philological Essays, p.* 108

It is doubtful whether such a principle would always apply in the case of a mute with a post-positive liquid. A Mochwana only knows of two combinations of this kind—viz., *tl* and *ts* (*tla*, come ; *tsimo*, garden); but if you give him a foreign word to pronounce, such as *Bethlehem* or *Esther,* he will invariably syllabicise every consonant or spiritus, thus — *Be-te-le-he-me, E-se-te-re*. At all events, he will only use such combinations as those to which he is accustomed in his own speech, and even interpolate these with vowels in some instances. This fact, crude and superficial as it may appear, ought not to be beneath the notice of the philologer. I know of no objectively true instance in which either of the Sechwana combinations *tla* or *tsa* can be explained by this principle, but it is possible some may yet be found.

A reference to my former remarks in the present work, in respect to the influence of syllabic *quantity* on combinations of consonants, will, no doubt, in connection with the above quotation, be suggestive.

A proof that *quantity* does give rise to certain combinations of consonants, is afforded by the following facts, which cannot be ignored in the examination of this important subject. In the English language there is very little difficulty in recognising the pronunciation of words when the vowels are all elided, and many persons avail themselves of this mode of writing as a means of short-hand. Take, for instance, the sentence—

*T rd th mntny lmst nsprbl frm sch sbjct.**

If we introduce only the accented or *long* vowel, in every instance, the pronunciation is indicated with double distinctness.

T róid th mnótny álmst nséprbl frm such subjct.

Note.—(*a*) It may be observed that where any *liquids*, faucal or nasal, occur as initials, the insertion of the preceding vowel is unnecessary, unless it is accented, as *nséprbl*, *álmost*.

(*b*) When a *mute* is followed by any post positive *liquid*, the intervening vowel, unless accented, is absorbed in the consonantal diphthong—*e.g., pr* and *kr* in *nséprable* and *máckrel*.

2. There are those instances of permutation in which *the organically distinct articulations* " *are in reality derivative sounds, descended from a more complex element capable of producing both*"— *e.g.,* Greek δις and Latin *bis*, in relation to Sanskrit *dwis;* Latin *bellum*, for ancient form *duellum*, &c., &c.† It is to such that

---

* This was sugested by the perusal of an article in "*Evangelical Christendom.*"

† Garnett.

161

Dr. Donaldson, who was the first to notice the principle, has given the name of "*divergent articulations.*" It cannot be better described than in the words of the learned discoverer, for appending which I make no apology, as they are contained in a concise form in the Encyclopædia Britannica, which may be inaccessible to some of my readers.

"The older grammarians had only one name, *metalepsis*, for all interchanges, whether regular and easily explicable, as from *p* to *b*, or irregular, and at first sight inexplicable, as from *p* to *k*. The present writer was led to an explanation of these divergent interchanges by an inquiry into the nature of the Greek letter called the digamma, which he proved to be a complex sound, consisting of a guttural combined with a labial (*New Cratylus*, p. 110), and he extended the same principle to all cases in which two words, undoubtedly of the same origin, exhibit articulations which could not have been interchanged. In all such cases, he concluded that the original form exhibited a combination of the two sounds. The brief but decisive induction by which this law was established, in 1839 (*New Cratylus*, 1st Edition, p. 136), was greatly extended by **Mr. Garrett** in his valuable paper 'On certain Initial Letter-Changes in the Indo-European Languages'—(*Proceedings of the Philological Society* for 1846, vol. ii., p. 233, *sqq.*) A simple example or two will show the application of this law. The Sanscrit *paktas* corresponds exactly in meaning to the Latin *coctus*, and the Greek πεπτός. But as *p* cannot pass into *k*, the Latin differs from the Sanscrit in the initial, and from the Greek in the included sound, or, in **Grimm's** useful terminology, they differ reciprocally in *anlaut* and *inlaut* Now the Latin *coquo* shows us that the guttural in this case was not pure, but that it was followed by a vocalised labial; and it is known that even in Cicero's time, *coquus* was pronounced *quoquus* (Quintil. *Inst. Or.* vi. 3, § 47.) The divergent articulations *p* and *k*, converge, therefore, in the compound sound *qv* = *kp*, and the three words are accordingly reducible to an identity of origin as well as of meaning. Again, we have in Greek κελαινός as a synonym of μέλας, μέλαινα, μέλαν; and with the exception of the initial or *anlaut*, the words are identical in root or crude form. But we cannot derive *k* from *μ*, or *vice versâ*; and, according to the law, we must assume the complex sound *kμ* as the origin of these divergent articulations. Fortunately, we are not left to an inference in this case, for Pamphilus, of the school of Aristarchus, recorded the fact, that μέλαθρα, meaning "the rafters blackened by the smoke," were anciently called κμέλεθρα (*Etymol. Magn*, p. 521, 33.) Lastly, to take an instance in which we have all forms of the process, the Latin *vivus* exhibits no traces of a guttural in combination with the labial. But the perfect *vixi*, from the corresponding verb *vivo*, shows that the *inlaut* at least involved a *k* sound; whereas a comparison with the Gothic *quios* = *vivus* indicates that *qv* was also the original type of the

M

anlaut, or initial articulation; and thus we arrive with perfect confidence at the conclusion, that *vivus* = *qviqvus* was ultimately identical in meaning, as it is in signification, with the old Norse *quikr*, old Saxon *quic*, and modern English *quick*."—*Ency. Britann.*, 8th Edition, vol. xvii., p. 540.

The above process was suggested to Dr. Donaldson by an inquiry into the nature of the *digamma*, which he concludes to be a combination of a guttural consonant with a post-positive *w*; in fact, a "palatal." And it is not improbable that many of these complex articulations referred to will be found to have been "palatals" (whether the post-positive letter was formerly *y* or *w*), as well as mere combinations of simple consonants. For instances of several languages having the *included* articulation, while others have both it and the *initial*, see Garnett (*Phil. Essays*, pp. 108, 250, 251, 258, 259, &c., &c.

I am inclined to apply the process detected by Dr. Donaldson in the Indo-European tongues, to the explanation of an anomaly occurring in the Sechwana system of permutation."— See table, p. 16, where I have

Verb.	Verbal Noun.	Verb with the Object-Particles.		Mutations.
		i = *self.*	m, n, n̄ =_*me.*	
16. **Sila**	**Tsilō**	**Itsila**	**Ntsila**	s to ts
22. **Tsenya**	**Tsenyò**	**Itsenya**	**Ntsenya**	ts immutable

NOTE.—Nos. 2, *Cola* (tsyola), and 17, *Shòka* (syòka, perhaps sy), are, so far as regards the simple consonants, in combination, precisely analogous examples, but, being *palatals*, I cannot notice them here.

It is true, in the Sechwana the mutation implies a diversity of grammatical relation; but, inasmuch as I have proved that the whole series of Sechwana permutations of simple consonants may be reduced to phonic laws, is it not legitimate to conclude that these laws will explain any anomalies in their compound forms? May we not presume that the complex form of *s* was *ds*,* and that the primary change is from *dsilo* to *tsilo?* It is possible that the former may yet be discovered in some interior dialects. The example cited by Dr. Donaldson is almost

---

* My reader may be inclined to insist on *dz*, but a perusal of the 5th chapter may convince him of the correctness of my conclusion.

analogous—viz., *m* and *km* in the examples μελαθρα, κμέλεθρα In the Sechwana examples, the mute which is elided is pre-positive to a *faucal* liquid ; in the Greek, to a *nasal* liquid. The Œolic βρόδον for ρόδον, βρίζα for ρίζα, are merely analogous phenomena. I have, in the preceding pages, attempted to prove that *s*, *z* (th), *f*, *q* (Oriental), are analogues of *r* and *l*, which appear to occur more frequently in European tongues as the included element; therefore the same explanation must apply to them. Of all these analogues, only *s*, *r*, and *l* occur in the language; and the only combinations in which a *liquid* is post-positive, are *ts* (see above examples), and *tl* in the following, as well as their aspirated forms—(*See* p. 16):—

Tlotla, Tlotlō, Itlotla, Ñtlotla, we have tl immutable.

In the Sechwana, however, we have no example of an *l* or *dl* being commuted into *tl*, so that there are no means of either proving or disproving above conclusions. They will, however, be suggestive to other minds. I am content to admit my ignorance of the consequences deducible from the mere statement of this anomaly, and from my lame attempt to explain it.

At pages 20 and 53 I have referred to the insertion of a *k*, in the case of verbs commencing with a vowel or *spiritus*—(*See* p. 16—

23. Ila, Kilo, Ikila, Ñkila,—is commuted into k ;)

and explained it on the principle of *euphony ;* but the following, from **Garnett,** may suggest a different course of speculation on the subject.

" Formerly the only method of connecting ἁλινδέω and χαλινδέω together, was by supposing that a guttural had been dropped or assumed. But the knowledge that the former anciently had the digamma, places the matter in a different light, and makes it at all events probable that they are in reality collateral formations."—(*Phil. Essays,* p. 248.)

I have also, in the course of this work, referred to another peculiar phenomenon in the Sechwana language, which may perhaps be included under the permutations observed by Dr. Donaldson—viz., the tendency to substitute the *spiritus* or pure aspirate for the aspirated mute or liquid, *i.e.*, *h* for either q̓ (gutt. *ch*), r̓, or b̓, —*e.g.*, *hòna* for 'q̓òna*(there); *hae* for 'q̓ae* (home); *he* for *r̓e* (we); *hèla* for *bhèla* (sweep). By the analogies pointed out, I conclude of course that the same will be found to apply to *l̓* (Zulu and Welsh), *f̓,* * *s̓, z* (th²), *d̓,* and *g̓.* In proof of this conclusion, however, I have not found any objectively true instances in Sechwana speech, but have little doubt of the probability of their occurrence to the students, on a comparative survey of cognate dialects.

Similar phenomena abound in the Indo-European tongues. In the Anglo Saxon *hræd,* according to Garnett, " *h* represents a more ancient guttural."† "The Slavonian *greblo* (an oar), would, in Bohemian, become *hreblo.*‡ " *S,* in Latin, almost invariably" corresponds with the *spiritus asper* in Greek—*e.g.,* ὑπερ and *super* are exactly equivalent."§ Dr. Prichard writes :—

" It is to be observed that *h* never stands as the initial of a word in Erse in the primitive form, or is never, in fact, an independent radical letter. It is merely a *secondary* form, or representative, of some other initial—viz., *f* or *s*. It must likewise be noticed, that the same words which begin with *s* or *f* as their primitive initial in the Erse, taking *h* in their secondary form, have in Welsh *h* as their primitive initial. This fact affords an instance exactly parallel to the substitution in Greek of the rough and soft breathings for the Œolic digamma, and in other words for the sigma. Οἰνῳ, as is well known, stands for Ϝοινῳ, ʽΕσπερος for Ϝεσπερος, and ἑπτα probably replaced a more ancient form of the same word, viz., σεπτά; ἑξ stands for σεξ; ὑs and ἑρπω for σῦs and σἱρπω."‖

In all such cases, it is frequently supposed that the *spiritus* is merely substituted for the simple consonant, but all such facts

---

* The Sesuto, an impure dialect, has *f̓* where the Sechwana has both *h* and the still purer form *bh* (*b̓*).

† *Phil. Essays,* p. 245.

‡ Ibid. p. 257. It is not stated whether the *g* in the Slavonian word is a *liquid* Germ. gutt. *ch* (*q̓*), or a mute.

§ Ibid. p. 107.

‖ Quoted by Garnett. Ibid. p. 83.

as I have met with in the Sechwana go to prove that the *spiritus* has lost its consonantal form—*i.e.*, the mute, which it formerly modified, has disappeared; in fact, that *s*, or *f*, or *th*, or *r*, or *l*, in all such cases, must have been aspirated consonants, and so far complex elements. To be more explicit: upon the basis of the Sechwana examples, *he* for *r̈e*, *hòna* for *q̇òna*. I believe that the fact of *h* being the secondary form, is a proof that the primary forms were not simply the *tenues r* and *q* (Oriental), but the *aspiratœ r̈* and *q̇* (gutt. *ch*); or, in other words, the former + the *spiritus*. In a comparison of dialects, it will not improbably be found that an aspirated consonant in the one will be represented by an aspirated consonant in the other—*e.g.*, *nari* (buffalo) is usually written by the missionaries *nari*, and the Isi-Zulu equivalent is written by the Zulu missionaries *nyati*, but I would venture to assert that it is pronounced *nyat'i*; for the Isi-Zulu equivalent of the Sechwana *r̈e* (we) is not, as usually written, *tina*, but rather *thina* (t'), as I have heard it distinctly pronounced. The importance of precision in these matters cannot be over-rated, as the following example will show, in any attempts to make a subjective use of the analogy. *UthiXo* is the Zulu name for Deity (not *Utiχo* as usually written). *Orija* is that mentioned by visitors to the lake *r̈-habi*,* as used by the natives there. If in this word the *r* is aspirated (*r'*), there can be little doubt that *Orija* and *UthiXo†* are cognate varieties of the same expression, and that neither has any connection with *Morimo* of the Sechwana, in which the *r* is a *tenuis*.

It would be an easy matter to carry the illustration further, and not an unprofitable task to attempt to arrive at other principles in a comparative survey of South African dialects; but when a student is acquainted with the actual pronunciation of

---

* Usually written *Ngami*, but pronounced as above.

† The *click* (χ) in the one is probably a substitute for the *palatal* in the other.

only *one* dialect in a comparative survey, there is much to detract from the pleasure of his researches.

I shall close by placing before the reader an extraordinary permutation occurring in the Sechwana language which may not be uninteresting—viz., the change of the tenuis combination *ri* to *ts* (*mocweri*, a fountain ; *mocwetsana*, a spring), and of the aspirate form *ṙi* to *tś* (*naṙi*, buffalo ; *natśane*, young buffalo). For instance, one would little have suspected that the verb *rusa*, to stock, of milk (of a cow before calving), was the causative form of *cwa* (come out), but for the above analogy. The occultation of the fact arises merely from the confusion of orthographies. Were *cwa* written with all its constituent elementary letters, *tsywa*, it would be more evident. Precisely by the same analogy is it that *rule* (has come out) is the perfect of *cwa*, and *burule* (ripe, ready) of *bucwa* (ripen). The Batlhapiñ have again *cona* (tsyona), for *ṙona* of the other tribes.

I shall not attempt to explain this phenomenon in the Sechwana, but leave it to the speculations of those who have more collateral knowledge at command. The following, from Garnett, may not be out of place :—

" We may here suggest that it would be a matter of curious speculation to trace the Indo-European words commencing with *r*, or its combinations, to their equivalents in the Tartarian dialects, supposing any to exist. It is clear that, if they are to be found, it must be under some other forms, and the identification of those forms could not fail to clear up points in philology which are at present involved in obscurity."—*Phil. Essays*, p. 258.

This able writer held that " an accurate knowledge of the permutations of sound in cognate languages is the very foundation of all rational etymology."[*] I trust that the few rays of light which I have attempted to throw on the subject, by a careful explanation of the phonology of this barbaric dialect, will introduce the Sechwana to the attention of those really able to make use of its stores of new material.

---

[*] Phil. Essays, p. 179

CHAPTER V.

COMBINATIONS OF SIMPLE CONSONANTS.

To the eye, the number of combinations of simple consonants may well appear infinite, because they are arbitrary; but to the ear, the laws of articulation will very materially prescribe their limits. I have in this chapter nothing to do with any combinations of consonants with vowels, a subject which will occupy the third and most difficult part of this work. This will alone materially limit the number for present consideration. Before proceeding to treat of such as really occur in the Sechwana language, I shall do what is practicable to every closet student—viz., to try the extent of the various combinations of which the simple consonants of my classification are susceptible, in order to arrive at the principles which regulate their use. Those of the *mutes* (*k*, *t*, *p* ; *g*, *d*, *b*) are as follows :—

kg	*kd*	*kb*	*gk*	*dk*	*bk*
tg	*td*	*tb*	*gt*	*dt*	*bt*
pg	*pd*	*pb*	*gp*	*dp*	*bp*
gd	gb	db	dg	bg	bd
kt	kp	tp	tk	pk	pt

In all, *thirty.** But it is usually held that, in attempting to articulate any one of them, it will be found that though it may be possible to make such combinations to the eye—to the ear the first " must assume the property (quantity) of the second." That is, with regard to these *mutes*, a principle is observed that

---

* Not including the double form of each consonant, making *six* more.

a *fortis* 'can only stand in opposition to a *fortis,* and a *lenis* to a *lenis,** or the corresponding aspirated forms of the respective instances, by which limitation all those represented in italics are usually excluded, and the remaining *twelve* combinations to be regarded as proper phonetic compounds.

Dr. Latham's "Law of Accommodation."

It is to this principle in the combination of the *mutes* that Dr. Latham has applied the term "law of accommodation," and others "law of homogeneousness." Even supposing it to be correct and constant in respect to the *mutes,* that learned writer, however, carries it to a far greater extent than I believe is warranted by legitimate proofs. Excluding his *liquids* and *semi-vowels,* the following is his system of consonants, all of which he calls *mutes.*†

Lene.		Aspirate.	
sharp.	flat.	sharp.	flat.
p	b	f	v
t	d	þ (th²)‡	ð (th³)
k	g	χ (q⁺?)	γ (q̊?)
s	z	σ (sh)	ζ (zh)

Now, of these he adds :—

"Certain combinations of articulate sounds are incapable of being pronounced. . . . . *Two (or more)* mutes, *of different degrees of sharpness and flatness, are incapable of coming together in the same syllable.* For instance, *b, v, d, g, z,* &c., being flat, and *p, f, t, k, s,* &c., being sharp, such combinations as *abt, avt, apd, afd, agt, akd, atz, ads,* &c., are unpronounceable. *Spelt,* indeed, they may be; but attempts at pronunciation end in a *change* of the combination "—*Eng. Lang.,* vol. i., p. lxiii.

So far as regards the first *three* pairs, which I have separated from the rest by a horizontal line, it would perhaps not be possible to contradict Dr. Latham ; and were he to use the word

---

* This would only be a more correct and concise rule than that in vogue among Greek grammarians—viz., " a *tenuis* can stand only before a *tenuis,* an *aspirata* before an *aspirata,* and a *media* before a *media.*"

† *Eng. Lang.,* vol. i., p lxiii. *Vide* my note in reference to this term.

‡ The explanatory letters in brackets I have inserted.

"*mutes*" in the proper and restricted sense, it might be proper
to endorse his remark further on—" It is only with the mutes
that there is an impossibility of pronouncing the heterogeneous
combinations above mentioned." That the law is in force in
Greek, in such examples as γδουπος; in Latin, in such as
scriptum, *rectum* (stems *scrib-*, *reg-*); and in English in *stept*,
pluckt, &c., &c., there is no denying. But in English we have
the combinations *kd* in *backdoor*, *pd* in *lapdog*, *kb* in *blackbird*, *tb*
in *nutbrown*, *dk* in *woodcock*, which are all pronounced exactly
as written, whether we accent the first or second syllable, and
show that such combinations are not phonically impossible ;*
therefore I rather think that an absolute rule does not exist, and
that the "law of accommodation" is guided by the particular
habit of any language. It is remarkable that, while in Greek
it occurs in the beginning and middle of words, in Latin it only
occurs in the middle, and in English most frequently at the end.
Dr. Latham himself admits that there are no general rules for
determining which of the two letters accommodates itself to the
other. The phenomenon must therefore be accounted for upon
some more satisfactory principle.

But when Dr. Latham extends the law to the *continuous*
sounds of other writers, it is time to demur. The following is a
case in which he applies it to such :—

"*The letter s.*—In a very large class of words the letter *s* is used in
spelling where the real sound is that of the letter *z*. Words like *stags*,
balls, *peas*, &c., are pronounced *stagz*, *ballz*, *peaz*. It is very important to
be familiar with this orthographical substitution of *s* for *z*.
"The reason for it is as follows :—

---

* The example *black-guard*, pronounced *blaggard*, is an exception ; but
we have *black-gum*, in which the articulations are distinct, though kindred.
The above examples may be spurned because in compound words ; but
surely they are quite as legitimate as the usual examples of *nuthook*, *uphold*,
&c., employed by scholars to illustrate to an Englishman the nature of the
aspirated *t*, *p*, &c., occurring in Oriental languages.

" The words where it is so sounded are either possessive cases, or plural nominatives; as *stag's, stags ; slab's, slabs,* &c.

" Now, in these words (and in words like them), the sounds of *g* (in *stag*), and of *b* (in *slab*), come in immediate contact with the sound of the letter *s*.

" But the sound of the letter *s* is sharp, whilst those of *g* and *b* are flat, so that the combinations *gs, bs,* are unpronounceable. Hence *s* is sounded as *z*."—*Eng. Lang.*, vol. ii., p. 69.

The tenor of this reasoning may be all very logical, but, upon the principle laid down in the preceding chapter, I am inclined to question the truth of part of the premises—viz., that *s* is *sharp* (or fortis). I would urge that the change of *s* to *z*, in the above examples, may be accounted for upon another ground, *i.e.*, there is nothing to disprove that *s*, in the words *stags* and *peas*, is a vocalised form of the letter; in the word *balls*, that either *s* itself, or the *l* in apposition, is also vocalised. In fact, a proof of this very argument forms the context to the above quotation from his work :—

" In the old stages of the English language, a vowel was interposed between the last letter of the word and the letter *s*, and when that vowel was sounded, *s* was sounded also.

" Hence *s* is retained, although its sound is the sound of *z*."—*Ibid.*

I have already attempted to prove that *z* (in my tableau *š*) is only a vocalised form of *s*. Is it not, then, as likely that the change of the sound in particular English words is to be accounted for by the fact of an indistinct vowel sound, or element of vocalisation, taking place of the old full vowel sound, and merging in the consonantal articulation, so as to form a vocalised consonant? That, in many cases, the permutation of *s* to *z* occurs in combination with the *lenes-mutes g, d, b,* I do not deny, and shall rather attempt to account for the fact; but would allege that, (1) there are other instances in which such changes take place without any other consonant in apposition, *e.g.*, *disable, dismal, prison, easy, cosmetic, visible, resemble, misery, reason, presence,* &c., in all which cases the *s* could be indicated by *z* (or *š* of my tableau); (2) there are also instances in which, after such consonants, the mutation does not take place, *e.g.*, *eggshell*, *absent, landslip, godsend, abstruse, nutshell. Rosetree*, again, is an example in which a *lenis, s*, precedes a fortis, *t.*

There is the more necessity for our arriving at correct views on this subject, inasmuch as, according to the principles of this treatise, what is said of *s* by Dr. Latham ought to apply to what I have attempted to prove are its analogues—viz., *q* (Oriental), *r, l, f, th*[1] (*z* of tableau). In the following table there are, for instance, *forty-two* combinations of the simple consonants of my tableau, in which a *mute* is the prepositive element:—

TABLE I.

kq	kr	kl	ks	kz (th′)	kf	kv (Mex.)
gq	gr	gl	*gs*	*gz* „	*gf*	gv „
tq	tr	tl*	ts	tz „	tf	tv „
dq	dr	dl	*ds*	*dz* „	*df*	dv „
pq	pr	pl	ps	pz „	pf	pv „
bq	br	bl	*bs*	*bz* „	*bf*	bv „

Now, according to Dr. Latham, all those combinations in italics are unpronounceable, because, in his system, the conjunct elements are of different quantities. But he holds that *gr, gl; dr, dl; br, bl*, are pronounceable, because both elements are *flat* (*lenes*); and here he has the testimony of Professor Max Müller, who says of *l* and *r*, " they are soft, like the mediæ, owing to the process of their formation." However, upon the basis of new materials in Sechwana phonology, I have already proved, satisfactorily I trust, that the *mutes g, d, b*, and the liquids *l* and *r*, are similar in quantity. I have also made an effort to show that *q* (Oriental) is an analogue of the elementary forms of both *r* and *l.* Moreover, by analogy, I have attempted to prove that both *s* and *th*[1] (*z* of tableau), as well as the labial *f*, are, in their tenues or elementary and unmodified forms (not usually admitted into

---

* These are in bold letters, as particular reference will be made to them in the sequel.

classification), analogues of both *r, l,* and *q* (Oriental); and, consequently, that the combinations of all these with the mutes g, d, b, are also pronounceable. As to *s,* the English examples

bigseat	gladsome	absent
not	not	not
bigzeat	*gladzome*	*abzent*
nor	nor	nor
bikseat	*glatsome*	*apsent*

will alone show that the combinations *gs, ds, bs,* are quite as pronounceable as *gl, dl, bl.* If the combinations of these *mutes* with the other *liquids, q, th*[1], and *f,* existed in English or in the Sechwana, it would no doubt be an easy matter to furnish similar examples.

But in maintaining that coincidence in quantity is necessary to the proper pronunciation of conjunct articulations, has Dr. Latham not utterly forgotten that in such combinations as *kl, kr; tl, tr; pl, pr,* which abound in the English language, in such words as *cloth, crown; little, tree; place, pride,* the elements, so far as regards quantity, are heterogeneous, as well as in such combinations as *ts* and *tf,* which he also sanctions?

In the following table, again, are *forty-two* combinations, in which the *liquids* are pre-positive:—

TABLE II.

qk	rk	lk	sk (th[1])	zk	fk (Mex.)	vk
qg	rg	lg	sg „	zg	fg „	vg
qt	rt	lt	st „	zt	ft „	vt
qd	rd	ld	sd „	zd	fd „	vd
qp	rp	lp	sp „	zp	fp „	vp
qb	rb	lb	sb „	zb	fb „	vb

Here, though Dr. Latham has above made such an oversight as that noticed in instances where the *mutes* are prepositive, he admits that the liquids *l* and *r,* though *flat (lenes),* may be followed by a *sharp* consonant, as *alp, alt.* The same is allowed on the principles of this treatise; but still more—viz., that, inasmuch as I have proved q, s, z (th'), and f, to be analogues of r and l, and therefore all *flat (or lenes)*, their combinations, with a sharp consonant, whether this be post or pre-positive, are all pronounceable.

This treatise not only holds that the *liquids* of its classification, although *lenes*, can be pronounced in apposition to the *lenes*-mutes (which Dr. Latham denies in considering all, except l and r, as *sharp*), but it also maintains that they are distinctly pronounceable in connection with *fortes*-mutes; in fact, that the liquids r, l, s, z (th'), q, and f, are pronounceable with any simple mutes (unmodified by either the *spiritus* or element of *vocalisation*), whether post or pre-positive. If this can be disproved, the conclusions at which I have arrived respecting the nature of these *liquid* elements are invalidated. If not, any conventional notions regarding our habitual use of only some of their combinations must fall to the ground.

Now, it must be borne in mind that, in the above groups of combinations, I have only had to do with the *tenues* forms of all consonants, *i.e.*, their absolutely simple or elementary forms, unmodified by either the *spiritus* or *vocalisation;* and, moreover, that among these consonants, those of s, z (th'), f, and q (Oriental), as *tenues* forms, are not usually admitted into classifications. Men are in the habit of looking at the *aspirated* forms of these latter consonants—viz., the common s, *th*, f, and the Germ. *ch* (gutt.), having only their *sonant* modifications z (common), th^3 (this), v (common), and the Arabic ع (Northumberland *burr*). It is possible that, by now considering all the *combinations* of these *tenues* forms, as affected respectively by the *spiritus* and element of *vocalisation*, we may be enabled to approximate to correct conclusions, and a satisfactory analysis of the difficulty.

Consonantal Diphthongs.

The remark of Dr. Lepsius, concerning " a complete and accurate theory of transcription" in respect to the vowels, is equally applicable to the consonants, inasmuch as it is necessary to make a distinction between what are and are not *diphthongs* among their compound forms. Even the subject of vowel *diphthongs* is involved in such confusion, that I need not wonder at finding myself in a labyrinth in the case of the consonants. The following quotation will display the unscientific and random style in which these are usually disposed of.

(*Here ends the Manuscript.*)

" The diphthongal consonants are *r, w, y, j, q, ch, wh.*"—*Author of Article*
" *Stammer*," *Penny Cyclopædia.*